DR. SHELTON J. GOODE

BEYOND INCLUSION

REIMAGINING THE FUTURE OF WORK,
WORKERS, AND THE WORKPLACE

outskirts
press

Beyond Inclusion
Reimagining the Future of Work, Workers, and the Workplace
All Rights Reserved.
Copyright © 2021 Dr. Shelton J. Goode
V2.0

The opinions expressed in this manuscript are solely the opinions of the author and do not represent the opinions or thoughts of the publisher. The author has represented and warranted full ownership and/or legal right to publish all the materials in this book.

This book may not be reproduced, transmitted, or stored in whole or in part by any means, including graphic, electronic, or mechanical without the express written consent of the publisher except in the case of brief quotations embodied in critical articles and reviews.

Outskirts Press, Inc.
http://www.outskirtspress.com

Paperback ISBN: 978-1-9772-4008-8
Hardback ISBN: 978-1-9772-4098-9

Cover Photo © 2021 www.gettyimages.com. All rights reserved - used with permission.

Outskirts Press and the "OP" logo are trademarks belonging to Outskirts Press, Inc.

PRINTED IN THE UNITED STATES OF AMERICA

ALSO BY THE AUTHOR

*Representative Bureaucracy: African American Mayors
and Municipal Employment*

*So, You Think You Can Teach: A Guide for the
New College Professor in Teaching Adult Learners*

Diversity Managers: Angels of Mercy or Barbarians at the Gate

*Crisis as a Platform for Social Change from
Strawberry Mansion to Silicon Valley*

*Winter in America: The Impact of the 2016 Presidential Election
on Diversity in Companies, Communities, and the Country*

PRAISE FOR

*Beyond Inclusion: Reimagining the
Future of Work, Workers, and the Workplace*

"*Compelling*!"

Many diversity professionals (myself included!) work hard to equip leaders with the tools to improve business performance—no one has done so with more clarity and authenticity than Dr. Shelton Goode. The practical insights in Beyond Inclusion: Reimagining the Future of Work, Workers, and the Workplace are critical to any leader looking to build and maintain a sustainable, inclusive workplace.

—*Nick Araco, Chief Executive Officer, AchieveNEXT*

"*Common-sense tools and direction from a top D&I leader!*"

"The advice in this book is key to helping our company improve our culture, embrace diversity, implement change, and facilitate healthy discussions. It has helped us have honest discussions and take positive steps to improve our teams' daily work-life."

—*Frank Jones, CEO and Chief Financial Officer, Stafford Development*

"Gripping!"

If you want to become an authentic leader within your company and with your customers, make reading this book a priority. Dr. Goode unveils the model companies should use to stay competitive and adapt to current leadership trends. This book will change how managers think about work, workers, and the workplace. This book is a MUST READ."

—*Andres Gonzales, Chief Diversity Officer, Froedtert Health*

About time! Diversity and inclusion from a business leader's perspective.

"Business is inherently conflicted between D&I and bottom-line results. In Beyond Inclusion, Dr. Goode provides a firsthand personal account of companies' attempts to wrestle with these business dilemmas. Dr. Goode uses his insights and experiences to offer powerful lessons for corporate executives and D&I professionals, as well as frontline managers."

—*Nat Alston, Chair, National Association of African Americans in Human Resources*

"I've been waiting for this!"

"Dr. Shelton Goode knows from firsthand experience how to leverage diversity and inclusion for competitive advantage. In Beyond Inclusion: Reimagining the Future of Work, Workers, and the Workplace, he provides a comprehensive and authoritative examination of companies' efforts to create a more diverse and inclusive culture. More importantly, he adds his unique insights and shares his practical experience from working with his clients. If you want proven methods for advancing diversity, inclusion, and equity in your company while avoiding the classic mistakes, this book is for you."

—*Robbie Bishop-Monroe, D.B.A, CPA, Assistant Professor, Loyola University Maryland*

DEDICATION

To the families of Ahmad Aubrey, Rashard Brooks, Breona Taylor, and George Floyd—your sacrifice will not be in vain. Remember the challenge Dr. Roosevelt Thomas issued to us: "Diversity—in action—is the painful awareness that other people, other races, other voices, and other habits of minds, have as much integrity of being, as much claim on the world as you do. And I urge you, amid all the differences present to the eye and mind, to reach out to create the bond that will protect us all. We are meant to be here together."

TABLE OF CONTENTS

FOREWORD i
PREFACE v
ACKNOWLEDGMENTS xvii
SECTION ONE: REIMAGINE WORK 1
CHAPTER 1: A CRISIS IS A TERRIBLE THING TO WASTE ... 3
   Introduction 3
      Crises Breed Change 4
      Economic Impact of the Pandemic 6
      Pandemics, Wars, and Workers' Rights 8
      A Once-in-a-Generation Opportunity 10
      The Future of Work 12
      Think About This 15
CHAPTER 2: THE BEGINNING OF TOMORROW 16
   Introduction 16
      Reimagining the Future of Work 17
      The Future Workplace 18
      Next-Generation Workforce 25
      The Need for A New Talent Management Model 26
      Workplace: Rethinking Where Work Gets Done 27
      Work in the Future Will Need to Be More Valuable and Meaningful 28
      Think About This 29

CHAPTER 3: INCREASING ECONOMIC INCLUSION BY DIVERSIFYING SUPPLIERS 31
    Introduction... 31
    The More Things Change.. 31
    Client Case Study... 34
    Think About This 35

SECTION TWO: REPOSITION THE WORKFORCE 37
CHAPTER 4: HACKING TALENT MANAGEMENT 39
    Introduction... 39
    Attracting Top Diverse Talent 40
    Leading Practices to Attract Diverse Talent 40
    Onboarding Top Talent... 43
    Managing Top Talent 45
    Rewarding and Recognizing Top Talent 46
    Retaining Top Talent... 47
    Think About This 49

CHAPTER 5: DEVELOPING A DIVERSE PIPELINE OF TALENT 50
    Introduction... 50
    Building A Diverse Bench Through Succession Planning.......... 51
    Cultural Fluency Training for Leaders.. 52
    Putting Theory into Practice 53
    The Icarus Multicultural Leadership Competency Model 55
        Leading Diverse Organizations 56

    Adapting to Employee Differences 58
    Tolerating Ambiguity 58
    Demonstrating Agility 59
  Cross-Disciplinary Collaboration 60
  Think About This 61

CHAPTER 6: DISRUPTING DIVERSITY AND INCLUSION TRAINING 63
  Introduction 63
  History of Diversity and Inclusion Training 64
  Shift to Multicultural Training 66
  Diversity Pioneers: Angels of Mercy or Barbarians at the Gate .. 68
  Intent versus Impact 70
  Valuing Diversity 72
  D&I Training in Higher Education 73
  Think About This 74

SECTION THREE: REINVENT THE WORKPLACE 75

CHAPTER 7: LEVERAGING EMPLOYEE RESOURCE GROUPS TO INCREASE EMPLOYEE ENGAGEMENT 77
  Introduction 77
  The Impact of ERGs on the Future Workforce 78
  ERGs: A Client Case Study 79
  Think About This 81

CHAPTER 8: EMPOWERING THE DIVERSITY AND INCLUSION COUNCIL TO TRANSFORM THE CULTURE 83
  Introduction 83

Defining Diversity and Inclusion Councils................................ 84
Executive Diversity Councils.. 84
Regional Councils 85
Advisory Councils 85
Establishing and Operating D&I Councils................................. 86
Building a Solid Council Structure.. 87
Defining Council Goals and Objectives 87
Developing the Council's Business Plan 88
Creating a Compelling Communications Plan 90
Developing an Evaluation Plan 91
D&I Council Governance... 93
Client Case Study... 94
Client Engagement.. 95
Moving from Awareness to Action 95
Methodology and Results... 96
Lessons Learned 97
Think About This 97

SECTION FOUR: RESET THE CULTURE 99
CHAPTER 9: LEADING TOMORROW'S WORKFORCE: THE CEO AS CHIEF TRUST OFFICER 101
Introduction... 101
The Intersection of Trust and Inclusion 101
Barriers to Trust: False Impressions and Cumulative Inequities
.... 103

    Trust and Diversity as a Leadership Competencies 106

    Trust as a Component of Authentic Leadership 111

    Best Practices.. 115

    Think About This 117

**CHAPTER 10: THE POWER TO BE BETTER:
THE GEORGIA POWER CASE STUDY**............................120

    Introduction... 120

    The Beginning of Never... 121

    Where there's Smoke.. 123

    Crisis as a Platform for Change 126

    Researchers Identify Underlying Causes 130

    Supreme Court Decision Creates a Duty to Act 132

    Enterprise-wide Mandatory D&I Training 134

    Communication as a Platform for Change 138

    What Gets Measure Gets Done.. 139

    Think About This 139

**CHAPTER 11: AUTHENTIC LEADERSHIP DURING
A TIME OF CRISIS**..142

    Introduction... 142

    Apples and Trees 144

    Leadership Philosophy and Management Style....................... 146

    A Crisis Is a Terrible Thing to Waste 148

    Implications for Crisis Leadership Theory 152

    Think About This 157

CHAPTER 12: CREATING A CULTURE OF CIVILITY, COMPASSION, AND COMMON SENSE.................................159
    Introduction.. 159
    Compassion and Civility versus Correctness and Comfort 160
    Facilitating Courageous Conversation 161
    Understanding the Barriers to Courageous Conversations 163
    Think About This 164

CHAPTER 13: THE FUTURE WORKPLACE: THE ROLE OF THE CHIEF DIVERSITY OFFICER 166
    Introduction... 166
    Angels of Mercy or Barbarians at the Gate? 167
    Ain't Such a Thing as Superman 170
    I Was In The Right Place—It Must Have Been The Wrong Time.. 173
    Hit the Road Jack 176
    Think About This 177

CHAPTER 14: INCLUSION THROUGH JUSTICE AND EQUITY 181
    Introduction.. 181
    Client Case Study.. 182
    Moving from Organizational Comfort to Cultural Competence.. 184
    Contributing to the Triple Bottom Line: Financial, Social, Environmental 186
    Changing Demographics and Customer Expectations 186

Preparing Workers to Reenter the New Workplace 189
Developing Sustainable D&I Strategies 192
Enhancing Talent Management Capability and Capacity 192
Increasing Trust by Reducing Bias 193
Optimizing High Impact Business and
Employee Resource Groups 193
Enhancing and Expanding the Company's Brand 194
Developing Realistic Metrics with Teeth 194
Enlisting the Board in Reimagining the Company 195
Some Final Thoughts 195

APPENDIX A: MY TOP FIVE FAVORITE BOOKS ON
DIVERSITY, EQUITY, AND INCLUSION 199
APPENDIX B: JUSTICE, EQUITY, DIVERSITY,
AND INCLUSION (JEDI) DEFINITIONS 203
APPENDIX C: NOTES 261
APPENDIX D: REFERENCES 287
About the Author 303
About Icarus Consulting 306
Index 309

FOREWORD

By Dr. Tana M. Sessions, Bestselling Author of "Working While Black: A Woman's Guide to Stop Being the Best Kept Secret"

The coronavirus pandemic exposed the country's class and racial divisions and tested the fragile social safety net like few events have in the last century. In *Beyond Inclusion: Reimagining the Future of Work, Workers, and the Workplace*, Dr. Goode, a Forbes D&I Trailblazer, explains how insecure jobs, a lack of paid sick leave, difficulties accessing unemployment benefits, challenges of finding affordable housing, battles of getting health insurance, and other issues have deepened the pain and potentially allowed the virus to spread faster and further. The service sector, retail, and restaurant workers, many with little savings and few benefits, have been hit hardest. Similarly, COVID-19 fatalities are impacting African Americans and poor communities disproportionately.

The most misleading cliché about the coronavirus is that it treats everyone the same. It doesn't, neither medically nor economically, socially, or psychologically. Covid-19 exacerbates preexisting conditions of inequality everywhere it strikes. In June 2020, this resulted in social turmoil, up to and including uprisings and protests.

Social unrest had already been increasing across the country before COVID-19 began its assault. According to the Brink Center at Boston University, over 100 large anti-government protests occurred between January 1, 2017, and December 31, 2020. Some of these protests toppled local, state, and national politicians.

The immediate effect of Covid-19 has dampened most forms of protest as many cities and states forced their populations into lockdowns, which kept people from taking to the streets or gathering in groups. However, behind the doors of quarantined households, in the lengthening lines of soup kitchens, in prisons and slums—wherever people were hungry, sick, and worried even before the outbreak—tragedy and trauma continue to build up. These also present a compelling business case for doing things differently after we emerge on the other side of the pandemic.

The coronavirus has thus put a magnifying glass on inequality in the country. There's been a move by some of the very wealthy to "self-isolate" on their Hamptons estates or swanky yachts—one Hollywood mogul swiftly deleted an Instagram picture of his $590 million yacht after a public outcry. Even the comfortable middle-class can feel safe working from home via Zoom, Skype, WebEx, and Slack.

But countless other Americans don't have that option. Indeed, the less money a person makes, the less likely they can work remotely. Because they lack savings and health insurance, these workers in precarious employment must keep their jobs, if they are lucky enough to have a job, to make ends meet. As they do, they risk getting infected and bringing the virus home to their families, which, like poor people everywhere, are already more likely to be sick and less able to access the complex and costly healthcare system. Consequently, the coronavirus moves fastest through neighborhoods that are cramped, stressful, and bleak. Above all, it disproportionately kills the poor and people of color. These facts are self-evident and true, which provides a clear mandate for change—starting with work, workers, and the workplace.

In a country with a long history of racial segregation, it should come as no surprise that the virus impacted some zip codes more than others. That's because everything conspires to make each neighborhood its own sociological and epidemiological petri dish—from average incomes and education to apartment size and population density, from nutritional habits to patterns of domestic abuse. For example, in the average urban metropolitan areas, low-income households have, on average, almost half the living space (500 square feet) as low-income households in the national average (987 square feet). The difference between large black cities and rural areas is even more significant.

To those living in black neighborhoods in New York, Philadelphia, Newark, Chicago, or Detroit, there's no such thing as "social distancing" because the whole family sleeps in a one-bedroom apartment. There's no discussion of wearing masks because they don't have masks. They ignore the advice to do more handwashing because they don't have running water.

And so, it goes, wherever COVID-19 shows up. The National Chamber of Commerce has warned that the pandemic will destroy over 25 million jobs nationwide and drastically cut another 75 million people's income. Most of these people were already poor. As their suffering worsens, so do other issues, from alcoholism and drug addiction to domestic violence and child abuse, leaving an entire generation traumatized, perhaps permanently.

In this context, it would be naive to think that individuals or communities can carry on as before once this crisis is over. Anger and bitterness make their way in both the virtual and physical workplace. Early harbingers include millions of New Yorkers banging pots and pans from their windows to protest their government or furloughed workers in Chicago marching in protest over the skyrocketing unemployment.

In time, these passions could become new populist, progressive, or radical movements, intent on sweeping aside both the Democratic and Republican parties they consider the working class's enemy. This pandemic is an ultimatum to those who reject diversity, equity, inclusion, fairness, and equality. It demands that companies think harder and more boldly, but still pragmatically, about the underlying problems the pandemic has exposed, including social disparities and racial inequality. *Beyond Inclusion: Reimagining the Future of Work, Workers, and the Workplace* is a wake-up call for all CEOs who hope not just to survive the pandemic but to thrive in a business world where all the rules have changed.

PREFACE

My name is Shelton Goode, and the book you hold in your hands is the product of numerous years spent writing, talking, obsessing, and, most of all, doing real work with clients and colleagues related to the topic of diversity, equity, inclusion, and culture. Over these years, I've had countless conversations like the ones around which this book is structured. I have worked hand in hand on real client situations as the CEO and President of Icarus Consulting. I tried to crystalize these ideas into a methodology and brought them to life situations. Before that, I spent over a decade as a diversity and inclusion executive for several companies ranging in size from 600 million to 18 billion. The culmination of my experiences helped me to bring these ideas and methods to life on these pages.

A powerful common thread links these challenges. When there is a significant change to make—a change of any type—powerful emotional forces in the organization seem, at first blush, to resist it. Under the surface, however, other psychological effects are also brewing and multiplying. And these forces are potential sources of catalytic strength. Over the past two decades, the leaders I have worked with have been successful because they could look past that initial resistance and tap those sources of power. They also avoided the urge to drown emotional responses to change in favor of more rational arguments. This, in a nutshell, is the fundamental lesson of this book, the "secret recipe" of my consulting practice. Diversity and inclusion are not about counting people. It's about making people count. Positive emotions matter enormously and can energize any organization. People must feel good about what is asked of them—and the only way to increase employee engagement is to help employees attach positive emotions to the (inherently frightening) idea of change.

Another secret is that what leaders first perceive as resistance might be a pace of change that isn't yet visible to the naked eye. The best leaders know that creating a diverse and inclusive company takes real-time and are adept at ferreting out and rewarding what is evolving, rather than throwing their hands in the air and despairing about how their organization is "stuck." The best leaders also know that looking at the organization only at the surface, as a totality, provides an incomplete picture and can consider their company as a collection of subcultures, competing with and cannibalizing each other. There is no such thing as a monolithic culture within any organization; most companies, regardless of size, by definition, are multicultural.

Facing backlash in February over a sweater that looked like blackface, Gucci followed a now-predictable course. Company officials apologized for appearing to mine demeaning imagery from the past, hired a chief diversity officer, and vowed to create multicultural scholarships and a more diverse workforce. Burberry announced similar efforts after it showed a hoodie that looked like a noose the same month, and Prada did the same in 2018 after it had unveiled a line of figurines that also resembled blackface.

This is not just the playbook of the fashion industry. Dozens of companies have sought to deflect controversy over embarrassing missteps or revelations of homogeneous boards and workplaces by launching high-profile initiatives or hiring a person of color as their chief diversity officer.

Research by Dr. Thomas Kochan discovered that companies were spending an estimated $8 billion a year on diversity and inclusion efforts. However, since Trump's election and the emergence of movements like #MeToo and Black Lives Matter, the industry has exploded. A 2019 survey of 234 companies in the S&P 500 found that 63 percent of the chief diversity officers had been hired or promoted to their roles during the past three years. In March 2018, the job site *Indeed* reported that postings for diversity and inclusion professionals had risen 35 percent in the previous two years.

The field of diversity and inclusion shows little sign of waning, given the spike in hiring chief diversity officers or external consultants. The buzzwords "diversity," "equity," and "inclusion" are emblazoned on blogs, books, and conferences—second only to #BlackLivesMatter. Thomson Reuters, a multinational mass media and information firm, even created a Diversity and Inclusion Index to assess the practices of more than 5,000 publicly traded companies globally. Nonetheless, while the business of marketing and targeting diversity and inclusion is flourishing, diversity is not.

People of color who make up nearly 40 percent of the U.S. population remain acutely underrepresented in most influential fields. From 2009 to 2018, the percentage of black law partners increased from 1.7 percent to 1.8 percent. From 1985 to 2016, the proportion of black men in management at U.S. companies with 100 or more employees barely budged from 3 percent to 3.2 percent. People of color held about 16 percent of Fortune 500 board seats in 2018. A 2018 survey of the 15 largest public fashion and apparel companies found that nonwhites had only 11 percent of board seats and that nearly three-quarters of company CEOs were white men. And in the top 200 film releases of 2017, women and people of color accounted for 7.8 percent of writers, 12.6 percent of directors, and 19.8 percent of lead roles.

A look at higher education—where, in fall 2017, 81 percent of full-time professors at degree-granting postsecondary schools were white while just 3 percent were Hispanic, and 4 percent were black—clarifies the forces that allow these disparities to persist. Though the 1960s saw the introduction of affirmative-action policies intended to address the history of slavery followed by centuries of discrimination against people of color, decades of legal challenges have undermined these measures. Since 1978, for example, Regents of the University of California v. Bakke has prohibited companies from using racial quotas or other remedies to address past discrimination.

In recent years, implementing diversity and inclusion programs has been touted as a feel-good exercise that includes gender and sexual orientation to body size. But while we should be concerned about discrimination against any group, the term has become such a catchall that we have lost focus on the original intent of anti-discrimination efforts.

Consequently, many whites now claim they are being disenfranchised as others are afforded undue advantage. A 2019 National Public Radio survey found that 55 percent of white Americans believe that white people are discriminated against, while, tellingly, a lower percentage said they had experienced discrimination. Moreover, renewed calls for diversity are playing out against resurgent white nationalism, a rise in bias crimes, and a president who has denigrated Mexicans, Muslims, and blacks, among other groups.

Although the worsening racial climate appears to power the diversity industry, several studies suggest that these initiatives can make matters worse by triggering racial resentment. Think of the Google engineer who was fired for writing a memo deriding the company's diversity efforts. He filed a class action claiming that Google discriminates against conservative white men before ultimately moving to arbitration.

For diversity and inclusion to become a reality in the nation's workplaces, companies need to do more than recycle costly and ineffectual initiatives. Companies need to analyze metrics related to hiring, pay, promotions, and bonuses along racial and gender lines to detect and disrupt patterns of bias.

Research conducted by the consulting firm Russell Reynolds Associates found that more than half of chief diversity officers do not have the resources or support needed to execute programs and strategies. Only 35 percent had access to company demographic metrics. Russell Reynolds surveyed 1,800-plus company executives and found that diversity and inclusion ranked last on a list of eight potential business priorities.

However, persistent failure appears not to have prompted many companies to change course. Although Google reportedly spent $114 million on its diversity and inclusion efforts, its most recent diversity and inclusion report showed that blacks made up just 3.3 percent of the workforce and held 2.1 percent of tech and 2.6 percent of leadership roles.

Why do companies spend so much to achieve so little? Courts tend to look for symbolic structures of diversity rather than their efficacy. In other words, the diversity apparatus doesn't have to work; it just needs to exist, and it can help shield a company against successful bias lawsuits.

Actual progress won't come without discomfort. It requires company leaders to change their behaviors. Companies must change incentive structures and interrogate their business policies, procedures, processes, and practices.

In the end, diversity and inclusion will not be ushered in by pledges, slogans, or quotas. It can only be achieved once white America has weaned off a prevailing narrative of racial preeminence, which can still be glimpsed in historical stories, film and literature, and racially offensive iconography like blackface. The seeds of this corrosive ideology are planted early, and a paradigm shift will require courageous leadership. Yes, the change will need resources and resolve, but no amount of money will succeed alongside our shared humanity's willful negation.

This book provides a framework for creating a diverse workforce and sustaining an inclusive workplace after the pandemic. The book's secret sauce is based mostly on productive working relationships with countless business leaders—some of them my clients and other individuals who have trusted me with the deepest hopes and fears about their organizations. These individuals have permitted me to share their experiences for two reasons. First and foremost, they wanted me to convey how common and universal leadership challenges are. They wanted me to share some practical ways for dealing with how these changes will affect the future of work, workers, and the workplace.

Chapter one discusses the future of the workplace. In several ways, this chapter provides a baseline or foundation for understanding the mega-trends that will occur in the next decade that will transform work, making it more valuable and meaningful. Additional insight into the pandemic's impact on the future of work, workers, and the workplace is provided by carefully analyzing selected studies.

Chapter two examines the future of work due to many change forces affecting organizations' three deeply connected dimensions: work, workers, and the workplace. The new realities created by these forces of change present business leaders with complex questions to consider—including the ethics around human and machine collaboration, the challenges associated with longer careers, and the uncertainties related to how to hire, develop, and retain the talent needed by companies after the pandemic.

In chapter three, we forecast efforts that companies will take to increase economic inclusion by diversifying suppliers. It envisions the process organizations will use in the future to select, contract, and interact with small vendors and disadvantaged suppliers in a manner that supports and enhances economic inclusion along the supply chain. It predicts organizations' recognition of their supplier base's diversity and sensitivity to the nuances of languages and strategies used to attract prospective vendors. It describes how organizations should attempt to ensure diversity in their procurement processes and enhance the performance of small and disadvantaged businesses owned by women, people of color, veterans, and individuals with a disability.

Chapter four helps business leaders assess whether their organizations have created an optimal environment for diverse leaders' successful performance by addressing the following questions: What can the organization learn from their leaders of color and women who have been successful? What are the factors that are contributing to the success of leaders of color and women?

The chapter will also help leaders pinpoint opportunity areas for recognizing and rewarding top performers within the organization by addressing the following set of questions: How is the organization demonstrating its value and commitment to diversity and inclusion through recognition and reward programs? Do the organization's diversity and inclusion accountability measures have teeth? And lastly, how is the organization rewarding exceptional performers and employees with high potential?

Chapter five predicts steps organizations will have to take to ensure they have a pipeline of diverse talent. The chapter provides a no-BS look at the odds stacked against women and people of color in professional settings, from the wage gap to biases and microaggressions, with actionable takeaways. The chapter looks into a crystal ball and provides the much-needed talent advice guide for CEOs specifically, finally ending the one-size-fits-all approach of large companies that lump employees together into a talent pool and overlook the unique barriers to success for women and people of color.

The chapter acknowledges the "ugly truths" that keep women and people of color from getting the proverbial seat at the table in corporate America: microaggressions, systemic racism, and white privilege.

Chapter six discusses the history of diversity, inclusion training, and its efficacy. The chapter also takes a close look at the backlash against diversity and inclusion training in organizations. The chapter deftly illuminates the phenomenon of "diversity backlash" and helps the reader understand "backlash" as a defensive move that people make when challenged by diversity and inclusion training. Backlash is further characterized by anger, fear, guilt, and behaviors, including argumentation and silence. These behaviors, in turn, function to reinstate white equilibrium and prevent any meaningful dialogue.

Chapter seven forecasts how organizations will leverage employee resource groups (ERGs) in the future. It predicts the efforts organizations will have to take to engage and invest in their employees. It also explores how ERGs can help advance and accelerate companies' diversity, equity, and inclusion efforts.

In chapter eight, we explore some of the ways organizations will leverage their diversity and inclusion councils so that the council will effectively support the organization's diversity and inclusion goals. Several companies' best practices are examined, and we look at how they measure their diversity and inclusion council's ability to support companies' D&I strategy and overall business goals.

Chapter nine covers the business case to transform the corporate workplace culture into a more inclusive environment. The chapter shines a bright light on diversity and inclusion and asks the tough questions about what has been effective and why progress has been so slow. The chapter also highlights some extraordinary success stories and speculates the valuable lessons other organizations need to learn from these case studies.

The chapter argues that despite decades of handwringing, costly initiatives, and uncomfortable conversations, organizations have fallen far short of their goals apart from a few exceptions. It incisively shows the vast gap between the rhetoric of inclusion and tangible achievements. It also starkly predicts that if organizations deliver on the promise of diversity and inclusion, they need to abandon ineffective, costly measures and commit to combatting enduring racial disparities, implicit biases, and systemic inequities.

Chapter ten examines a case study of one company's efforts to create a culture of trust by reducing bias. It covers the organizations' specific actions in shaping, guiding, and sponsoring diversity and inclusion programs and initiatives to increase employee engagement and trust. It also includes methods the CEO put in place to ensure accountability and sustainability in the organization.

Chapter eleven describes how even the most skilled leaders can be challenged during a time of crisis. We analyze two leadership case studies in the chapter. The first case study focuses on a CEO known for his systematic approach to problem-solving who must act quickly in response to the crisis. The second involves a CEO who chose not to wait until the legal strategy was finalized before implementing several sweeping culture and organizational changes.

Chapter twelve explores that in organizations, everything happens through communication and, more specifically, conversations. Whether it is a manager conveying performance expectations to an employee, checking for understanding of an assignment, recognizing someone for a recent accomplishment, or laying out a strategy for penetrating a new market, a courageous conversation is at the center of it.

Chapter thirteen discusses the chief diversity officer's (CDO) role in reimagining the future of work, workers, and the workplace. Diversity and inclusion experts have consistently emphasized the importance of assigning accountability for guiding the organization's strategic diversity and inclusion efforts. According to these same practitioners, appointing a chief diversity officer (CDO) is crucial to ensuring an organization's diversity and inclusion strategy. This person can ensure that managers in the organization are trained to create inclusive work environments and lead diverse work teams. Moreover, chief diversity officers can advocate that the organization make managers' performance ratings and compensation dependent, in part, on their success in achieving diversity and inclusion goals.

Chapter fourteen concludes the book by discussing the challenges ahead for work, workers, and the workplace. It describes realistic short-term and long-term goals and challenges business leaders to set and stretch the company to thrive in the post-pandemic world.

ACKNOWLEDGMENTS

From the length of these acknowledgments, it may read more like an Academy Award acceptance speech than a simple thank-you. I know my editor is rolling her eyes because she is always counseling me to be brief, but I must thank the many people who helped me bring this vision to reality. Whether it was emotional support, interviews, editorial help, research, or supplying the thousands of pieces of information that make a book like this possible, I could not have accomplished it without the people listed here.

While the final product's responsibility is my own, I am indebted to numerous scholars and diversity and inclusion professionals for their helpful comments and critical suggestions on various aspects of the book. This final product's journey has been informed mainly by my professional experiences and personal perspectives presented here and input from several top thought leaders on managing diversity in companies and communities.

There would be no book, of course, if not for the family, friends, and professional colleagues who were generous and brave enough to share their personal views on diversity in America with me. This kind of honesty and courage is a lot to ask for and even harder to repay. The practical insights helped me write several chapters. In no order, these include the following contributors: Jim Rogers, Jennifer Brown, Steve Paskoff, and Bill Proudman. Special thanks go out to my wife, Pamela Goode, who inspired me to write this book and offered valuable insights and encouragement.

I presented an earlier version of the book to some of my former students from Troy University, Georgia State, and Duke University. Their critique and feedback helped shape several of my conclusions. As an adjunct professor at several colleges and universities, I have the privilege of interacting with some of the brightest and most energetic students I have encountered in my twenty years of teaching. They forced me to rethink several ideas, and they constantly challenged my underlying assumptions about the concept of diversity in America.

I am especially indebted to my friends and colleagues I have had the privilege of working and laughing with. Over the years, my family, friends, and colleagues have helped me hone my ideas and improve my writing and teaching diversity management. As a result, I have contributed more fully to developing a new generation of diversity management leaders.

Thanks to my client organizations. While consulting and facilitating diversity and inclusion strategic planning sessions, I had the opportunity to work with some of the most enlightened leaders in the country.

Every author needs practical help in addition to inspiration and encouragement. I am blessed to have had so many publishing professionals who dedicated many hours to this project. Betty Waiters deserves special mention for her meticulous editing of the manuscript and critical feedback throughout the final draft preparation. The final stages of permissions, copyediting, and meeting the publisher's deadlines would have been impossible without her help. I also thank her for her critical comments on sections of this book and on related research work.

A special shout-out goes to the team at Outskirts Press, who provided critical counsel during the hectic process of finalizing this book for publication. The entire team provided me much-needed guidance and professional expertise. I was thrilled to work with this team of professionals who often used their humor, warmth, and knowledge to guide me through the often stressful and confusing process of publishing a book.

Special appreciation goes to my team at Icarus Consulting, whose expert and sensitive advice enhanced both the text's readability and value.

Finally, I would like to thank my family, my pride and joy, and whom this book is dedicated to. I love you all.

SECTION ONE: REIMAGINE WORK

CHAPTER I
A CRISIS IS A TERRIBLE THING TO WASTE

Introduction

This chapter discusses the future of the work. In several ways, this chapter provides a baseline or foundation for understanding the megatrends in the next decade that will transform work, making it more valuable and meaningful. Additional insight into the intersection of work and diversity is provided through leadership interviews and case studies.

Two additional significant findings emerged from this investigation. First, some organizations have repackaged their traditional equal employment opportunity and affirmative action programs. These organizations have not, and it would seem, fully embraced the broader concept of diversity and inclusion. Second, some organizations do not address some of the most basic and traditional dimensions of diversity, such as race, ethnicity, or gender. This raises several fundamental and intriguing questions about diversity and inclusion programs and their purpose.

It is too soon to say with any precision how the pandemic will shape the future of work. It seems the changes will strengthen the public healthcare system, making it more affordable and easier to access. There may be new laws to address the disparity between salaried employees who enjoy paid benefits and those who rely on freelance work to get by. Perhaps scientists and other experts will be more closely heeded when they speak of climate change and its dire effects. However, there is no doubt that the pandemic's political, economic, and psychological effects on workers and the workplace will be transformative and long-lasting. Not necessarily in partisan terms—those red versus blue lines seem too deeply entrenched, but rather in the way government touches our everyday lives. If this country's history holds to course, this crisis will serve as a platform for change like the ones before it.

To understand why it helps to go back to the country's founding. After throwing off a monarchy, the Constitution's architects were deeply wary of creating a strong, centralized seat of power. They designed a federal government that will be difficult to bring about bold changes on a national scale. According to James Madison, "In framing a government which is to be administered by men over men, the great difficulty lies in this: 'you must first enable the government to control the governed. And in the next place oblige it to control itself.'" Add to that structural impediment the human tendency to put off difficult choices, and the result is institutional inertia that tends to favor the political status quo.

Crises Breed Change

It takes something dramatic to shake things up in this country. Take Social Security, which may be the most popular program born of the Depression, and the vast expansion of the federal government that followed. An "old age" pension was part of the 1912 Progressive Party platform, the goals laid out by Bull Moose candidate Theodore Roosevelt in his unsuccessful bid to reclaim the White House. Yet it wasn't until August 1935, after the economic ravages of the country's near-collapse left millions of Americans destitute, that President Franklin D. Roosevelt signed the Social Security Act into law. It wasn't like the idea was born in crisis, but its implementation became more feasible and urgent. Other crises had such horrific consequences; they, too, overrode the inclination toward governmental inaction. The outbreak of World War II underlined the dangers of America's insular foreign policy. The Great Recession showed, again, the dangers of unbridled financial speculation. The Katrina Hurricane resulted in remedies that compensated for failings, and in some instances, overcame long-standing bureaucratic and political intransigence. The Boston Marathon Bombing forged a network of international alliances to prevent further terrorist attacks. The 9/11 attacks highlighted weaknesses in the country's domestic security programs. They resulted in the Homeland Security Department's creation and a vast government surveillance program and those cumbersome security lines—to thwart further hijackings. The Financial Crisis resulted in regulations to provide stronger financial oversight and put a brake on risky investments.

If we think some things could have been done better and should have been done better, we tend to make changes. Put another way, crises create opportunities to do something different and better. They don't end partisanship, but they push aside some of the impediments to big ideas. In the shorter term, at the ballot box, political crises inevitably result in a voter referendum on the one man, and they have all been men that Americans look to for leadership, the United States president. Some fare better than others.

Abraham Lincoln was reelected during the Civil War. Herbert Hoover was tossed from the White House amid the Great Depression. Roosevelt was returned to office three times during the Depression and World War II. The major tumult surrounding September 11 and the great recession had largely receded for Presidents George W. Bush and Obama, respectively, by the time they faced voters. Both won second terms. American workers rendered their verdict on President Trump in November 2020, and the impact, like the long-term impact of the pandemic, is unknowable at this time. Nevertheless, whatever happens on election day, changes will come to America, and they will endure well after the pandemic has ended. It is one certainty in these gravely uncertain times.

Economic Impact of the Pandemic

Crises like pandemics, economic collapses, natural disasters, social unrests, financial collapses, and world wars have at times ended up reordering societies throughout history—shrinking the gap between the rich and the poor or empowering the working class. The Black Death helped end feudalism. The Great Depression helped lead to the New Deal. Extreme economic inequality has never shrunk in a meaningful way without a major crisis.

The coronavirus pandemic is not on the order of the plague, but it's hitting the country during a period of agitation about worsening inequality. Already, it has unveiled how precarious life is for many people of color, causing some to protest. How employers and policymakers respond could improve work in the United States for the long term or worsen existing problems.

Pandemics are a social shock that gives workers more leverage to demand concessions from their employers. Crises like the pandemic reveal what is already broken or in the process of breaking. They are attacks on a socioeconomic system that force corporate and political leaders to address the underlying issues and make things happen collectively.

The United States is distinctive among wealthy countries in its lack of worker protections like nationwide paid sick leave, paid family leave, and universal health insurance. Many employers expect workers to be on call around the clock for both high and low-wage earners. Companies typically put shareholders and investors first, ahead of employees, customers, and communities.

But the coronavirus pandemic has shown the flaw in that logic: workers' well-being is the foundation for everything else.

Already, Congress has given some workers paid sick and family leaves for the first time. Companies have started to offer paid leave, subsidized childcare, and flexible work schedules. Millions of Americans are working from home, which could reset workplace practices even when they return. People recognize the importance of many jobs that have long been undervalued, like janitors, childcare providers, teachers, health aides, delivery people, and grocery store workers.

There is no guarantee of a positive outcome for workers; it depends mainly on the next twelve to eighteen months' choices. Even if some past crises have ultimately given workers more leverage, the opposite could be true this time, given the high unemployment levels. The American response has been less generous than countries like Demark, Britain, and Germany who are paying large portions of wages while people aren't working so that companies can keep them employed.

Nonetheless, if more Americans perceive that the system has fundamentally failed them, experts say it could lead to widespread demands for better protection. Millions of people have suddenly lost their jobs, along with their health insurance and other benefits. The partisan disagreement has slowed government assistance, and many workers are excluded from the support Congress has authorized. In many ways, the pandemic exacerbates inequality: staying home or seeking health care is easier for the rich than the poor. Research by the CDC confirms that the COVID-19 virus is disproportionately impacting African Americans and Latinos.

The country has experienced a reduction in the economic inequality gap since the pandemic outbreak because of the stock market. Still, there are potential longer-term effects for the working-class poor. The poor will only be better off if the pandemic crisis results in long-term and substantial policy changes.

Pandemics, Wars, and Workers' Rights

When the bubonic plague killed an estimated 30 percent to 60 percent of the European population in the mid-1300s, it became an extreme example of how pandemics can rebalance societies. Ultimately, it helped serfdom in parts of Europe. Since so many people died, labor became scarce, and workers had more sway with landowning lords. Many peasants could, for the first time, own land or move for opportunities. It's embedded in a more extensive series of economic shifts in Western Europe. Still, the Black Death's economic impact cannot be overstated because it was a shock to labor supply and demand.

It appears the coronavirus pandemic will be nowhere near as deadly as the plague. But even a relatively small-scale shock like this reopens the realm of the possible. Six centuries later, in the United States, a growing labor movement before World War I culminated, after the war, in stronger unions, widespread strikes, and the end of the twelve-hour workday. In addition to the Spanish flu pandemic of 1918, the war resulted in a shortage of working men and so many of these jobs opened to women for the first time. In turn, women gained more power to argue for higher wages and the right to vote.

The Great Depression led to the creation of America's safety net with the New Deal. The only time the United States had universal public childcare was during World War II, when the country needed to make it possible for women to work while men were at war. The process hasn't been smooth or without disagreement and setbacks. Many of the gains won by the labor movement in the 1920s were eventually reversed. New Deal policies faced significant political resistance from critics who said they raised the deficit too much and veered into socialism. From the start, those policies excluded women and people of color.

A crisis on its own has not been enough to start a labor movement, but if a movement has been simmering, a crisis can make it boil over. For example, the conditions weren't right for workers to revolt during the 2008 recession, but this time they might be. We have had more than a decade of agitating, planning, and think-tanking on the need to solve inequality and workplace imbalance problems. So, these ideas are more prominently on the plan because of the pandemic crisis.

A Once-in-a-Generation Opportunity

Since the start of the COVID-19 pandemic, workers in the United States have organized strikes and protests asking for protections like hazard pay, gloves, and sick leave. Congress has passed policies, albeit temporary ones, that would have been politically unthinkable before now, including paid leave and direct payments to individuals. Congress has introduced bills to make some of the benefits permanent. Some companies have permanently given workers paid sick leave. Other companies have offered paid leave but made it temporary.

This is a once-in-a-generation opportunity. Corporate leaders and policymakers need to focus on restructuring the economy in a way that rebalances power between workers and their employers. For hourly workers, the importance of paid sick leave has become more evident. Just one in three service-sector workers have it. According to research from the University of California, a survey of hourly workers in California found that 60 percent of workers felt compelled to work when sick. The COVID-19 crisis is an opportunity for change because public health care is so evident and strong. We've never had such evidence for how this impacts communities and the country. It's not just the corporate bottom line.

For white-collar, salaried workers, coronavirus is, in a way, offering a natural experiment by forcing companies to let people work from home, create their schedules, and spend more time with their families. It could convince companies that constant face time is unnecessary. My extensive experience as an HR executive leads me to believe that part of why companies haven't changed is its shift in mindset to not focus on hours and be instantly responsive to a text at 9 p.m. It's a shift to working on the assumption that employees should decide when, where, and how they do their work.

An abrupt shift to working from home with schools closed is in no way a perfect experiment; people may feel less in control of their lives than ever, and most have no childcare. But now, it's forcing companies to innovate. It's no longer whether they want to. Companies must think of new ways of working, and sometimes a crisis can be a platform for change.

The policy changes that have already happened in response to the COVID-19 virus have come very quickly. They have illuminated how relatively easy it would be for workers to have these rights—employers or policymakers would just have to say so. It may be hard for companies to take back benefits, even those they have said are temporary. You can't put the Genie back in the bottle once you clarify that these things are within the company's capacity to do; workers' baseline expectations change. That was true of the New Deal, the Great Society, and Obamacare. The pandemic crisis has clearly shown that companies can do a lot more than they thought they could do. They are proving once again that crises are a useful reminder, even in a tragic kind of way—of what we could do if we wanted to or had the will to do it.

The Future of Work

Since the pandemic, the country seems to appreciate the value of on-demand or "gig" job workers more than ever—especially jobs like delivery couriers, cashiers, and customer service reps, who have become a lifeline for people stuck at home. In some cities on lockdown, delivery workers have been classified as "essential." That is thrown into sharp contrast to the nature of their work and their lack of protections like health care, sick leave, workers' compensation, and stable pay. The country is paying unprecedented attention to gig workers.

We are absolutely at a fork in the road. The conversation is at a turning point now, where we're shifting from talking about the future of work to realizing it's not about the future. It must change right now. Benefits like unemployment insurance arose in the 1930s in response to the Great Depression crisis. Employer-sponsored health insurance came later, as did federal requirements to give employees time off for family and medical leave. These systems provide a safety net to people who work, but they reflected the needs of a twentieth-century workforce when far more people worked for one employer for most of their careers. Today, tens of millions of people with nontraditional work arrangements are left out.

Some parts of the workforce have gone without traditional benefits for decades, long before "the gig economy" existed: house cleaners, nannies, plumbers, electricians, tutors, and even real estate agents, many of whom are self-employed or lack a full-time employer who would administer benefits. There's a lot of commonality between driving for Uber and someone working as a tutor or a subcontracted worker providing cleaning services for Google. These workers have slightly different work arrangements, but their inability to access benefits is similar.

When the economy ground to a halt in 2008 after the Financial Crisis, most people without W-2 jobs didn't qualify for unemployment benefits because they couldn't claim an employer who had paid unemployment taxes. Now, legislators have temporarily changed that policy, allowing freelancers and self-employed individuals to claim unemployment benefits for the first time. I believe this can be attributed to the increased visibility of gig workers that came from the pandemic. It's raised awareness that if you provide unemployment insurance benefits only to the people who have traditional employers, you will leave tens of millions of people.

The increased visibility means the public may finally be tuned in enough to force even broader regulatory changes. For the first time since the gig economy has become a household term, around 2009 or so, legislators are thinking very actively that the benefits being provided are not just going to employees but also self-employed individuals and those who are part of the gig economy. This is a clear example of a crisis being used to bring about social change.

There have been previous attempts at so-called portable benefits, which are tied to individuals rather than the corporations they work for. In 2018, the National Domestic Workers Alliance piloted Alia. This program pools clients' voluntary contributions that domestic workers can then redeem for disability insurance, accident insurance, life insurance, or paid time off. Clients make small, recurring payments—the recommended amount is about $5 per house cleaning, and workers can access their accrued funds in an online dashboard.

There hasn't been much urgency around providing these benefits until very recently. As more portable benefits are emerging, it will be essential to use the momentum to catch on. With the coronavirus crisis, I think we're going to see public opinion change very quickly. A large part of what we needed was visibility. We have that now.

Legislation has started to emerge that would address some of those needs. Senator Mark Warner (D-Virginia) reintroduced a bill in February 2020 that would earmark $20 million for states and nonprofits to offer benefits like workers' comp, disability coverage, and retirement savings to people without traditional employers. The coronavirus is underscoring how vulnerable some workers are without access to a safety net. This crisis demonstrates why we need a portable benefits system for gig workers, independent contractors, and other contingent workers. In May 2020, Philadelphia became the first city in the country to pilot its portable benefits program, which affords domestic workers up to forty hours of paid time off each year.

And while companies remain unlikely to offer benefits freely, some gig workers find themselves with more leverage than ever. In March 2020, Instacart announced that it would hire 300,000 more workers to meet demand. Workers could secure better treatment, including the promise of protective supplies like masks and hand sanitizers and a higher raised tip amount. Workers for Shipt, a Target-owned grocery delivery company, followed suit within a week.

Significantly, you see more of this type of activism at this moment than we've seen in the past. Workers feel they're in a strong enough position to make these types of demands. Still, even if Instacart met all its workers' needs, it wouldn't do much for the millions of other workers with similar types of jobs. If you're giving workers benefits while preserving outdated business models, then you're allowing companies to get away with not providing protections to long-overdue workers.

Some states are pushing for companies to reclassify their workers as employees, not contractors. California recently passed legislation that defines Uber drivers, DoorDash delivery workers, and similar roles as employees; in New York, a court recently ruled that Postmates workers cannot be classified as independent contractors despite strong opposition from many companies.

Think About This

The coronavirus crisis may divert attention away from those recent regulatory decisions, but I argue that long-term change will ultimately require legislation. We see temporary solutions, but that invites the broader question. Are we going to be able, as a country, to take some of these temporary solutions and make them more permanent? If that push for more durable solutions doesn't happen now, while public sympathies for gig workers are exceedingly high, then it may never happen at all.

CHAPTER 2

THE BEGINNING OF TOMORROW

Introduction

It's the first day after the first dose of the COVID-19 vaccine has been administered. Now what? The pandemic brought with it forces of change that have affected three significant work dimensions: the work itself, who does the work, and the workplace, or better yet, where work is done. To be successful, companies must have a new business plan, not only for today but for a decade from now.

This chapter examines the future of work due to many forces of change affecting an organization's three deeply connected dimensions: the work, the workforce, and the workplace. The new realities created by these forces of change present business leaders with complex questions to consider, including the ethics around human and machine collaboration, the challenges associated with longer careers, and the uncertainties related to hiring, developing, and retaining the talent needed after the pandemic.

What does the future of work mean? Much discussion has focused on artificial intelligence and whether robots will take our jobs, but implicit technologies are only one aspect of the massive shift underway. To understand what's going on and, more importantly, what we can do about it, it's essential to consider multiple converging mega-trends and how they are already fundamentally changing all aspects of work—with implications for companies, communities, and the country.

Reimagining the Future of Work

This isn't the first time organizations have entirely changed the cultural idea of work. In the preindustrial economy, work was synonymous with craftsmanship, the creation of products, or the delivery of complete outcomes. The craftsman took end-to-end responsibility for delivering the product or result—a cobbler, for instance, would do everything from measuring the customer's feet to making final adjustments in the finished pair of shoes. The industrial revolution changed this conception of work, as industrialists realized that products could be manufactured faster and cheaper if end-to-end processes were atomized into repeatable tasks in which workers (and later, machines) could specialize. The notion of a "job" became that of a collection of tasks not necessarily related to each other, rather than an integrated set of actions that delivered a complete product or outcome.

Now, as we step rapidly into the post-pandemic revolution, we once again appear to be redefining work to create valuable human-machine collaborations, shifting our understanding of work from task completion to problem-solving and managing human relationships. Technology has already begun to change the way we organize tasks into jobs. For example, robotics and robotic process automation have transformed manufacturing and warehouses, and digital reality technologies help workers transcend limitations of distance and who is assigned to which task. Research suggests that labor division between people and machines is expected to shift toward machines, especially for repetitive and routine tasks. The U.S. Chamber of Commerce indicates that this shift could eliminate upward of 14 percent and disrupt 32 percent of today's jobs.

However, there is evidence that these technologies could be used to augment the workforce's efforts rather than replace them. In fact, in a 2018 report, the World Economic Forum projected that while nearly 1 million jobs may be lost, another 1.75 million will be gained. The jobs of the future are expected to be more machine-powered and data-driven than in the past. Still, they will likely require human skills in problem-solving, communication, listening interpretation, and design. As machines take over repeatable tasks and the work people do become less routine, roles could be redefined to marry technology with human skills and advanced expertise in interpretation and service. Technologies such as design thinking can help organizations define roles that incorporate the new types of capabilities, skills, activities, and practices needed to get the work done.

To make all of this happen successfully, organizations will need to change how they think of work and develop the training their workforce needs to take on these new roles. Otherwise, these same companies could find themselves weighed down, trying to apply legacy concepts and skills to the new and quickly emerging world of human-machine integration.

The Future Workplace

For Milton Friedman, it was simple, "There is one and only one social responsibility of business," the Nobel economist wrote in 1970: to "engage in activities designed to increase its profits. Companies must obey the law. But beyond that, their job is to make money for shareholders."

And Friedman's view prevailed, at least in the United States. Over the following decades, "shareholder primacy" became conventional business wisdom. In 1997, the influential Business Roundtable (BRT), an association of the chief executive officers of nearly 200 of America's most prominent companies, enshrined the philosophy in a formal statement of corporate purpose. "The paramount duty of management and boards of directors is to the corporation's stockholders," the group declared. "The interests of other stakeholders are relevant as a derivative of the duty to stockholders."

Times change. On August 19, 2020, the Business Roundtable announced a new purpose for the corporation and tossed the old one into the dustbin. The original statement is 300 words long, and shareholders aren't mentioned by name until the end of the document. Before that, the group refers to creating "value for customers," "investing in employees," fostering "diversity and inclusion," "dealing fairly and ethically with suppliers," "supporting the communities," and "protecting the environment."

The new statement results from a yearlong reexamination that began with a testy dinner attended by a group of journalistic critics and involved a comprehensive survey of CEOs, academics, NGOs, and political leaders who focused on the fundamental questions well capitalism is serving society. The statement confirms that something fundamental and profound has changed how CEOs approach their jobs in the past few years.

If you were to trace the history of that change, you might start with the speech Bill Gates gave in Davos in 2008, in his last year of full-time service at Microsoft, calling for a new "creative capitalism." As Gates told the World Economic Forum, "the genius of capitalism" lies in its ability to "[harness] self-interest in helpful and sustainable ways." But its benefits inevitably skew to those who can pay. "To provide rapid improvement for the poor," he said, "we need a system that draws in innovators and businesses in a far better way. . . Such a system would have a twin mission: making profits and improving lives for those who don't fully benefit from market forces."

Over the next few years, Harvard Business School professor Michael Porter began pushing what he called "shared value capitalism" and "conscious capitalism." Salesforce CEO, Marc Benioff, wrote a book on "compassionate capitalism;" Lynn Forester de Rothschild, CEO of family investment company E.L. Rothschild, started organizing for "inclusive capitalism;" and the free-enterprise-championing Conference Board research group sounded a call for "sustaining capitalism." It seemed capitalism was desperately in need of a modifier.

Setting all this grammatical soul-searching in motion was a global financial convulsion. The financial crisis of the late 2000s shook the foundations of the sprawling market economy. It bared some of its uglier consequences: an enormous and widening gulf between the über-rich and the working poor, between the ample rewards of capital and the stagnating wages of labor, between the protected few and the vulnerable many. Moreover, compounding these inequities was a sweep of disruptive business technologies that began to come of age in the wake of the crisis—from digitization to robotics to artificial intelligence (A.I.) and that made vulnerable workers feel even more so.

The reaction against "the system" was broad and shocking in scale— particularly among younger people. A 2016 Harvard study found that 51 percent of U.S. respondents between the ages of eighteen and twenty-nine did not support capitalism; one-third, meanwhile, favored a turn to socialism. A 2018 Gallup poll of the same cohort found a similar rejection—only 45 percent viewed capitalism positively, a 23-percentage point drop from 2010 when Americans were still in the murky shadow of the Great Recession. Even a sizable chunk of Republicans was suddenly wary of the free market, other polls suggested.

The system's rejection manifested in the 2016 Brexit vote when the British masses flouted corporate and political leaders' collective wisdom. It was there in plain view during the bruising U.S. presidential election, when the leading Republican, Donald Trump, attacked the globalization and free trade that had driven U.S. business growth for three-quarters of a century—and as Democrats nearly drove socialist Bernie Sanders to the top of their ticket.

Capitalism, at least the kind practiced by large global corporations, was under assault from all sides, and CEOs were getting the message loud and clear. In December 2016, after the presidential election, Fortune assembled roughly 100 big-company CEOs in Rome, at the encouragement of Pope Francis, and spent a day in working-group deliberations on how the private sector could address global social problems. The group proposed ways that business could help reach the billions of people in the world who lacked essential financial services, support the effort to fight climate change, expand training programs for those whose jobs were threatened by technological change, and provide critical community health services to the half-billion people who had no access to health and medical care.

In a very un-Milton Friedman way, the gathering aimed to maximize not shareholder value but rather a social impact. And many of the CEOs seemed genuinely eager to use their business platforms to make a difference. However, I believe the main reason was that, in general, CEOs were worried public support for the system they have operated is in danger of disappearing.

What's driving this fear isn't just an ominous "what if" but also an outspoken "who." Public interest in corporate responsibility is unusually high: A July 2020 survey of 1,026 adults for Fortune by polling firm New Paradigm Strategy Group found that nearly three-quarters (72 percent) agree that public companies should be "mission-driven" as well as focused on shareholders and customers. Today, many Americans (64 percent) say a company's "primary purpose" should include "making the world better" in addition to making money for shareholders.

Another force that is genuinely driving this newfound social activism is employees. Younger workers expect even more from their company on this front. For example, according to the Fortune/NP Strategy poll, more than half of Americans overall (56 percent) say CEOs should take a stance on public issues; support for such action is overwhelming among those ages twenty-five to forty-four. Millennials may be driving the change more than anyone—and, more importantly, they are choosing to work at companies that are driving change too. Among those aged twenty-five to thirty-four in the Fortune/NP Strategy poll, 80 percent say they want to work for "engaged companies."

In that light, it's perhaps no wonder that Salesforce's Benioff publicly took on a "religious liberties" law in Indiana that he viewed as discriminating against gay people. Or that Bank of America CEO Brian Moynihan publicly objected when the legislature in North Carolina, the bank's home base, passed a bill limiting transgender access to public bathrooms. Or that Delta CEO Ed Bastian battled with his home-state Georgia legislature when he discontinued a discount program for the National Rifle Association. Or that Merck CEO Kenneth Frazier withdrew from President Trump's advisory council after the President's equivocal comments about the Charlottesville riots. In my view, the CEOs in each case took courageous moral stands, but it's also likely their workforces and a good chunk of their customer bases—were rooted in support.

That said, based on my experience as a chief diversity officer (CDO) for several companies, I can confidently state that none of these actions would have happened a decade earlier. When faced with a controversial social issue that didn't directly affect the bottom line, the standard CEO response was to stay quiet and insist that all his or her direct reports do the same.

Of course, not everyone sees this new social consciousness on the part of business as an authentic change—or even necessarily a good one. Several chief diversity officers I interviewed for this book shared their first-hand observations.

For example, one CDO stated, "I see the change. It has become socially unacceptable for a company or a rich person not to be doing good. But I do not see many CEOs asking the question, 'What can I do to make the world better?'"

A CDO of a publicly-traded energy company added, "But what many are failing to do is ask, 'What have I done that may be drowning out any of the good acts I'm doing? For example, the tax bill supported by my company resulted in the lion's share of the benefits going to corporations and increasing the income inequality underlying many social disparities and problems.'"

A CDO of a large financial institution argues, "What I see are well-meaning activities that are virtuous side hustles. While key activities of their business are relatively undisturbed... many of the companies are focused on doing better but less attentive to doing less harm."

These observations may be accurate. But given the immense power large companies exercise in society, the new social consciousness of business surely should be a step in the right direction. At a time when the nation's political leadership is tied in knots, more interested in fighting partisan battles than in uniting to solve public problems, some corporate leaders are trying to fill the vacuum.

Next-Generation Workforce

Not only have workforce demographics changed over the last thirty years—collectively making the workforce older and more racially and ethnically diverse, but the very social contract between companies and their employees has altered dramatically as well. Companies now have a broad continuum of options for finding workers, from hiring traditional full-time employees, partnering with employment agencies through managed services agreements, securing independent contractors, allying with gig workers, outsourcing, and crowdsourcing. These newer workforce options are available to solve problems, get work done, and help company leaders build more flexible and agile organizations. Alternative workers are growing in number; currently, according to the Society of Human Resource Management, approximately 35 percent of the U.S. workforce is in supplemental, temporary, project, or contract-based work. This percentage is expected to increase. For example, the freelance workforce is expected to grow faster (8.1 percent) than the total full-time workforce (2.6 percent).

As labor-sourcing options increase, it opens the possibility for more efficiency and creativity in composing an organization's workforce. But with more options often comes more complexity. Companies will have to consider how roles are crafted when pairing humans with machines and their human workforce arrangement. What type(s) of employment is best suited to ensure the creativity, passion, and skill sets needed for the work at hand? Orchestrating this sophisticated use of different workforce segments might require new workforce planning and hiring models. It will fundamentally change the view of the employee life cycle from the traditional "attract, develop, and retain" model to one where the key questions are how organizations should access, develop, and engage workforces of all types.

Organizations have an opportunity to optimize each type of talent relationship's organizational benefits while also providing meaningful and engaging options for a wide variety of worker needs and motivations. However, making the most of the opportunity will require a complete rethinking of talent models in a way that allows organizations to carefully match workers' motivations and skills with the organization's work needs.

The Need for A New Talent Management Model

Organizations have long thought of talent management as attracting, developing, and retaining top talent. As new, alternative work arrangements come on the scene, I predict that next-generation talent management models will focus on:

- **Access**

Next-generation models will address how companies tap into capabilities and skills across their internal and external talent landscape. This includes sourcing from internal and external talent marketplaces and leveraging and mobilizing full-time and contingent workers.

- **Develop**

Future talent management models will address how organizations provide employees with the broadest and most meaningful training and development range. This includes work experiences integrated into the flow of their work, careers, and personal lives.

- **Engage**

Talent management models for the future workforce will have to figure out how organizations interact with individual employees and support business teams. This includes multidirectional careers in, across, and outside the company and for business leaders and teams, providing insights to improve productivity and impact while taking advantage of new teaming and working ways.

Workplace: Rethinking Where Work Gets Done

As the "who" and "what" of work shift, so does the workplace. Physical proximity was once required for people to get work done, but the advent of digital communication, collaboration platforms, digital reality technologies, and societal and marketplace changes have allowed for and created the opportunity for more distributed teams. Organizations can now manage various options as they reimagine workplaces, from the more traditional co-located workplaces to those entirely distributed and dependent on virtual interactions.

Again, changing the physical workplace should not be seen merely as an opportunity to increase efficiency or reduce real estate costs. Workplace culture is highly connected to both innovation and business results, and as teams become more distributed, organizations might need to rethink how they foster both culture and team connections.

The importance of these connections should not be understated. For example, in previous generations, people would spend decades and even their entire careers in the same organization. In those cases, the sense of membership reinforced employees' identities and their psychological health. This will require more intentional efforts to create connections and community as workplaces become more virtual and filled with more contingent workers.

Work in the Future Will Need to Be More Valuable and Meaningful

Shifts in work, the workforce, and the workplace are deeply interrelated. Changes in one dimension can have significant consequences for workers and employers that have not been considered before.

What the future of work ultimately looks like isn't a foregone conclusion. Organizations are at a crossroads in redefining what it means to work, being an employer, contributing value, and managing talent in newfound ways. The purpose will bring the future into focus. Companies can choose to use advances in technology merely to drive more efficiency and cost reduction or consider more deeply how to harness these trends and increase value and meaning across the board—for business, customers, and workers. Companies that take a narrow approach will put themselves at risk.

To succeed, organizations will need to take a broader view and imagine the possibilities to manage work, the workforce, and the workplace to increase value and meaning while taking advantage of efficiency opportunities. Companies will need to take three actions to direct the forces of change profitably:

- **Plan**—Organizations will need to reimagine future possibilities by leveraging industry-specific data analytics and insights to define the organization's aspirations, ambitions, and strategies for transforming the workforce for the future. Companies will also need to set goals for the future of work beyond cost and efficiency, including value and meaning.

- **Compose**—Companies will need to analyze and redesign work, workforce, and workplace options that take advantage of the value of automation, alternative talent sources, and collaborative workplaces.

- **Activate**—Organizations will need to align organization, leadership, and workforce development programs to access skills, develop next-generation experiences, and engage the future workforce in long-term relationships and train business leaders in new ways of working. To do these things well, we, as employers, should activate the workforce and use technology in ways that generate broad and valuable benefits for organizations and society.

Think About This

In this chapter, we looked into a crystal ball and predicted the forces of change that will drive the evolution of work, workers, and the workplace; we also offer a perspective on how organizations should begin to respond to these new emerging challenges. Organizations today appear to have an unprecedented window of opportunity to shape what ultimately becomes the future of work.

CHAPTER 3

INCREASING ECONOMIC INCLUSION BY DIVERSIFYING SUPPLIERS

Introduction

This chapter forecasts efforts that companies will take to increase economic inclusion by diversifying suppliers. It envisions the process organizations will use in the future to select, contract, and interact with small vendors and disadvantaged suppliers in a manner that supports and enhances economic inclusion along the supply chain. It gauges organization's recognition of the diversity of its potential supplier base and its sensitivity to the nuances of languages and strategies used to attract prospective vendors. It describes how organizations attempt to ensure diversity in their procurement processes and enhance the performance of small and disadvantaged businesses owned by women, people of color, and veterans.

The More Things Change

One of the things that I am trying hard to eliminate is the term 'supplier diversity.' I think it is out of date. At one point, wealth and jobs were created in the supply chain, but that has changed. According to Forbes's research, the percentage of jobs created in financial services, professional services, and technology is now 40 percent of our economy. Since this is the case, companies need to make sure that women and people of color participate in the economy where wealth and jobs are created. Pigeon-holing small, disadvantaged, and diverse suppliers in supply chain management, construction, and commodities, while white men are the heads of hedge funds, private equity, and investment banks, is a clear and present danger to the economy.

Today's companies are just not focused on this. They are used to how diversity used to be talked about forty years ago and haven't transitioned. The amount of money and wealth created in private equity aligns with the amount of power and influence one has. Companies should ensure that women and people of color are also included in the economy where wealth and jobs are created. In 1967, Dr. King said, "I cannot see how the Negro will be liberated from the crushing weight of poor education, squalled housing, and economic strangulation until he is integrated with power into every level of American life." And that is where we are failing with supplier diversity. Women and people of color are being left out of opportunities to accumulate wealth and power.

Companies must move beyond supplier diversity and do a better job of keeping track of their spending by category. Companies need to track all their spending by category. They need to track mainly how much they spend with women-owned and minority professional services companies, advertising agencies, financial services companies, and public relations firms—places where influence and power are today.

Most companies look at total revenue being spent and how much goes to firms owned by women, people of color, veterans, or differently-abled, but don't consider spending by category. The problem with only looking at total spending is that it can skew the results. For example, company A spent $50 million on investment banking fees in a year with zero dollars going to women or people of color. Company B gave a $500-million contract for desktop computers to a women-owned wholesaler who buys them from IBM and sells them to you at a small mark-up. There was a significant revenue in both cases but little in profit or even fewer jobs. That is a huge mistake in how companies keep track of spending with diverse suppliers. This needs to be transformed to see wealth and jobs created in communities of color.

Very few companies track their spending by category and race. I often talk to CEOs who boast about their use of minority firms for catering and janitorial work. But when I look at their board of directors, I find they favor people with experience as venture capitalists, hedge fund managers, private equity managers, investment bankers, and the heads of law firms because that's where the wealth, power, and jobs are found. I interviewed several CEOs to determine how to challenge the status quo. According to the CEO of a major energy company,

"I have found works in changing the mindset are first to articulate the case that my job as the CEO is to help the company publicly declares values. Almost every company has made a public commitment to diversity and inclusion. It's on their websites and annual reports. They talk about how important it is. My job as the CEO is to help make sure we do what we say we're going to do and live the values we say we care about. I believe that I am not doing my job if I don't remind the company and nudge my fellow executives toward living the values we say we care about. I find that argument to be persuasive."

According to the CEO of a large company in the quick-service restaurant industry, "I believe that if you are going to work on diversity and inclusion, you've got to spend money with businesses owned by women and people of color in ways that will generate wealth and jobs. That seems to resonate. However, there are a lot of companies that don't want to hear about it and just wish you would go away."

Client Case Study

I have found an incredible success story with one of my clients in the energy industry, where I've been able to work with both the CEO and the head of diversity and inclusion. They are now doing business with roughly sixty minority professional services firms. It is such a remarkable success story because it illustrates that board members need to work effectively with their senior executives to make things happen.

The company has a robust program for minority-owned businesses, and they also treat their diverse suppliers as partners. To make these changes happen, the CEO had to have uncomfortable conversations and fight for the right thing and remind board members and other company executives that they are accountable for results. Additionally, the CDO had the ear of the CEO and other company executives. Too often, the person responsible for advancing supplier diversity efforts is buried in procurement, has no access to the CEO, and, consequently, can't affect the things the company is trying to accomplish.

Think About This

Unless opportunities and gains are shared equitably among all workers, owners, and business leaders, the country will not have strong, ongoing economic growth. Inequality among ethnic groups, women, LGBTQ, and people with disabilities hinders prosperity for all and fuels the need for safety nets instead of self-empowerment, independence, dignity, and respect. Much of this inequality stems from long-standing, systemic and structural inequities in the economy that have kept women and people of color who own businesses from having a fair chance to get ahead. The playing field is not level if we are to reimagine the future of work, workers, and the workplace. In that case, CEOs must correct these debilitating norms by changing the status quo and developing sound business practices to ensure a sustainable, healthy economy for an increasingly diverse global marketplace. For example, in most cases, it falls on the chief diversity officer to influence other senior executives and convince them the status quo isn't working. The CDO must provide the data. For example, at the top 300 companies on Crain's list, there are no African Americans on top construction, law firms, accounting firms, banks, etc. There are no African Americans who have made the top twenty-five with very few exceptions. When looking at Crain's top fifty publicly traded firms, there's not one African American CEO. Several private equity firms in the country have never had an African American professional, let alone an African American partner.

Business and the broader economy work best when prosperity is widely shared, especially among historically marginalized populations or those who have faced barriers to opportunity. An inclusive economy represents all interests in society—major and minority population groups, women, and men of every generation. Bringing about an inclusive economy requires a systematic approach that brings together government, the private sector, and communities.

SECTION TWO: REPOSITION THE WORKFORCE

CHAPTER 4

Hacking Talent Management

Introduction

This chapter examines if senior leaders assess whether their organizations have created an optimal environment for diverse leaders' successful performance by addressing the following questions: What can the organization learn from their leaders of color and women who have been successful? What are the factors that are contributing to the successful leaders of color and women?

The chapter also explores opportunity areas for developing top performers within the organization by addressing the following set of questions: How is the organization demonstrating its value and commitment to diversity and inclusion through talent management programs? Do the organization's diversity and inclusion accountability measures for developing women and people of color "have teeth?" And lastly, how is the organization taking steps to promote exceptional performers and employees with high potential?

Lastly, the chapter will help senior leaders learn how to stay close to the progress and outcomes attained through succession management by addressing questions like: What proportion of the organization's high potential talent pool are people of color and women? Does that percentage of succession candidates mirror the organization's internal availability? And lastly, who, if anyone, on the executive team is sponsoring people of color and women?

Attracting Top Diverse Talent

Much of the research on developing future executives highlights the importance of looking at character, competency (or specific skills and abilities), and competence (or achievement of results). Additionally, it is critical to consider the organizational context—the changes or challenges being faced right now, and the type of leader who can be instrumental in helping the organization achieve its vision. Considering the organizational context means being clear on the strategic direction in which the organization is heading and whether it is moving or stalled to ensure it can get the company to its destination. This premise does not change in any manner when considering diverse talent.

The rationale to explain the lack of racial diversity in the executive ranks generally includes statements like, "We don't have any internal candidates who are ready," "We can't find anyone," or "Those we can find are in such demand that we cannot practically lure them away." This limited qualified candidate pool dilemma has been at the core of many discussions on the absence of racial diversity in corporations, even in corporations headquartered in cities that boast a healthy supply of diverse talent.

Leading Practices to Attract Diverse Talent

The path to attracting diverse talent at the executive levels and within the leadership pipeline is not a secret, nor is it innately mysterious. Many organizations hailed for best diversity practices have created integrated solutions for sourcing top talent. The methods and strategies associated with yielding optimal results are straightforward, realistic, and implementable. They include expanding external networks, leveraging internal networks, shaping the employer brand, building cultural competence in external-facing roles (e.g., sales representatives, recruiters, public/community relations, etc.), holding search firms accountable for producing a diverse slate of candidates, recognizing that excellence has many forms (i.e., the traditional style of leadership is not the only style of administration), leveraging social media for outreach to candidates of color, and focusing on competencies, experiences, and demonstrated outcomes vs. stylistic issues and fit.

The organization that excels at recruiting the top, diverse talent has a disciplined process of continuously checking the pulse on the efforts and progress in attracting women and people of color by asking the following questions:

- Do we have talent goals? How are we communicating our talent goals internally?
- Where do we see success, and where do we see resistance or cooperation?
- What recommendations are we putting in place?
- Are our recruitment and selection methods bringing us a broad enough pool of qualified diverse candidates to enable us to have options?
- Who are our recruiting partners? What is our search firm's

success record with sourcing and presenting us women and people of color?

- Are we insisting that our search firm provide a diverse slate, and are we holding them accountable?

- At what schools are we recruiting to fill the pipeline, and why? Have we looked at others that might provide a more diverse candidate pool?

- Do we have up-to-date role descriptions for our positions that clearly outline the competencies and experiences required? Are any of these requirements artificial barriers to acquiring diverse talent?

- Do we have a diverse interview team (function, gender, race)? Are the team members senior to the candidate so they can assess the appropriate competencies? Have they been trained or coached on sound interviewing practices?

- Are we leveraging our business resource groups' leadership and diverse suppliers to identify and source diverse candidates? What kind of outcomes/referrals are we receiving through this process? And are we recognizing and rewarding employees for referrals?

- How are we onboarding our leaders? What role should I and my direct reports play?

- Are we fully leveraging external organizations (e.g., professional associations and networks) to identify and source diverse candidates?

- What feedback have we obtained on our employer brand from employees and various groups within the community? Are

there differences in perception given one's demographic group?
- How are we leveraging social media, and who is monitoring it?
- Are we fully leveraging our internal organizations (e.g., and Employee Resource Groups (ERGs) to identify and source diverse candidates?

Onboarding Top Talent

Inclusion—the full integration of an employee into the life of the organization begins with onboarding. Studies show that a person's first ninety days are critical in onboarding a newly hired person. This is especially true if it is a woman or a person of color.

Therefore, the organization should be prepared with rigorous and consistent onboarding processes designed to bring diverse employees into the company culture over that crucial ninety-day period and enable feedback and "course corrections" after that. This onboarding shouldn't merely be designed to accommodate transition generally for diverse employees, but to accommodate them according to the specifics of the change—the onboarding, for example, of a middle-aged employee into a culture dominated by younger people, an academic into a commercial culture, and so on.

During the recruiting process, let candidates know that a careful onboarding process has been designed to set them up for success in their new surroundings. Throughout onboarding, the CEO and head of HR should be alert for implicit biases among colleagues, which could lead to the microinequities that cumulatively demoralize new hires who differ from the organization's dominant group. Begin the process by explaining honestly what they can expect in terms of hierarchy, decision-making, openness, and collegiality. Introduce them to key decision-makers as well as members of the team with which they will be working. Arrange nonthreatening settings where they can ask fundamental questions without embarrassment about how things are done in the company and expectations regarding performance.

Assign them a mentor, someone who can help them through the apparent challenges of connecting successfully with superiors, peers, and subordinates, and guide them through the organization's folkways and culture.

Those who serve as mentors should be widely respected in the organization, with high visibility, a real commitment to diversity, and a nuanced understanding of the dynamics of fundamental attribution errors. You might also consider assigning an "onboarding partner" who has successfully made the same transition to the organization that the new hire is expected to produce.

Without a proven, comprehensive onboarding process, the new hire may perform ineffectively during the first months or year on the job. New hires who feel isolated or face a wall of bias may grow frustrated and depart. The company loses its considerable investment in the person and must redo the search, but the departed person's area may lack direction until the position is filled. Most importantly, the company misses out on the business benefits that might have been generated by that executive and earns a reputation as a place where inclusion is more illusion than reality.

Managing Top Talent

Research by social scientists suggests that between one-third and one-half of all managers fail upon taking a new position. While failure may not result in termination, this number is astounding. There are several underlying reasons:

- **Contextual Nature of the Job**—Factors that impact senior-level roles in the organization's external environment and episodic events.

- **Predictability**—Results in a new position cannot always be linked to past behaviors, given the nuances of different company cultures, politics, and challenges.

- **Equifinality** (several approaches may lead to success)—If the organization is focused on "one right way" in demonstrating leadership, there may be difficulty recognizing and appreciating factors leading to success for one person who may differ. With leaders of color, the issue may be stylistic. Consequently, traditional metrics for evaluation might be challenged.

An added challenge for leaders of color stems from their managers' lack of comfort, giving them candid feedback. Everyone around that leader may sense a problem in some scenarios, but feedback is not provided until it is too late. Feedback is withheld for several reasons, including fear of being misunderstood, labeled a racist, or lack of information. This ineffective practice of withholding feedback can result in the self-fulfilling and perpetuating prophecy that leaders of color will not excel in the organization.

Traditional performance-management tools are not always leveraged at the leadership level. However, performance management provides a necessary structure for evaluating individual performance and organizational effectiveness. Performance management provides a tool for outlining accountability, shaping behavior, tracking results, and creating and sustaining a multicultural work environment. Leading practices include having a performance management system that is fully aligned with individual pay and the company's business strategy.

Rewarding and Recognizing Top Talent

Many senior leaders ponder whether they will take their diversity and inclusion efforts to the next level or why it takes so long for them to see visible progress, particularly in representation and retention in senior ranks. One missing or often diluted piece of the puzzle is the accountability component. What gets measured and rewarded gets done. In addition to verbal commitment and performance management programs, organizations that see results have a strategic plan to recognize and reward desired behavior within the organization. The link to compensation is being made in many organizations. However, some of these efforts are half-hearted and leave room for escape. Better practices involve developing detailed specifications for expected behaviors in various areas so that one component of D&I does not compensate for another.

Another qualitative practice involves establishing programs and communication vehicles that recognize and showcase excellence to internal and external stakeholders. This recognition reinforces behaviors that facilitate creating a culture that demonstrates its value of diversity and inclusion.

While the strategies for creating recognition of and accountability for D&I are easy to understand, their implementation often requires transformative change within the organization's culture. Specific leading practices include ensuring that managers are trained to provide relevant performance feedback and timely recognition.

Retaining Top Talent

Retaining the best talent in the future will depend on the extent to which emerging leaders see tangible career advancement possibilities within their companies aligns with their willingness to stay with the organization. For many, a typical career advancement strategy involves moving out to move up. This strategy is used quite often by employees of color. Employees also leave their organizations for pay increases that are not accompanied by title changes. This turnover can be quite costly for organizations, mainly if a revolving door phenomenon operates in parallel. According to the Society for Human Resources Management (SHRM), the cost of turnover can be between six to nine months of an individual's salary. That means if an employee is making $100,000 annually, the cost to replace him/her could range from $50,000 to $75,000. Additional research suggests that the costs are even higher; they are not static and appear to vary by their role and wage. In that case, the cost of replacing a professional with a $100,000 salary would range from $150,000 to $213,000. According to a 2019 survey conducted by the Society for Human Resource Management, several factors contribute to the turnover cost: the cost associated with job posting, advertising, screening, interviewing, onboarding, lost productivity, lost engagement, customer service errors, training, and severance pay.

What contributes to the revolving door in organizations? Possible practices or gaps that warrant attention include:

- **Underutilization**—Companies may not be fully leveraging the capabilities of their talent. Women and people of color may not be receiving assignments that enable them to demonstrate their strengths and grow. Lastly, diverse talent may not be placed in roles that optimize their skill sets and position them for advancement.

- **Fishbowl practices**—Some companies may be overly scrutinizing the behaviors of women and people of color to the extent that they become hesitant to act.

- **Incomplete onboarding**—Most companies have implemented a comprehensive plan to onboard new talent, including connecting them with mentors and sponsors, resources, ongoing communication, and tools to help them become successful. However, many of these same companies fail to communicate some of the culture's unspoken or unwritten rules and political considerations. Managers and mentors are not providing detailed feedback (in the moment) so that individuals have a good sense of how they are doing that is effective within the business culture and/or how it may be missing the mark.

- **Biased evaluations**—Finally, companies may not have made a wise choice on an individual. They failed to ask questions such as: did he or she demonstrate what was needed for this position? Did we rush to fill the opening with a racially diverse candidate? Did we have a wide enough pool from which to choose?

Think About This

We have provided a road map for organizations to assess whether they have created an optimal environment to attract and retain their top performers. This information will help leaders pinpoint opportunity areas to attract, manage, reward, and retain top performers by intentionally and proactively addressing specific questions. Having been properly armed, CEOs can now implement and monitor talent management accountability measures that have teeth!

Optimizing a diverse, equitable, and inclusive talent-management process requires individual, team, and enterprise-wide efforts. It is an ongoing and dynamic process for which organizations can never assume that one year of excellent results will be replicated in the following years. Practices that contribute to talent management include demonstrating visible leadership commitment to diversity, equity, and inclusion and creating a culture of inclusion, particularly for women and people of color.

It is not enough to get diverse individuals in the door. Many companies have mastered the talent attraction element by leveraging professional organizations and networks, branding, etc. The organization must execute well-conceived strategies and consistent practices to retain new hires to minimize the "revolving door" phenomenon.

CHAPTER 5

Developing a Diverse Pipeline of Talent

Introduction

This chapter predicts steps organizations will have to take to ensure they have a pipeline of diverse talent. The chapter provides a no-BS look at the odds stacked against women and people of color in professional settings, from the wage gap to biases and microaggressions, with actionable takeaways.

The chapter looks into a crystal ball and provides the much-needed talent advice guide for CEOs specifically. It finally ends in the one-size-fits-all approach of large companies that lump together employees into a talent pool and overlook the unique barriers to success for women and people of color.

We conclude the chapter by acknowledging the "ugly truths" that keep women and people of color from getting the proverbial seat at the table in corporate America: microaggressions, systemic racism, white privilege, etc.

The chapter validates that women and people of color are not "imagining" the discrimination they feel, even if it isn't always overt. The chapter gives a straight talk on how organizations will need to address these issues head-on to succeed and provide a roadmap to organizations to make real change.

Building A Diverse Bench Through Succession Planning

A powerful mechanism for increasing diversity within senior leadership ranks is an effective succession management system. Succession management provides a company an enterprise-wide pathway for development. This system, however, must include checks and balances at every stage and candid dialogue around diversity. The process may become as subjective and biased as those using it. Overemphasis on style and fit often have disappointing implications for people of color and women.

For example, managers may unconsciously fall prey to using succession management to clone themselves. The rationale is, "I will feel comfortable leaving my position in the hands of someone like me, someone who will carry out my legacy." This often creates artificial barriers for diverse candidates who do not look like or communicate like the incumbent.

Due to the organization's historical hiring practices and resulting talent pool, an additional challenge may be an insufficient supply of diverse talent in the "ready now" or "ready in one to three years" pool. Consequently, organizations must ensure the development of those in the "ready in three to five years" pipeline and consider them an ongoing priority.

Succession management is an ongoing process and dialogue, not an event. It benefits from the input of multiple perspectives as much as it benefits from structured guidelines and tools. One of the best practices for increasing diversity within the talent pipeline is ensuring that a formal and structured succession management process occurs. It includes diagnostics, gap analysis, clear metrics, and checkpoints.

Cultural Fluency Training for Leaders

Leadership development is one of the outcomes of the succession-planning process. It is typically integrated and aligned with talent management strategies and business imperatives. Do the development strategies that work for white males and females work for aspiring leaders of color? It can be argued that they do; however, the jury is still out on how often equal opportunities are provided. The variables that enable individuals to advance within their organizations are individual effort, networking, access to developmental resources, and credible assignments valued within the organization. Some of the factors to consider when developing leaders of color include:

- **Depth and breadth:** individuals are given tasks that enable lateral movement to improve the big-picture view and upward mobility within a specific discipline.
- **The "right" jobs at the right time include:** challenging and developing skill sets, engendering credibility, and affording visibility to and interaction with senior leaders throughout the organization. Additionally, these assignments may consist of a temporary dedication in a specific functional area to address the individual's skill gaps. They ultimately provide access to

roles with profit and loss accountability as well as those in operations management.

- **The myth of the "right credentials:"** includes examining if the organization is fixated on promoting its leaders from a finite pool of business schools. This can limit the supply of diverse talent. These credential requirements may not guarantee success or advancement within a leadership position as they contribute to the current management team's comfort level.

- **Avoiding the career path maze**: too often, diverse talent has been moved repeatedly into lateral positions and staff roles that do not strengthen their chances of being considered for the executive ranks.

Many corporations are multicultural at either the domestic level or international level. Consequently, it can be stated that leadership takes place within a multicultural context. Multicultural environments include employees that represent different ethnicities, geographies, generations, religions, genders, etc. There are varying degrees to which work teams and organizational units will reflect this spectrum of diversity. However, whether one leads a multicultural team directly or has ultimate accountability for a multicultural organization, understanding and effectively addressing issues and opportunities within this context is inextricably linked to leadership and organizational effectiveness.

Putting Theory into Practice

Numerous models and frameworks have been developed to characterize cross-cultural competence. These frameworks have been developed, built upon, and repurposed by practitioners, academicians, and consultants. In general, these models address either the developmental stages of competence, typically moving from limited capability to full competence, or the components of cross-cultural competence, namely the knowledge, skills, abilities, and other characteristics an individual should demonstrate. Additionally, the cultural leadership competency models are often rooted in expertise and attributes relevant to entering new markets and leading diverse cultures in multiple locations.

Obviously, there is an overlap between the frameworks that define leadership competence in general and those that define cross-cultural competency. Specifically, the ability to demonstrate self-awareness, emotional intelligence, and adaptability is foundational to strong leadership and navigating a multicultural environment.

How do we translate these models into usable tools for performance management, succession planning, or career mapping within our organizations? There are specific behaviors aligned with each competency in comprehensive competency models and expected performance levels spelled out for job levels or roles. Breaking down a competency model into these behaviors helps leaders understand their values and interprets each competency within its organizational context. This can be a useful tool for many areas, including performance management, leadership development, and talent acquisition.

It is the expanded definitions of these competencies that guide employee behavior. Insights from chief diversity officers, chief human resource officers, and other executives support the notion that cross-cultural competence comes to life through consistent and visible actions. The company's standards for success will vary by company and reflect where they are relative to implementing a diversity and inclusion strategy.

The Icarus Multicultural Leadership Competency Model

Multicultural competency models can be readily compared to general leadership competency models. Ask an industrial-organizational (I-O) psychologist or organizational development (OD) practitioner what leadership competencies refer to. You will most likely get a robust framework that includes knowledge, skills, abilities, traits, and other characteristics. However, some schools of thought describe competencies as merely the technical expertise sets that a leader demonstrates. As an example, in a 2013 article in Forbes, entitled "The Most Common Leadership Model—And Why It's Broken," the author asserts, "Any organization that overweighs the importance of technical competency fails to recognize the considerable, and often-untapped value contained in the whole of the person. It's the cumulative power of a person's soft skills, the sum of the parts, if you will, that creates real value."

A term receiving increasing attention, especially within the healthcare industry, is "cultural humility." Cultural humility, in contrast to cultural competence, does not focus on achieving mastery or full proficiency. Instead, it is a continual process of self-reflection and self-critique that addresses power inequities between groups.

Attaining cultural humility is not only a goal but also an active process, an ongoing way of being in the world and being in relationships with others and self.

In our consulting practice, Icarus Consulting, we have a model and a framework for evaluating cross-cultural competency. The competencies and behaviors noted are general (portable across industries) and relevant to managers and senior leaders. In our model, all individuals within the organization would be held accountable for behaviors. While the list of behaviors offered is not exhaustive, it provides a solid foundation for defining cross-cultural competence. Corporate leaders and D&I practitioners can leverage these as a launchpad or comparison point and customize the behaviors to align more closely with their respective organizations' nuances.

At Icarus Consulting, we have developed a more holistic multicultural leadership model. Our model includes fifty skills that fall under five main competencies that address different focal points for a leader's behaviors and efforts. We believe the following competencies are critical to the leaders of organizations during times of chaos, transformation, or disruptive change.

Leading Diverse Organizations

- Demonstrates awareness of the cultural norms of the organization.
- Configures teams that reflect balance in terms of strengths, diverse and unique insights.
- Delegates work that compliments each direct report's strengths

BEYOND INCLUSION

and capabilities to contribute to team goals successfully.

- Crafts developmental and stretch assignments for direct reports to help them improve their level of contribution and performance.

- Holds direct reports accountable for creating a diverse and inclusive team environment.

- Contains direct statements responsible for maintaining inclusive work practices within their teams.

- Demonstrates an understanding of the need to balance individual values with organizational values.

- Mentors others and encourages dialogue to help employees understand the unwritten and unspoken rules of the culture

- Actively seeks an understanding of how traditional practices impact different groups.

- Challenges practices, policies, and behaviors that do not promote an inclusive work environment.

- Remains aware of how biases manifest in the organization's various systems and methods (e.g., interview process, performance management, succession planning, etc.)

- Challenges practices, policies, and behaviors that do not promote an inclusive work environment.

- Ensures there are forums and mechanisms in place for all employees to ask for support or provide information.

Adapting to Employee Differences

- Models open-mindedness and demonstrates curiosity by asking questions to understand different concepts and ideas.
- Listens attentively to differing points of view.
- Hires individuals from different backgrounds (culture, functional, etc.) to stimulate learning and new ways of thinking.
- Understands the levels of engagement, retention, and performance of varying demographic groups within the organization.
- Encourages peers and reports to look at issues from different perspectives.
- Leverages multilevel and cross-functional groups to address organizational challenges.
- Invites employees, customers, suppliers, and other stakeholders to participate in advisory councils and roundtables to bring new and varied perspectives into the organization.
- Keeps up to date with industry-leading practices and helps identify those that have relevance for the organization.

Tolerating Ambiguity

- Seeks new experiences outside of one's comfort zone to facilitate personal development.
- Reaches out to others with known differences in perspective to help identify oversights or blind spots.

- Demonstrates vulnerability by acknowledging what one does not know or would like to learn more about.
- Confidently leads the organization through change times (clarifying the rationale, vision, and implications for diverse stakeholders).
- Demonstrates the capacity to take calculated levels of risk to implement new approaches.
- Provides opportunities for groups who have not been traditionally underrepresented in the workforce.
- Uses data from risk assessments to inform D&I strategies and consult with leaders.
- Challenges the team's status quo by encouraging others to think differently and find new ways to accomplish tasks.
- Invites the group to address conflict openly and respectfully.
- Addresses disrespectful team behavior immediately.
- Speaks up in a supportive manner when specific individual's views are being ignored or disrespected.
- Encourages the team to challenge their assumptions before drawing conclusions.

Demonstrating Agility

- Demonstrates the ability to adapt one's behavior to the cultural context in which one is working.
- Identifies positive aspects related to internally or externally driven changes that impact the organization.

- Focuses on quality of contributions and results versus stylistic differences.

- Conducts conversations with direct reports to understand the strengths and unique contribution potential of team members.

- Provides constructive feedback to those from different cultural backgrounds and does so respectfully, mindful of individual needs.

- Facilitates discussions in a way that enables all team members to contribute.

- Identifies optional methods for helping employees/managers build cross-cultural competence, keeping in mind differing learning preferences and cultural backgrounds.

Cross-Disciplinary Collaboration

Another pathway to building cross-cultural competence is through cross-disciplinary collaboration. Leaders benefit individually through these interactions, and our consulting experience validates that the most innovative solutions often come when leaders solicit insights from multiple heterogeneous sources. Intuitively and intellectually, this makes sense; leaders should anticipate that one source will look at a problem or opportunity from a different angle than another source. This is essentially the business case for diversity and inclusion. Team diversity sparks optimism around leveraging cross-functional taskforces, cross-regional councils, or advisory committees comprised of employees from multiple levels. This practice results in groundbreaking outcomes and disruptive solutions—especially in technology, operations, customer service, product design, consumer goods, and service delivery.

The existence of cross-disciplinary teams and seeking multiple perspectives also distributes ownership and accountability throughout the organization. This is especially important in advancing the D&I strategy. Diversity and inclusion teams often have one or two individuals, and it becomes necessary to leverage the vast amount of work that needs to be done through others. This practice creates multiple ambassadors, champions, and advocates for D&I work and helps ensure inclusive practices take root in other areas, are aligned with business practices, and are sustained. This outcome is often the by-product of setting up D&I councils comprising leaders from each business unit or functional area.

It is important to note that even though cross-disciplinary collaborations may be more creative or relevant to the customer, achieving results or reaching decisions may not run as efficiently as a leader would experience on a more homogeneous team. Research and anecdotal insights from our clients speak to the challenges of managing diverse teams and supporting organizations' need to help build this competency among their front line, middle, and senior leaders.

Think About This

Senior leaders must learn to stay close to the leadership-development and talent-management processes to ensure the organization effectively cultivates and grows its internal leaders of color. When it comes to attracting and retaining top, diverse talent, organizations must ask two key questions: Have we included a substantive amount of diverse talent in our leadership assessment and executive coaching programs? What are the development gaps for our diverse talent?

Organizations must remember that it takes a diverse team time to reach optimal performance. There are different schools of thought on the extent to which managers should facilitate diverse teams' performance. For some, the ability to motivate, manage, and lead a diverse team is viewed as merely being part of effective management. For others, managing diverse teams is bringing an added layer of complexity. Diverse team members may bring expectations, needs, or modes of expression rooted in cultural differences unfamiliar to the manager. Applying this logic, a manager who feels comfortable and competent in interacting with different groups will probably be more successful in leading diverse teams.

CHAPTER 6

Disrupting Diversity and Inclusion Training

Introduction

This chapter discusses the impact of diversity and inclusion (D&I) training on the future of work, workers, and the workplace. It explores the efficacy of D&I training over the last two decades.

D&I training refers to educating employees to improve their awareness, attitude, knowledge, and skills. D&I training is a combination of best practices to improve diversity, equity, and inclusion. In most companies, supervisors and managers offer diversity and inclusion training to develop their capacity to lead diverse work teams. Today, most companies are focusing on training to increase awareness of implicit bias. Still, other companies find D&I training essential to increase productivity in their multicultural organization and address the challenges of increasing collaboration between employees from different generations. Companies have offered D&I training for decades, although the rationale for D&I training has changed over time.

We discuss the history of D&I training and take a close look at the backlash to D&I training in some organizations. In addition to illuminating the phenomenon of "diversity training backlash," we explain that "backlash" is a defensive move that white people make when challenged by D&I training that focuses on race. This backlash is characterized by emotions such as anger, fear, guilt, and behaviors such as arguments and silence. These behaviors, in turn, function to reinstate white racial equilibrium and prevent any meaningful cross-racial dialogue.

We also examine how diversity training backlash develops, perpetuates racial inequality, and what organizations can do to deliver diversity and inclusion training effectively.

History of Diversity and Inclusion Training

Companies have been conducting diversity education since the 1960s. Businesses started teaching D&I training in earnest in the late 1980s and throughout the 1990s to protect against and settle lawsuits. Many companies now assume that D&I training can boost productivity and innovation in an increasingly diverse workplace. The assumptions about D&I training's value have evolved over the decades because of its changing functions and uses.

D&I training started as a reaction to the civil rights movement and demands from equal opportunity activists determined to send a clear message to corporate America that black employees would no longer remain voiceless regarding unfair employment practices. Cultural sensitivity was the goal of initial D&I training efforts, which focused on increasing sensitivity and awareness of racial differences.

Focus groups and "fishbowl" discussions became a popular training method for bringing black and white employees together for emotional conversations about race relations. As a member of the Air Force, I witnessed first-hand how the military employed "fishbowl" discussion groups in what is perhaps the most extensive scale of diversity training ever conducted. Many of the Defense Equal Opportunity Management Institute (DEOMI) facilitators viewed the fishbowl discussions among black and white participants attending the diversity training as successful only when at least one white participant admitted that they were racist and became tearful about racial discrimination and white supremacy.

Employing a black-white pair of facilitators was considered essential for exposing participants to the two-race relations perspective and cross-racial collaboration. The DEOMI facilitators were typically men, and the white participants were most valued if they could openly show emotions about their journey in discovering their deep-seated racism.

DEOMI facilitators often viewed their role as trying to rebalance equality in a world that had historically oppressed those with less social, political, and economic power. Confronting white participants who made excuses for or denied their racism was common in the DEOMI's training approach. The goal was to increase white participants' sensitivity to the effects of racial inequity.

White participants tended to respond to confrontation in sensitivity training in three different ways. Some white participants became more insightful about race relations barriers because of being put on the hot seat during the two-day workshop. Some white participants became more resistant to racial harmony, and they fought against accepting the facilitators' label of them as "racists." And some white participants became what the DEOMI referred to as "fanatics." These individuals began advocating against any forms of racial injustice after completing the 2-day training.

As a person who attended DEOMI's diversity training, I can attest to its effectiveness. After several complaints from white participants, DEOMI reduced the number of training hours and curtailed using the "hot seat" or "fishbowl" techniques in response to negative evaluations by many participants who completed the training.

Diversity training in corporations also began to change as the federal government was curtailing affirmative action laws. Gender diversity training began to emerge during the 1970s and 1980s, just as diversity training expanded in the 1990s to focus on other areas, including ethnic, religious, gay, and lesbian perspectives and ability differences.

Some diversity and inclusion practitioners argue that the broader view of diversity began to "water down" the focus on race to the extent that it is no longer seriously dealt with within D&I training. They argue that focusing on implicit bias toward other groups does not activate the visceral reaction needed for individuals, organizations, and society to deal with racial discrimination.

Shift to Multicultural Training

Multiculturalism refers to the inclusion of the full range of identity groups in the organization. The goal is to take into consideration the different ways people identify as social beings. This perspective has become the most widely used approach today in diversity and inclusion training. However, the inclusion of other identity groups poses the challenge of maintaining focus on unresolved racial discrimination and effectively covering the many different identity groups.

The continuing focus on white privilege training work maintains a focus on racism in diversity and inclusion training. White privilege education involves challenging white people to consider the benefits they reap individually as racial group members with the most social, political, and economic power.

While white privilege, multiculturalism, and implicit bias training are significant individually and collectively, diversity and inclusion professionals must keep in mind that organizations vary in D&I education needs. Determining how to meet these needs requires the trainer to possess critical thinking skills and facilitate issues outside of their cultural experience. The capable chief diversity and inclusion officer (CDIO) can determine when race education is a suitable intervention.

Discussions about gender differences, sexual orientation, Native American identity, Latino empowerment, white privilege, etc., provide a rich context for understanding diversity's complexity. Today's savvy D&I trainer has the expertise to take a multicultural perspective in facilitating and training, and he or she must command a knowledge of the range of identity groups. As a result, giving each identity group the attention it deserves is no small matter.

The reality of global mobilization has required an even broader view of diversity and inclusion work due to working with an increasingly cross-national audience. The use of the label African American, for example, is complicated by the migration of white and black Africans to the United States. An organization may have employees from the former Yugoslavia, refugees from Somalia, workers from India, and people with limited English-speaking skills—to name a few modern diversity challenges. Religious diversity accompanies globalism, which is also included in contemporary diversity and inclusion training.

This complexity of identity group likely needs prompted D&I professionals like Al Vivian, CEO of Basic Diversity, to promote inclusive organizations. The objective is to remove the barriers to productivity for every organization member with particular concern for historically excluded group members.

Another recent change is the emphasis on inclusive leadership development. Inclusive leadership development broadens the focus of diversity and inclusion training programs and avoids the often-negative connotation of D&I training. Perhaps more importantly, inclusive leadership development builds on fundamental management training and aligns more closely with the talent management programs of organizations.

Diversity Pioneers: Angels of Mercy or Barbarians at the Gate

D&I professionals that lead D&I programs for organizations may have the title of chief diversity officer or vice president of diversity, while others are considered D&I leaders or managers. Regardless of what they are called, these positions are becoming increasingly prevalent in organizations. There was a time when the chief human resource officer (CHRO) would hire a consultant or trainer to handle diversity-related issues, focusing on sensitivity-awareness training as the expected solution.

Diversity pioneers in the late 1990s and early 2000s laid the foundation for today's D&I professionals' emergence. These diversity pioneers have been in the profession for more than twenty years, including those who have served as in-house or consulting professionals.

The individuals most considered to be a pioneer in the field of diversity and inclusion include Dr. Roosevelt Thomas, Ted Childs, Al Vivian, Dr. James O. Rodgers, John Fernandez, C.T. Vivian, Dr. Lee Gardenswartz, Dr. Ed Hubbard, Mary Frances-Winters, Fred Miller, Patricia Pope, Frank McCloskey, and Dr. Ann Rowe. This list is based on my professional experience, research of archival records, data collected from the American Institute for Managing Diversity, Society for Human Resource Management, and the Conference Board's Diversity and Inclusion Leadership Council.

Some of the D&I pioneers had specialized training when starting in diversity (management) and inclusion. Some had focused on race relations training, while others taught Human Relations courses in higher education before entering the field of diversity and inclusion as full-time consultants. Still, others were trained as applied research psychologists or taught cultural competency. Each diversity pioneer had to learn about navigating the landmines in corporate America's diversity work while on the front lines as consultants, trainers, and educators. The pioneers not only had excellent business and higher education credentials, but they also were battle-test professionals who had the bumps and bruises that come from being in the trenches of "just doing the work."

Intent versus Impact

By the mid-1980s, affirmative action was at its height, and many companies used external diversity consultants to help increase the numbers of women and African American employees. Some organizations used diversity training to safeguard against civil rights suits during this time. Much of the training focused primarily on black-white racial issues and discrimination, with little if any attention given to discrimination faced by other underrepresented groups, women, employees over the age of forty, or people with disabilities.

Some of the early diversity pioneers like Dr. Jim Rodgers also noticed that the business case in those days emphasized "diversity as doing the right thing" rather than as a business imperative. Women and people of color were expected to fit into the existing organizational culture, making it difficult to effect real organizational change.

Because of the work of Dr. Rodgers, Ted Childs, and others, today, diversity (and inclusion) is now accepted as a critical business driver rather than "diversity for diversity's sake." This was accompanied, in part, by a shift away from the singular focus common on compliance with equal employment laws in the early stages of diversity and inclusion.

Early on, diversity was about compliance because of the fear of discrimination lawsuits. And for others, it was about increasing the representation of African Americans and women in the workforce. Early approaches to increasing racial representation and individual awareness of individual and systemic bias did not create long-term sustainable organizational change. Some individuals became more aware, but the same policies, processes, practices, and behaviors often remained unchanged. Although some organizations still approach diversity from a compliance perspective, most organizations moved well beyond that. They came to understand that a company must leverage its diversity for competitive advantage by ensuring all employees' full inclusion to win in today's business game.

I had a chance to interview several of the early pioneers for this book, and collectively, they expressed concerns about the challenges chief diversity officers have today when advancing or accelerating their organization's diversity and inclusion posture.

At the top of the list, most diversity leaders must contend with organizational leaders who only give lip service to diversity and inclusion efforts without putting their hearts and souls into it or offering it the necessary resources for success. As a result, today's chief diversity officer too often must shoulder the full weight of the diversity and inclusion strategy. They can also get buried too far in the weeds to be effective. They are expected to partner with talent acquisition, talent management, supplier diversity, and other organization departments, which adds to the stress. In most companies, the diversity leader works alone or with a small team, and results are expected in a short time frame with a limited budget. Lastly, they are expected to manage a highly political role in a very bureaucratic environment while legally protecting the organization.

The result is that leading diversity and inclusion initiatives can be challenging, demanding, and frustrating. As a former chief diversity officer, who now consults with dozens of organizations, I can confidently say that organizations need to raise the bar for results. For example, the CEO should make all leaders accountable for contributing to and promoting diversity and inclusion, especially middle managers and frontline supervisors. Linking bonuses and merit pay to clear diversity and inclusion metrics is seldom given serious consideration in even the top companies recognized for their diversity and inclusion programs.

Valuing Diversity

"Valuing diversity" is a term used quite a bit these days when describing one of the aspirational outcomes of D&I efforts. When the phrase was coined in the early 2000s, some people thought it was "too touchy-feely" because it wasn't affirmative action or equal employment opportunity language. Some early diversity pioneers resisted the language because they thought corporate America was not ready to value their employees for their differences.

Dr. Jim Rodgers was one of the first to develop training based on the concept that valuing individual differences was essential to "getting 100 percent out of employees 100 percent of the time." He created the groundbreaking "Valuing Diversity" and "Managing Differently" workshops, which helped organizations understand the link between respect for employees and productivity. Thanks to Rodgers, increasing numbers of organizations have embraced the idea that we need to value employees' differences.

D&I Training in Higher Education

Colleges and universities began offering diversity courses as a part of their management curricula in the early 2000s. For example, Stanford University and the California State University at Fullerton had the foresight to offer cultural diversity courses to fulfill general management requirements. However, there was considerable debate among academicians about whether the management field needed to include diversity courses.

In the middle of this culture war, I was an adjunct professor teaching graduate courses in human resource management and public administration. My corporate background enabled me to interweave diversity and inclusion in the management courses I taught. The students were very receptive to the classes. Students accepted the diversity principles integrated into the curricula and understood the importance of valuing different values and beliefs.

Recruitment of historically excluded group members, especially women and students of color, was the primary focus at most universities. No one would seriously listen to creating an inclusive organization before increasing the numbers of women and students of color. The attitude was, let's get as many women and students of color in as possible and worry about retaining them later.

Think About This

Diversity and inclusion training has helped organizations achieve incredible gains in attracting and retaining women and people of color and creating an inclusive environment—only to see those gains undermined by leadership and economic climate changes. The lesson learned is that sustainable diversity and inclusion initiatives require an ongoing commitment to removing all the barriers that can lead to reverting to old business ways. Diversity and inclusion training must, for example, be embedded into the organization's policies, processes, and practices to prevent the organization from regressing to earlier inclusion stages.

As economic, political, and global changes required new ways of solving old problems, the early diversity and inclusion pioneers experienced many road bumps. This brief history suggests their sheer determination and commitment built an invaluable foundation from which we all can draw meaningful lessons. This chapter reminds us that we must continue to build on the pioneers' foundation to better manage the inevitable organizational impact that diversity and inclusion training will have on the future of work, workers, and the workplace.

SECTION THREE: REINVENT THE WORKPLACE

CHAPTER 7

Leveraging Employee Resource Groups to Increase Employee Engagement

Introduction

Chapter seven forecasts how organizations will leverage employee resource groups (ERGs) in the future. It predicts the efforts organizations will have to take to engage and invest in their employees. It also explores how employee networks will need to be organized to benefit from these networks' efforts.

As we all know, the demographic profile of the United States is shifting rapidly, with women and people of color expected to reach majority status by 2044 due, in part, to the projected growth of Asian, Hispanic, and multiracial populations, according to the Census Bureau. As a result, companies will have to leverage their employees to reach diverse customers and communities. They will need to accomplish this through the innovative use of employee resource groups (ERGs)—voluntary, employee-led groups made up of individuals who joined based on shared interests, backgrounds, or demographic factors such as gender, race, or ethnicity. These groups are also known as affinity groups or business resource groups.

This chapter provides advice on how organizations can effectively leverage their ERGs for competitive advantage and meet their employees' specific needs and concerns.

The Impact of ERGs on the Future Workforce

As a former chair of the diversity and inclusion leadership council for The Conference Board—a global, nonprofit business and research association, I worked with diversity leaders whose companies took full advantage of their ERGs to identify gaps in their business strategies.

That experience motivated me to research the potential impact of ERGs on the future workforce. I discovered that more than half of the companies with thoroughly developed diversity strategies use their ERGs to improve the business in three ways.

First, ERGs make sure employees have an opportunity to be heard, valued, and engaged.

Second, they help their organizations gain a better understanding of employee needs. Finally, they give a unique insight into employee engagement and performance.

More than 70 percent of the organizations I studied relied on their ERGs to build a workforce that reflected their customer base. The thinking was that customers would be more loyal and feel more comfortable if they did business with people who understood them. Almost 30 percent of the companies I studied got assistance from their employee resource groups to increase their spending with diverse suppliers.

At 90 percent of the companies I examined, ERG members helped new employees get acclimated during the onboarding process. My research confirmed that the first 60 to 90 days of employment are critical for any new hire, and they can be particularly challenging for women and people of color. That short window of time can mean the difference between whether an employee stays for the long run or leaves the organization before the year is out. ERGs were also leveraged to acclimate employees and engender a sense of loyalty and belonging to their new company.

ERGs can also be an excellent resource for identifying gaps in an organization's talent development process. Sixty-three percent of the companies I surveyed have an employee resource group focused on young professionals. Given how fickle Millennial employees can be when it comes to staying at a job, ensuring they have access to a group to network and grow with is a great way to increase retention.

Many companies also successfully use their ERGs to improve the organization's leadership development process, drive results, forge relationships, and ensure alignment between their business and diversity strategies. The data suggest that ERGs are not only good for business but also essential!

ERGs: A Client Case Study

One of my clients is a supermarket chain in California. As this case study will illustrate, there is strong evidence to support the business case for ERGs. California has the sixth-largest economy in the world. There are more Latinos (48 percent) in California than Caucasians (38 percent). So, if you look at consumption patterns in driving business and growth in California, it also involves looking at the Latino community. California's largest trading partner is not China or Canada, it's Mexico and Latin America. California's largest trading partners speak Spanish, and 40 percent of the state's population also speaks Spanish, and they are a natural ally for increasing Latino customer business.

The supermarket chain engaged my firm, Icarus Consulting, to advance and accelerate its efforts to target stores in the Latino community. Of the company's 300 stores, only 20 percent were in Latino neighborhoods. The CEO explained that Latinos have a smaller basket size, but instead of going to the supermarket four times a month, they shop eleven or twelve times. If you look at their total basket every year, they bring $3,500 more per person into the supermarket than any other customer group. This is significant given there are tiny margins, 1 percent to 2 percent, in the supermarket business.

Icarus Consulting helped reorient the company's marketing strategy to be the "supermarket of choice in the Latino community." To achieve this goal, the company enlisted the help of their Hispanic employee resource group. After five years, the supermarket chain's highest sales per square foot were Latino stores. The Hispanic ERG helped educate senior leaders that it was not about diversity and inclusion or multiculturalism, but about mathematics, and the CEO is compensated based on driving growth and earnings.

When the CEO started seeing the results, the company adopted several Hispanic ERGs recommendations and initiated many changes.

For example, they played Spanish music in the stores. They also advertised the store's circulars in Spanish and hired store managers from the surrounding bilingual community who brought preexisting customer relationships. Based on their Latino ERG recommendations, the supermarket chain also initiated something that no other competitor was doing at the time: the company created a place in each store where mothers could have their kids taken care of for half an hour while they shopped. The company also put an indoor playground in each store with a professional daycare provider and a nurse. The company also put a coffee bar in each store where mothers could come together and watch while their kids played. With the combination of these initiatives and other operational changes, sales went through the roof!

Initially, persuading the CEO and other senior leaders in the company was a challenge! However, when you present a strong business case, people start to listen. One of the company's Hispanic ERG goals was to help the company increase sales and profits.

Icarus Consulting had to educate the CEO and other senior leaders to change their mindset and provide a different framework for the ERG's recommendation because most company leaders thought the Hispanic ERG was just a "social club." They had been led to believe that diversity, inclusion, and ERGs were about helping the company "look like this or that because it's a good thing to do."

Think About This

Diversity and inclusion are crucial issues if you want to be a talent magnet for Millennials. Millennials are a purpose-driven generation.

They want to be happy, and they want to be part of an organization that values people's differences in everything. That's the way they grew up. So, when they come to a company that's not like that, it's a culture clash for them, and they are not going to be happy. If you can't recruit those people, then you're in big trouble. Your ERGs are an untapped resource that should be unleashed so you can get your fair share of the top talent in the emerging workforce. That's one of the most important messages I share with my clients.

CHAPTER 8

Empowering the Diversity and Inclusion Council to Transform the Culture

Introduction

This chapter explores how organizations will leverage their diversity and inclusion (D&I) councils so that the council can effectively support its diversity and inclusion goals. Several companies' best practices are examined to study how they leverage their diversity and inclusion councils to support their diversity and inclusion (D&I) strategies.

D&I councils are a valuable component of a company's D&I strategy because they provide an inclusive and effective mechanism for managing and initiating D&I programs. The best councils successfully align efforts with the company's operations, strategies, missions, and objectives. They also help assess the effectiveness of the D&I strategy, monitor efforts, and report progress. D&I councils also demonstrate the company's commitment to D&I.

This chapter looks at various types of diversity councils, their strengths and weaknesses, and how they are structured and governed. It also provides recommendations on how to design, create, and establish a council for your company. Lastly, it discusses how companies can promote their D&I council and support them by providing the necessary resources to ensure their success.

Defining Diversity and Inclusion Councils

It is important to clarify terms before getting too deep into the chapter process because one person's D&I council is another individual's "social club." D&I councils come in many forms and have various structures and names, but most diversity professionals agree that there are three basic types.

Executive Diversity Councils

Executive diversity councils are composed of executive leaders responsible for aligning the D&I program with the company mission and strategy. Executive diversity councils demonstrate the company's commitment to diversity, equity, and inclusion by ensuring the application of the D&I process at all levels of the organization. A company's CEO usually chairs this council and appoints its membership, which generally includes C-suite executives and other senior managers. This approach demonstrates that the company sees D&I as a high priority.

This type of D&I council is highly effective when led by the chairman, CEO, or chief diversity officer. Council members are senior vice presidents, vice presidents, business-unit heads, or other high-level leaders from all the company's business functions or core businesses. In general, this council develops a comprehensive, integrated D&I strategy and integrates best practices.

Regional Councils

Regional D&I provides a greater representation of a company's workforce, and they are usually larger than executive diversity councils. Regional D&I councils often implement the D&I strategy and policies established by the executive council. They are also responsible for advising company leadership on the company's D&I needs and the progress of diversity initiatives throughout the organization.

An organization may create several regional councils to represent multiple business units, locations, or operational components. Georgia Power adopted such a structure following an intensive D&I benchmarking process, which included best-practice visits to other organizations. The benchmarking team discovered that one of the hallmarks of embedding diversity, inclusiveness, and cultural competence into an organization is by establishing regional D&I councils. Consequently, the company made regional D&I councils a central component of its D&I strategy by encouraging each business unit to create a council.

Advisory Councils

An advisory council's role is to ensure that its D&I initiatives align with a "specific business unit's business goals. Advisory D&I councils are also formed to improve teamwork, enhance creativity, and increase productivity by ensuring employees feel valued and respected. Sodexo North America has a sophisticated structure of advisory councils. Its parent, the French-based Sodexo Group, is a leading provider of on-site services, benefits and rewards services, and personal and home services to companies, hospitals, schools, individuals, and communities.

Sodexo North America's cross-market diversity council (CMDC) is an example of an enterprise-wide advisory D&I council responsible for developing effective, culturally competent D&I programs. The CMDC is comprised of managers who want to foster a more diverse and inclusive company. Its charge is to collaborate and operationalize the D&I strategy within each business line, serve as thought leaders to advance the D&I, and implement D&I within a specific line of business.

Establishing and Operating D&I Councils

Before forming a D&I council, the company should invest time to conduct research and benchmark councils at similar organizations and analyze their impact. This effort provides an excellent opportunity to socialize the idea with key stakeholders.

Companies that do not benchmark their D&I council limit the council's possibilities. Consequently, the council often fails to thrive and can lose focus. Benchmarking enables the council to evolve, quantify its contributions to the business, measure itself against other councils, and break free from habits and practices that have outlived their usefulness.

Also, the company should look outside itself to gain information about D&I council best practices, reviewing articles in diversity and inclusion magazines, and visiting competitors. Putting all the data and thoughts in order will make the D&I council more efficient and effective.

Building a Solid Council Structure

Once the initial information-gathering phase has been completed, it is time to focus on structure. The company should design and construct a framework that will synchronize every council element and integrate them with its D&I strategy. Successful councils leverage robust organizational, governance, and communications processes that engage company leadership, other stakeholders, and local, regional, or global operations. They also capitalize on clear authority lines, designations of responsibilities, communication links, and feedback loops that facilitate interaction between D&I council leaders, organizations, and employees.

Defining Council Goals and Objectives

Of course, the company must ensure it has established D&I council goals and objectives when beginning the planning process. However, the company needs to allow the data-gathering process to inform its selection and ensure it understands the opportunities and pitfalls of creating a D&I council. A central aspect of this process is deciding the council's attributes that will help ensure continued success. More specifically, the company should want to determine the characteristics that will make the D&I council successful. In general, the most effective D&I councils adhere to a set of common guidelines. They include:

- Align their council programs with business needs, practices, and strategies.
- Develop a long-term strategy, stated purposes, goals, objectives, and a mission statement.
- Collaborate with the executive leadership team, D&I staff, and human resources leadership.
- Develop links with outside D&I, industry, professional, and community groups.
- Recruit diverse membership and actively engage with employees in field organizations.
- Earn senior leadership support and participation.
- Demonstrate the importance of D&I to the success of the organization.
- Communicate council goals and objectives, program efforts, and achievements.
- Build a reputation as a source of competent counsel, support, and advocacy.

Developing the Council's Business Plan

Achieving council goals and objectives depends, largely, on the council's success in supporting the needs of the company. Consequently, the council must develop a business plan that connects its objectives, activities, and programs to its strategic goals and business objectives. The council's plan should clarify how it will advance the company's business strategy in:

- Business development, product innovation, and marketing intelligence.
- Employee engagement, innovation, recruitment, and retention.
- Diversity and inclusion awareness and alignment with company goals.
- Brand enhancement.
- Public relations and public affairs communication.
- Community development and economic inclusion (supplier diversity).

The council's business plan should focus on how it can help (1) drive company's growth, (2) enhance the company's reputation as an industry or market leader, (3) create a supportive and innovative workplace, and (4) strengthen the company's ability to be a socially responsible company. Also, the business plan should enumerate the impacts of the council on reducing costs and improving efficiency. Another focus should be its role in raising professional standards and its part in attracting talented professionals, reducing turnover among high-performing employees, and facilitating employee communication, interaction, and engagement. The plan also should explain the council's role in tackling problematic workplace issues, such as working with a disability, achieving work-life balance, illuminating unwritten rules, identifying barriers to inclusion and equity, and increasing employee engagement.

A practical, aligned business plan—one that includes budgets, nonfinancial costs, timelines, performance-management tools, and

ROI analyses, will demonstrate the D&I council's professionalism and thoroughness. An effective plan will help convince senior leaders that the D&I council will help advance its business goals and why their participation in the council would benefit their professional reputations.

Creating a Compelling Communications Plan

The D&I council's hard work will be diminished if no one knows what the council is doing. Consequently, the council should create a communications strategy to ensure it informs the people who need to know, wants to know, and do not know they want to know. The D&I council should base its plan on public relations and marketing communications' best practices. Effective D&I council communications plans have common attributes. They are:

- Focus on the needs and wants of their company.
- Provide an authentic and convincing message.
- Captivate and break through the clutter of the messages that constantly bombard employees.
- Differentiate and specify why the current D&I council initiatives are better than past efforts that may not have delivered on their promises.
- Motivate and persuade all stakeholders to act.
- Create a memorable and lasting impression.

The D&I council's communications plan should focus on developing a focused set of creative messages that speak directly to employees, managers, and senior executives in personal ways. That is, they should touch on needs and desires. This *insightful* approach demonstrates that the council understands and appreciates the different audiences, circumstances, and perspectives.

The council's communications plan should *captivate employees*, getting their attention with an innovative theme to unify its components and leverage original and provocative messaging to *differentiate* the council's programs from other initiatives. The D&I council's communication plan must target specific employees carefully and be persistent, using the power and reasonableness of their arguments to educate about the program's value in employees' minds while motivating them to support the council's efforts.

Developing an Evaluation Plan

It is common to view metrics and measurements as necessary tedious tasks, but the effort can be rewarding. Understanding where the council stands, weighing successes, identifying shortcomings, and plotting the future is energizing. Being uncertain of the council's situation and confused about the path forward can be disquieting and enervating. Moreover, the benefits of benchmarking easily outweigh its challenges.

D&I councils should develop an assessment model that focuses on the council's success in meeting the company's needs. When creating a D&I council assessment plan, consider the following:

- Assess what the council is willing to change.

- Understand and believe in the value of metrics and let this knowledge shape the development and implementation of D&I council initiatives.

- Create processes for identifying D&I issues and commit to correcting them.

- Measure everything of significance; the council cannot improve what it does not measure.

- Focus on evaluating business impact, which has the most significant influence on the success.

- Be attentive to the essential subjective elements that cannot be quantified.

The next step to ensuring accountability is establishing the measurements for the activities the D&I council wants to measure. In developing an evaluation process, the council should include all relevant stakeholders, be holistic in approach, and measure the council's impact on the business, the workforce, the marketplace, the community, or the industry.

The need for an evaluation system that measures the progress the D&I council is making in achieving its goals and objectives is essential. The council's metrics must be credible, provide subjective and objective results, and make a strong case for the council's value to the company in terms of business needs (i.e., revenue growth, expense reduction, workplace improvement, brand enhancement, and advancing the company's D&I mission).

D&I Council Governance

After the D&I council has developed its business, communications, and assessment plans, the next step is to formalize ideas, decisions, and projects in a charter.

The D&I council's success depends on its ongoing effectiveness and its ability to demonstrate value to the company and its leadership. The D&I council's governance plan should also provide open and honest communications, periodic reporting on activities and accomplishments, and opportunities for feedback and input.

The charter will form the blueprint that defines the council's organizational structure (rules, practices, and procedures) and delineates operation and governance modes. The charter defines the D&I Council's purpose, goals, objectives, and mission. The charter indicates how the D&I council will align its actions with business practices and strategies; work and communicate with D&I staff, senior leadership, and the workforce; and operate and govern the council (officers, elections, membership, powers, voting, amendments).

D&I council charters are unique to each company; however, there are several common elements:

- **Organization**—Describes how the D&I council chair will appoint the committee members; what constitutes a quorum; when the committee will meet; how the plan will be established; how minutes will be written, distributed, and approved; how the council will report back to the executive sponsor and senior leadership team; how the charter will be reviewed on an annual basis; and delineates the committee's leadership positions and their responsibilities.

- **Responsibilities**—Establishes the review, counsel, and evaluation functions of the D&I council, which include support of the D&I team, human resources department, D&I policies, procedures, practices, and activities; the identification of specific D&I issue and problem and amelioration efforts; the legal, regulatory and compliance issues with potential material impacts; and the development of new policies, programs, actions, and procedures.

- **Scope**—Provides an overview of the council's ability to access company records; meets with employees and senior leaders to support these council activities.

Client Case Study

Icarus Consulting was engaged by one of our clients in the beverage industry to conduct a company-wide D&I assessment, analyze the results, and report back to senior leadership with our findings. The company's goal was to make sure they asked the right questions about its diversity and inclusion performance, commitment, and involvement. As a result of this assessment, we helped company leaders understand how employees felt about the culture and work environment. We also informed senior leaders of what they did well and where they needed to improve their D&I efforts.

Client Engagement

The company had a strong focus on D&I. A D&I executive steering committee comprised of senior leaders was in place, along with a D&I council. Ongoing D&I training and education were offered to all employees. However, D&I became less of a strategic priority due to other competing priorities, and the D&I executive steering committee disbanded. While the D&I council remained intact, they lost support, had little influence, and offered no real D&I programs or initiatives.

With the hiring of a new VP of Human Resources (HR), there was a renewed commitment to D&I. Based on previous experience, the VP of HR realized the importance of having a diverse workforce and the necessity of having a culture of inclusion. Given the organization was going through a culture change, it was a perfect time to position D&I as part of the change efforts.

Moving from Awareness to Action

Our client selected four areas to focus on to help employees understand the benefits of building a diverse, highly-skilled, and qualified workforce and advance their diversity and inclusion strategy. One of those focus areas was enhancing its D&I council's capacity and capability. The goal was to explore ways to help the D&I council support the D&I strategy and foster an inclusive, high-performing team. With the help of Icarus Consulting, the D&I council:

- Explored how the D&I council could achieve a more significant impact by leading important initiatives that engage more people.

- Analyzed the mission and goals of the council to ensure alignment with the company's business goals.

- Assessed current activities and initiatives for impact and explore ways to move them from *events* to sustainable *results*.

Methodology and Results

Icarus Consulting helped the company expand the D&I council membership and recruited a senior leader to serve as the council's Executive Sponsor. A formal charter was created, and five subcommittees were formed, each focusing on a critical D&I initiative. The D&I council members took the Icarus Diversity and Inclusion Leadership Assessment™ to gain insight into individual perceptions regarding diversity, equity, and inclusion.

Icarus Consulting helped the D&I council achieve several key results:

- One hundred percent of D&I council members completed the D&I council self-assessment.

- A snapshot of D&I council members' perceptions of the current organization was presented and discussed with council members.

- The analysis showed differences in attitudes based on individual D&I council members' experiences within the current culture, which led to meaningful discussion.

- The report identified areas to enhance and develop the D&I competence and capabilities of the council.
- Data from the D&I council assessment was used to direct and guide the D&I council strategy.
- The D&I assessment expanded and reinvigorated the D&I council to focus efforts.
- One hundred percent of D&I council members attended the D&I council Certification Course™, which enhanced the council's ability to support the D&I strategy.

Lessons Learned

Icarus Consulting helped the company leverage its D&I council to help drive employee engagement and innovation. The company effectively used its D&I council to gain a snapshot of its culture and used it as a baseline to measure future progress. Our clients effectively used a D&I council self-assessment tool we designed for them to gain a clear picture of the D&I council's strengths and challenges. Assessing organizational culture and D&I council competencies provided developmental opportunities for both the organization and the D&I council to become more inclusive and culturally competent.

Think About This

Today there is much more focus on measuring the impact and demonstrating the value of the D&I council. While more companies measure the impact of the D&I council, it's important to remember that it's not a "one size fits all" approach. Organizations should approach the measurement of the D&I council in different ways and at their own pace. It may begin with something as simple as measuring the impact of D&I council training. With more evidence of the D&I council's impact on organizational business objectives and outcomes, more leaders will support the D&I council.

D&I councils are well established throughout the private and public sectors. D&I councils represent one of the best and surest ways to integrate the company's D&I activities, demonstrate its executive team's commitment to diversity and inclusion, align D&I to business priorities, and enable councils, senior leaders, D&I staff, employee resource groups, and other employee teams, business units, and departments to work together effectively, honestly, and openly to advance D&I initiatives throughout the company.

SECTION FOUR: RESET THE CULTURE

CHAPTER 9

Leading Tomorrow's Workforce: The CEO As Chief Trust Officer

Introduction

This chapter covers the business case to transform the organization's workplace culture into a more inclusive culture. It starts by shining a bright light on diversity and inclusion and ask the tough questions about what has been effective—and why progress has been so slow. It argues that despite decades of handwringing, costly initiatives, and uncomfortable conversations, organizations have fallen far short of their goals apart from a few exceptions. We incisively show the vast gap between the rhetoric of inclusion and real achievements. Lastly, it starkly predicts that if organizations deliver on the promise of diversity and inclusion, they need to abandon ineffective, costly measures and commit to combatting enduring racial attitudes, bias, disparate treatment, and systemic inequities.

We also highlight the extraordinary success stories and speculate about the valuable lessons other organizations need to learn to match those gains.

The Intersection of Trust and Inclusion

In the past decade, diversity and inclusion efforts have grown from mostly a matter of compliance to an urgent matter for company success. It's no longer an issue confined to the HR function; it has become top-of-mind for CEOs who understand its long-term implications for their businesses. The work of creating diverse, equitable, and inclusive companies is proving harder than ever. Why? The answer lies in deep-rooted implicit biases that few people recognize.

As diversity and inclusion have moved to the front burner for CEOs, the concept has also broadened from familiar categories of gender, geography, race, and the like, to an understanding of difference as any characteristic that the dominant group in a context might consider "other." That dominant group could be the usual suspects—white males seemingly partial to people who look just like them, or it could be an engineering culture uncomfortable with people's ideas and business orientation from customer-centric backgrounds. In yet another organization, the diversity problem might be a shortage of people with a genuinely global outlook. In this broader understanding, true diversity is a difference of perspectives. It is a range of informed opinions, educated views, and ideas, and it is perhaps the best source of innovation and organizational creativity.

This broader understanding involves considerable nuance. It acknowledges that people from diverse backgrounds and orientations are often more varied because of different assumptions and norms. However, it also insists that the focus on the diversity of ideas, as opposed to the background, should not become an excuse for recruiting only those who look like the hiring manager and who, in the worst case, turn out to lack even the diversity of ideas that is the business value of diversity in the first place.

Moreover, leading companies now understand that diversity, by itself, is not enough. It must be accompanied by inclusion—a company culture that genuinely welcomes, values, and leverages diversity advantages. That does not mean merely assimilating different employees into the culture—in effect, making them clones of the dominant group, but enabling their differences to flourish, complement each other, and be put to work. Think, for example, of the way leading orchestras, distinguished theater companies, and top sports organizations put diversity and inclusion to work in high-performance teams capable of greatness.

Barriers to Trust: False Impressions and Cumulative Inequities

Merely creating a diverse workforce without harnessing its virtues to the business may satisfy compliance mandates, but it fails to meet the many business reasons that drive diversity today. Innovative companies understand that, and they must embrace the compelling business case for diversity and inclusion—at least in principle.

In principle, despite the almost universal acceptance of the business case, even the most well-intentioned companies often run into great difficulty in achieving diversity and inclusion in practice. Why, despite apparent goodwill and genuine desire to put diversity to work, is it so hard to do? A large part of the answer lies in the implicit biases that prevent us from accurately interpreting the behavior, character, motives, and worth of people who differ from us.

Social psychologists tell us that we invariably make the same mistakes in interpreting other people's actions. We overestimate the importance of fundamental character traits as a cause of the behavior, and we underestimate the context and situation. For example, a person studying diligently for an exam attributes their success to being intelligent, while an observer sees the person as "hard-working." The psychologists call such mistakes "fundamental attribution error" or "actor-observer bias."

By any name, this deeply ingrained habit of thought can be highly destructive when it involves people the observer regards as "other." If someone else fails to complete a task, we will likely attribute it to a character flaw like laziness rather than extenuating circumstances. Conversely, if we fail to complete a task, we tend to blame someone else. When such judgments are generalized to cover all the diverse group members, the result is "ultimate attribution error," or what is commonly called stereotyping or biases.

Insufficient attention to biases can lead to an organization being permeated by "microinequities": small slights, subtle insensitivities, and little daily acts of often unconscious exclusion that cumulatively demoralize and often derail employees. These systematic implicit biases and errors can wreak havoc with an organization's ability to create an inclusive environment for people whose backgrounds and perspectives differ from the majority (i.e., women, people of color, gay, differently-abled). For example, if a woman succeeds in an effort, some people might attribute such success to external circumstances—a good economy or a lucky break. If the diverse member fails at a task, it is often attributed to some structural deficiency of character or ability.

Some employees expect a woman or person of color to have specific characteristics from a broader perspective, even though these same employees have no information about the individual being judged.

These biases lead, in turn, to discriminatory behavior such as in-group bias—the tendency to give preferential treatment to others perceived to be members of the group or to the setting up of formal and informal groups that might exclude employees who may represent differences. The dangers of this are evident in recruiting, retention, promotion, and succession planning—that is, on the frontlines of diversity.

More insidiously, insufficient attention to these biases can lead to an organization being permeated by microinequities. For example, men habitually bantering about sports before meetings may subtly exclude female employees. A condescending tone, a name repeatedly mispronounced, implicit signs of low expectations for the other person's performance—any of these can send negative signals and create a competitive atmosphere. Those on the receiving end may eventually find it intolerable and leave the company.

All these inequities, big and small, visible and not so apparent, add to a failure to capitalize on diversity's business promise. Because they are deeply rooted in human cognition, they are complicated to see and even more challenging to address. They are the proverbial elephants in the room that no one wants to acknowledge. After all, who wants to admit to a bias of any kind—or is even capable of recognizing it, since it is so deeply ingrained in the thought processes we experience as entirely rational and irreproachable?

This is the great unspoken in too many approaches to diversity. Bypassing over in silence the real roots of the challenge, we minimize its difficulty. Not surprisingly, the result is often suboptimal diversity and inclusion efforts. It demoralizes employees and produces disappointing business results that undermine the organization's commitment to diversity and inclusion in the future. Until this reality is acknowledged and addressed, the benefits of diversity and inclusion will remain elusive.

Trust and Diversity as a Leadership Competencies

A sustainable diversity and inclusion strategy starts with the understanding that the ability to work across differences is a crucial leadership competency for chief diversity officers and top executives. CEOs should insist that it be a well-developed skill set of the executives on their teams and probe for it when hiring top executives, just as they probe for technical expertise or strategic insight. Only then will diversity genuinely start at the top, not just because there is a C-level executive responsible for it but also because it is a competency required of everyone in the C-suite. Just as important, everyone aspires to the C-suite.

The ability to handle diversity is as concrete and measurable as any of the more familiar leadership competencies. Based on experience working with senior management teams across industries and on more than 25,000 management appraisals, including appraisals of CEOs, CFOs, COOs, and CIOs conducted during the past five years, Icarus Consulting has developed a comprehensive model of leadership that encompasses ten core competencies of senior executives. One of those competencies explicitly focuses on diversity.

The other competencies are results orientation, team leadership, collaboration and influencing, strategic orientation, market orientation, change leadership, developing organizational capability, customer impact, and market knowledge. The model provides a baseline measurement of how leaders evaluated as "outstanding," "good," and "average" scored on our scale for measuring each of the competencies.

A score at the lower end of the range indicates purely reactive behaviors with short-term impact. Ratings in the middle indicate more proactive action. A top score represents highly dynamic behaviors focused on broad, long-term implications.

The differences in scores and what they mean in concrete terms can be significant. Executives who score poorly accept the validity of other cultures and other viewpoints, but they don't act on that understanding. They understand that a specific business area may have unique operations and people who differ from the larger organization's mainstream. They understand cultural differences between regions or organizations and realize that sociopolitical factors in other countries or organizations influence business opportunities. But they do not view tackling diversity and inclusion as an imperative, and their response to it is mostly passive.

Executives who score in the middle reaches of the scale go beyond understanding to action. They demonstrate their acceptance of other points of view by changing their own and advocating "other" business approaches because of the perceived superiority of those approaches. Further, they get results working with diverse colleagues (again, defined in terms of the relevant difference from the majority, whatever the difference might be). They seek out differing views and anticipate how diverse colleagues and groups will respond to their opinions. As managers, they can make appropriate decisions tailored to the sociocultural circumstances in which they are operating. These are all laudable and valuable behaviors, and companies who have such executives are fortunate.

Executives who score in the upper reaches of the scale possess a deep understanding of diversity and inclusion. They take proactive steps to put diversity and inclusion to work for the company, and they act as facilitators between different groups and cultures. They are not only able to leverage diversity but also able to educate others in the organization about how to do so. There is friction; they can guide those with differences to work together to produce results more smoothly. They understand the power of diversity both internally and in markets, and their competency in diversity is integrated with their skills in strategic orientation and market orientation. Leaders consciously use appropriate influencing approaches to negotiate across differences and agendas to create and maintain momentum for a common purpose.

It is essential that, when considering new members for their team, CEOs discuss diversity and inclusion with senior job candidates, both to signal how seriously the company takes it and to make sure firsthand that the candidate has the degree of competency required.

As with any essential leadership competency, understanding diversity and the typical behaviors for each performance level is valuable in three critical ways. First, it provides an assessment tool for CEOs and heads of HR looking to hire the right executives for the executive team. Second, it provides an additional and increasingly important criterion that CEOs and other senior leaders can use to select, promote, and develop team members. Third, it offers a personal development roadmap that executives and managers can use to improve their behavior and performance regarding diversity and inclusion.

It is essential that, when considering new members for their team, CEOs engage candidates on diversity and inclusion, both to signal how seriously the company takes it and to make sure first-hand that the candidate has the degree of competency required. That includes new members who might be promoted from within as well as external candidates.

If the candidate is internal, the CEO might know specific situations and ask even more probing and pointed questions. Similarly, with an external candidate found through executive search firms, the CEO should be well supplied with interview questions, assuming the executive search firm has done its homework.

Diversity and inclusion are essential leadership competencies on which every top executive should be expected to perform well. The key to interviewing is not merely to ask candidates how they feel about diversity and inclusion. It is far more revealing to ask interviewees to tell stories about their experiences. For example, "Tell me about a time that you felt yourself in conflict with a definable group or someone you regarded as fundamentally different from you in your company. What was the nature of the conflict, and what was your part in it? How was it resolved?" Ask them to describe instances in which they saw diversity and inclusion contribute to business value—precisely, the nature of the contribution, such as an idea, a way of working, or a perspective that would otherwise have gone unconsidered.

Conversely, ask for instances in which diversity and inclusion issues hindered the realization of business value and what role the candidate played in addressing the situation. The goal is to talk about behavior, which is far more revealing than an abstract discussion about attitudes. And no one is likely to have a better view of the big picture—the entire fabric of diversity and inclusion throughout the company, than the CEO, who is ultimately responsible for making it work.

Many companies realize they must address diversity and inclusion processes and infrastructure. However, fewer understand that diversity is an essential leadership competency on which every top executive should be expected to perform well. And fewer still are fully aware that the real root of the problem lies in our implicit biases—the fundamental errors of attribution, the unjustified assumptions, and the reflexive stereotyping that form blind spots when it comes to those who differ from us.

As individuals and organizations, we need to continually remind ourselves that implicit biases are hard to see and even harder to eradicate. Those who are not convinced can try this quick thought experiment: Did you unconsciously assume that the candidates reflected the company mainstream in the discussion above about probing diversity and inclusion? Why couldn't the candidates just as well be women or people of color? Why shouldn't they be put to the same test? It's a relatively good error; the assumption that diversity candidates don't need to be examined for their diversity competency indicates why it is essential to approach diversity with great care.

CEOs who understand the nuances of implicit bias, nip microinequities in the bud, and hire for diversity and inclusion competency will find it is well worth the effort. With the commitment to diversity and inclusion—and leadership competence in addressing it—flowing from the top, such CEOs create the potential for a wealth of business benefits. The organization becomes open to infusions of fresh ideas and new perspectives that can lead to previously unrecognized opportunities in products, services, and markets. Operations across borders and cultures benefit from greater understanding and cooperation, boosting productivity and effectiveness. The company earns an excellent reputation that strengthens the brand, appeals to increasingly diverse customers, attracts top talent from whatever source, and energizes all employees. And the CEO succeeds where many others have struggled because he or she has started by grasping the real roots of the challenge—making diversity and inclusion work.

Trust as a Component of Authentic Leadership

As a diversity and inclusion professional who has dedicated almost two decades to helping leaders manage diverse work teams and create inclusive workplaces, I offer some thoughts of what CEOs can do to develop and sustain diverse, equitable, inclusive, and profitable companies. After all, the workplace is where people spend most of their waking time and given the uniqueness of a group of people connected by a common purpose. There is an opportunity to take advantage of this unique context in certain places to leverage trust as an inclusion multiplier.

Lead inclusively: Leaders should acknowledge that the concerns of all parties are real. Employees experiencing emotional issues outside the company's walls are not left behind as they arrive at work and swipe their ID badges. The sense of threat and insecurity is an underlying tension that saps productivity, and things only worsen when leaders don't acknowledge this reality. Our times call for leaders with the courage to speak about these polarizations and forge a third way. Omission through passivity is not a neutral stance. It can contribute to greater divisiveness.

Today's polarized environments can stir more blaming than bridge-building. Leaders can help all sides listen to one another to acknowledge and own their parts in forging new solutions rather than merely blaming those with different points of view.

As I shared in my book, *Winter in America: The Impact of the 2016 Presidential Election on Diversity in Companies, Communities, and the Country*, so much of the 2016 presidential election was fueled by fear caused by economic dislocations for so many and exacerbated by scapegoating that has given way to ugly and frightening exhibits of hate. But most people are not haters. Most are scared and at a loss of what will restore their livelihoods, whether in the neglected inner cities or the overlooked countryside. However, when leaders offer comfort and compassion and encourage teams to take time out to talk about what is going on for each of them and be heard by those who voted for a different candidate, it can lead to healthier companies and communities.

Lead authentically: CEOs can engender trust by demonstrating authentic leadership and making it personal, first through transparent reflection and then action. Leaders, like everyone else, are personally affected by the social justice movement. To be an effective leader in this context, it is helpful to pause and reflect on exactly what these effects are. This entails a process in which leaders connect with their core values, principles, and beliefs. Authentic leadership begins with this kind of centering. Only by admitting to ourselves that we feel vulnerable, afraid, and even angry, and then doing the work of gathering perspective and strength from our core beliefs, can we begin to offer genuine empathy and clearer thinking that will nurture trust and more inclusive environments within our organizations.

From here, leaders can speak publicly and personally to create more relevance and connection. The most authentic stance to offer insight is from the vantage point of one's personal story. How did the social justice movement affect each person emotionally and practically? Opinions can be debated as right or wrong—personal stories much less so.

Lead boldly: Leaders should project a willingness to change. My colleague offered this one, Jim Rogers, author of numerous books on leadership, including *Managing Differently*.

Rogers suggests that anxious employees will look toward leaders who can adjust to change quickly. Inclusive leaders understand they need to include others and include themselves as the first movers of change. It is paramount for leaders to change strategies, systems, and cultures to transform organizations. But too often, we forget the foundational, most fundamental aspect of change: changing our leadership style. According to Rogers, CEOs who lead boldly accelerate positive, compelling, inclusive change. When robust and inclusive leadership is needed, corporate leaders should not forget to change what they want to see and accelerate it.

Lead confidently: On the protective side, of course, you want your organization to be vigilant about any hate speech and acts and be swift in addressing them. With the three principles described here, on the proactive side, get practical and act confidently by simply getting groups of employees talking. First, provide ground rules such as: don't debate policies; instead, talk about needs and aspirations. Don't attack the person; discuss perspectives. Listen to understand rather than listen to the debate. Have a skilled facilitator lead a session where each person in the conversation shares what they hope to get out of life personally and for their family. The facilitator should capture all responses once everyone has shared, start with the commonalities that emerged, and slowly move into the differences. The group size should be limited to ten to twelve people, and the group should have a skilled facilitator. Then replicate this throughout the organization.

The ideas here are modest compared to what will need to be done to address the high-stakes battles fought in the public square with dramatic livelihood and even life-threatening implications for individuals, families, and communities. But suppose we can get people who have become antagonistic, fearful, and suspicious of one another due to their differences talking with each other, then, each time we do, we can declare a small victory and build from there.

Best Practices

Our political leaders do not demonstrate the concept of civility, compassion, and common decency that we expect from our coworkers. It concerns me to see how far that will go in the workplace. So, what can we realistically do about it? How can we reduce stress in the workplace and mitigate the emotional exhaustion felt by most of our employees?

In my book, *Crisis as a Platform for Social Change from Strawberry Mansion to Silicon Valley*, I suggest that "change starts with leadership." Leaders need to model positive behavior to help people work through their anxiety. This starts with acknowledging the unsettled feelings some people may be experiencing.

In research for this book, I surveyed over 100 companies in the Atlanta metro area. I discovered that well over half (60 percent) of respondents said their companies hadn't communicated to their employees' potential changes to health care, work visas, or international travel. But staying silent or hoping that everyone works through it on their own is not an effective strategy.

Social crisis events like the #MeToo and the #BlackLivesMatter movements require that we create a safe space to talk about social justice without inciting conflict by focusing on its feelings, such as anxiety and uncertainty. This begins by asking front-line managers to identify precisely what employees need to hear from the CEO and other senior leaders to settle their apprehension and anxiety. Focus on the things you can control, such as employees' workload, the tone and tenor of team discussions, and how you react to the unexpected. Organizations should create a strategy and communication plan that acknowledges what people may feel and includes consistent messaging across the organization.

Simple steps can make a big difference. Some best practices include organizations starting the workday with brief meditation exercises to help employees focus on the work at hand. Another popular best practice includes organizations insisting that employees step away from their desks intermittently for quick deep-breathing breaks or encouraging them to take a walk or refuel in the breakroom. At one of our client companies, the chief human resource officer leads daily five-to-ten-minute dance breaks, inviting employees to participate in HR's version of the Soul Train Line or participating in line dances like The Wobble. Some other actions to consider:

- If your company offers EAP benefits, be sure that employees know their benefits and how to access the confidential services.
- When necessary, call for a time-out on a political discussion in the office. Such boundary-setting by managers can help team members who are still recovering from postelection stress and fatigue.
- Dial back the pressure on projects that don't demand it. Not everything is urgent. Revisit and reset, where appropriate, your

team's priorities and communicate the new expectation.

- If your workplace deals directly with customers, consider tuning TVs and radio stations in common areas to neutral stations such as cooking or home and garden programming. The same goes for TV monitors that may be in common areas shared by employees. One CHRO recently shared with me that there was minor conflict over setting the channel to a specific cable news station at her company. If you need to take a time-out and turn TV monitors off altogether, do it.

Think About This

Building an inclusive culture is no small undertaking. CEOs are very protective of their cultures, as they provide a blueprint for how to behave. Cultures create norms for operating and enable some level of predictability in an uncertain and competitive marketplace. Changing culture may require uprooting beliefs and practices with which employees have become comfortable. CEOs have the primary role of creating and sustaining the company's culture. This is done through the leader's ongoing communications, advocacy, sponsorship, and personal interactions with others. Additionally, whether focused in one area or enterprise-wide, culture transformation efforts should be done incrementally and address all systems within the organization, e.g., talent management systems, etc.

A survey conducted in August 2020, three months before the presidential election, by the American Psychological Association found that one in four U.S. employees reported being negatively affected by political discussions at work. Younger workers especially reported diminished productivity and increased stress. And many employees reported feeling distanced from their colleagues and having more negative attitudes toward them, and an uptick in workplace hostility, all due to political conversations.

In research for this book, I conducted a survey of 100 companies in metro Atlanta on the Georgia election's impact for two Senate seats on the workplace. More than 25 percent of respondents said they experienced a negative effect on workplace productivity. Another 43 percent said they were undecided or didn't know the overall impact; they conceded the election created uncertainty, which undoubtedly contributed to a degree of distraction.

In October 2020, I spoke at the MRA Annual Conference, and the personal stories and observations shared by conference participants I talked to reflect these themes:

- "The election is impacting workforce productivity. Suddenly there is confusing guidance or lack of clarity on the practical applications of several employment laws. The Trump administration has created a tremendous amount of work. It has heightened anxiety across a huge population of employees who don't know how they will be impacted by immigration changes, health care, etc. It has created a distraction," noted a participant.

- "The presidential election is creating uncertainty for our employees and job candidates with nonimmigrant work visa status, which serves as a distraction," said another conference participant.

- "Those who are not directly impacted by the election have expressed that they have family members who are impacted, close and distant. This causes added stress to their lives, affecting health and well-being. Others who are reminded of their immigrant experience fear that their country could be added or have empathy for current immigrants and refugees' plight. The sense of helplessness and frustration in our company is palpable."

Almost everyone agrees that in the months following the 2020 presidential election, the country collectively experienced subtle and not-so-subtle social changes that have unavoidably carried over into the workplace.

We continue to witness the emergence of a growing community of dissenters; protests, rallies, and other public demonstrations are regular occurrences. There have been calls for a nationwide strike. Over two dozen groups have announced plans for protests.

In general, we seem to be more tuned in to what is happening and consuming more news. The New York Times reported record growth in readership, adding 276,000 digital-only subscribers at the start of the 2020 presidential election cycle. Cable and network news viewership is up as well. And if it's possible, we're checking our Twitter accounts even more frequently than usual. But all this close attention to the latest news updates, tweets, or alerts feels like a Groundhog Day-like a loop of waiting for the other shoe to drop (and there are many shoes). It isn't helping with most employees feeling less positive or productive. More likely, we are exhausted and a little depressed by it all.

CHAPTER 10

The Power to be Better: The Georgia Power Case Study

Introduction

This chapter examines the case study of a large organization's efforts to create a trust culture by reducing bias. It covers the organization's specific actions in shaping, guiding, and sponsoring diversity and inclusion programs and initiatives to increase employee engagement and trust. It also includes methods the CEO put in place to ensure accountability and sustainability in the organization.

The Georgia Power case depicts the company's efforts to transform its culture and describes its detailed steps to manage a complex culture-change initiative. It also discusses the company's business rationale for the diversity and inclusion initiatives, identifies roadblocks encountered by the company during implementation, and explores how the barriers were managed.

The case study's specific situations are based on archival data and first-hand experience with the events described in the case study. The goal is to help you obtain an integrative and systematic perspective about complicated change-management efforts to creating and sustaining a diverse, equity, inclusive workplace based on justice.

The Beginning of Never

It was the summer of 2000, and things were going exceptionally well at Georgia Power. A heatwave had air conditioners humming and electric meters spinning. The company's 8,000- plus employees were executing the business fundamentals, meeting a record demand for electricity, and serving the needs of almost two million customers. In other words, the company was doing everything possible to meet its commitment of "keeping the lights on" and "being a citizen wherever the company served," philosophies put forth many years earlier by Georgia Power's first president, Preston Arkwright Sr.

Amid all this success, on July 27, 2000, three African American employees filed a racial discrimination lawsuit against Georgia Power and its parent, Atlanta-based Southern Company, in Fulton County Superior Court. Four more employees eventually joined the original three and alleged that the company "systematically discriminated against African American employees" in pay and promotion and maintained a racially hostile work environment.

The lawsuit against Georgia Power was one of several lawsuits at the time against some of Georgia's largest corporations. In April 1999, for example, eight African American employees at Coca-Cola filed a lawsuit accusing the company of discriminating against its African American employees in pay, promotions, performance evaluations, and terminations. In June of that same year, the second group of workers filed a race discrimination suit against Coca-Cola; the company tentatively resolved the first case on the same day. In July 2000, African American employees at Home Depot also filed a lawsuit claiming the company fostered a "pattern of discrimination against African-Americans and showed reckless indifference to a hostile work environment."

During this same timeframe, African American employees had also filed discrimination lawsuits against several large Atlanta-based companies. The accusations ranged from discrimination in job responsibilities to retaliation for filing discrimination complaints. The trend was not unique to Atlanta, but some lawyers and diversity experts conceded that the city was ripe for race-discrimination lawsuits because of its image as a Mecca for African Americans, intense competition for top-paying jobs, and the fact that African American employees at Atlanta's premier corporation, Coca-Cola, had filed the first major suit, setting the example for African American employees at other Atlanta companies to follow.

Just weeks after filing the lawsuit against Georgia Power, the Equal Opportunity Commission announced actions taken against twenty companies across the United States because of racial discrimination incidents. The Equal Employment Opportunity Commission also confirmed it was investigating dozens of other complaints involving racial discrimination. According to the Equal Employment Opportunity Commission, charges of racial harassment were on the rise. In 1999, the Equal Employment Opportunity Commission received 6,249 charges alleging racial harassment, accounting for eight percent of all charges filed with the agency. During the 1990s, the Equal Employment Opportunity Commission received a cumulative total of 47,175 such charges (six percent of all charges filed), compared to a cumulative total of 9,757 racial harassment charges in the 1980s (almost two percent of all charges filed). Retaliation charges also increased to the point where they represented 25 percent of all costs (19,694) filed in 1999.

Where there's Smoke

For several years, internal employee engagement surveys had indicated that employees throughout all levels of the company had a fear of sharing unfavorable information and had a concern about what they could and could not say to senior managers. For example, the company's 2006 employee engagement survey asked employees to respond to the statement, *"I can share my opinion without fear of retaliation."* Almost 60 percent of employees who responded indicated "never," "seldom," or "sometimes." This response was consistent across all employee categories and demographics, including gender, race, ethnicity, job classification, job tenure, and department. The problem was especially acute in the management ranks, where 33 percent of managers responded on the survey that they were uncomfortable sharing their opinion and unfavorable information with their immediate supervisor because of a fear of retaliation.

The company had processes, policies, and a code of conduct that explicitly prohibited discrimination, harassment, and retaliation; however, employee fear of retaliation had emerged as a barrier preventing Georgia Power from achieving a diverse and inclusive workplace.

Compounding the problem was the disturbing fact that employees did not trust the company's employee concerns process to resolve issues like retaliation. The company's employee concerns process, considered by senior leaders as the "crown jewel" of the company's D&I initiatives, was based on best practices learned from other companies and had been in place for over five years. The workplace ethics department, created in the lawsuit's wake, had responsibility for the program, which included well-publicized reporting procedures, a twenty-four-hour helpline for employees, and trained workplace ethics coordinators devoted to hearing and investigating employee concerns.

The company's previous employee concerns process and the Equal Employment Opportunity department were restructured in the wake of the lawsuit and a subsequent internal investigation, which discovered a substantial lack of trust in the company's Equal Employment Opportunity department and how they handled employee concerns. As a result, the company revised the process. It implemented a new method for investigating employee concerns and creating new avenues of appeal for employees after an investigation had been completed and a decision reached.

The company had made several other substantive enhancements to the Workplace Ethics department and employee concerns process. However, employee surveys conducted after a company reorganization revealed, surprisingly, that despite a seemingly excellent workplace ethics department, many employees had continued to report a fear of retaliation concerning using the company's internal procedures for filing claims of mistreatment, challenging leadership behaviors they believed were unfair, and reporting concerns of retaliation.

Providing employees with a safe, effective, and robust means to report suspected misconduct and other concerns is one of the most critical and challenging components of changing a company's culture. Creating a culture where most employees speak up and feel compelled to do so was one of several paradigms Georgia Power acknowledged it had to change to create a diverse, equitable, and inclusive workplace.

There are myriad challenges for companies attempting to create an effective employee concerns process. Perhaps none is more challenging than a fear of retaliation. Add to this the perception that reporting may be futile, and it is easy to understand why it was hard for the company to create a culture in which employees felt comfortable reporting their concerns.

The difficulty of establishing a culture that welcomes speaking out and challenging the status quo was a prominent finding in the Ethics Resource Center's 2008 National Business Ethics Survey.

In a nationally representative survey of employees at all levels, the study found a tremendous amount of observed misconducts in the workplace that go unchallenged and unreported. For example, according to the survey, more than 40 percent of employees who observe misconduct do not challenge or report it. The main reasons for the failure to report were the feeling of futility and the fear of retaliation. The survey also found that approximately 13 percent of employees who filed a concern believed they experienced some form of retaliation for reporting their concerns.

Like most companies, Georgia Power found that it was a continuous challenge to get employees to the point where they were comfortable speaking up, challenging things they believed to be wrong, and reporting misconduct. But more than most companies, Georgia Power took an aggressive and creative approach to combat employees' fears of retaliation. The ambitious culture change initiative was designed to create a culture of inclusion through justice by reducing employees' fear of retaliation.

Crisis as a Platform for Change

The company's first move was to get at the root of employee discomfort and identify why employees were not comfortable reporting their concerns. To ascertain how employees perceived and understood retaliation, the company hired an external consultant. In part, the external consultant was selected because of their expertise in human capital risk management and their ability to help companies diagnose complex cultural, ethical, and related risk-mitigation issues. The external consultant was asked to accomplish three specific objectives:

1. Analyze the previous D&I culture audits, employee surveys, and work environment assessments to confirm and identify the root cause(s) of retaliation in the culture.

2. Identify the specific behaviors employees perceived as retaliatory and delineate the fears and perceptions by job level within the company.

3. Provide analysis and recommendations as to what specific actions the company should take to address the problems.

The consulting firm reviewed the internal company information and conducted focus group meetings with employees. External consultants also studied employee engagement survey results and analyzed data from dozens of different sources. The external consultants reviewed over 2,000 company documents and correlated over 110,000 data points in performing a statistically significant Gap Matrix as part of their audit.

The consultants assigned to the project established a 95 percent confidence bandwidth and a .70 correlation coefficient in identifying the factors that could explain the level of variation in the percentage of employees who feared retaliation. The assessment methodology included the four organizational development consultants reviewing the theme filters, data, and findings independently and jointly. As a result of this comprehensive and scientific investigation, the consulting firm was able to define with a high degree of confidence what retaliation behavior looked like from the perspective of Georgia Power employees:

Retaliation within Georgia Power is demonstrated by a pattern of unwelcome, unjust, unreasonable behavior that intentionally or unintentionally creates feelings of humiliation, hurt, embarrassment, and degradation. Although these behaviors do not meet the legal standard of retaliation, they create a work environment where employees do not feel valued, respected, or productive. Consequently, these subtle and specific behaviors and communication patterns eventually reduce employee trust in leadership, undermine employee engagement, and retard organizational effectiveness. Retaliatory behavior in the Georgia Power culture is often linked to both informal and formal forms of power in the workplace. Peers-toward-peers, employees-toward-

managers, and managers-toward-employees can exhibit it." (Excerpt from Executive Summary of Final Report Provided to Georgia Power Management Council, 2006)

The external consultants identified ten specific behaviors perceived by employees to be retaliatory in order of pervasiveness:

1. **Rewarding conformity**—Consistently rewarding and recognizing only those who conform and who "do not rock the boat."

2. **Limiting development**—Deliberately derailing a person's career by continuously isolating them to hold them back or slow their advancement.

3. **Applying selective memory**—Continually bringing up adverse events in the past, even if the event is ten years old, as employees believed one adverse event would permanently damage a person's career.

4. **Isolating employees**—Continually overlooking a person for developmental assignments or opportunities to take on additional responsibilities.

5. **Withholding information**—Deliberately withholding work-related information or resources, including emails.

6. **Using harsh body language**—Constantly engaging in subtle body language or using a tone of speech that could be interpreted as threatening, disapproving, or abusing.

7. **Encouraging public ridicule**—Consistently making someone the ongoing brunt of jokes, pranks, or practical jokes.

8. **Using vague communicating**—Repeatedly failing to communicate the "real" reasons for actions or decisions.

9. **Ostracizing challengers**—Excluding a person from formal and informal meetings.

10. **Pressuring nonconformists to comply**—Exerting subtle pressure to go along with something that the person feels is not right.

The company's senior leadership team was surprised that employees interpreted the concept of "retaliation" much more broadly than lawyers or the courts had previously done. Senior leaders in the company were equally surprised to learn that very subtle perceived slights could impede employees' desire to report concerns just as much, if not more, than a manager's intentional conduct or behavior.

The external consultant's audit confirmed that the fear of retaliation inhibited the company's diversity and inclusion efforts. Moreover, the consultants were able to identify the flow of retaliation and delineate which employee groups had the greatest fear of reprisals. Before the external consultant's investigation, it was widely assumed by senior leaders in the company that the most significant percentage of employees who feared retaliation were those employees covered under the company's collective bargaining agreement (union employees). Although this was true (26 percent), the next most significant gap was seen between the officers, directors, and frontline managers who reported directly to them.

The magnitude of the problem for this group (20 percent) suggested that managers feared retaliation from the executives they reported directly to, at a rate like that of the frontline union employees. The latter reported directly to a first-line supervisor. A forensic study of the situation by the outside consulting firm revealed that the fear of retaliation potentially contributed to several other problems for the company, such as communication.

Many middle managers were not telling the executives they reported to the things they needed to know for fear of how they would react. The external consultant conducted focus group meetings with employees from the company's customer service department and discovered that some employees were reluctant to tell their manager about specific customer complaints. The consensus sentiment was, "If I tell the manager what customers are saying, my career will be over." The external consultant cautioned the company that, "If retaliation is this large of an issue at the top of the company—those who are to set the proper example—it goes to follow that it is an issue throughout the company."

The company's top executives spent a day at an offsite location reviewing the external consultants' findings and determining what steps were needed to create the company culture and atmosphere where all employees wanted to work by building trust between employees and their managers.

Researchers Identify Underlying Causes

During this period, Georgia Power was not the only company whose culture was afflicted with this unhealthy organizational behavior. From the rank and file right up through senior management, employees in several other companies feared retaliation. Numerous research studies empirically identified the factors that caused employees to bring ideas to their supervisors and managers or withhold them from management. The research discovered that many organizations had formal mechanisms, such as an ombudsperson and grievance procedures, for encouraging employees to speak up about serious problems. However, almost 50 percent of the employees who responded to the survey revealed they "felt it was not safe to speak up or challenge traditional ways of doing things."

The research also revealed that although employees were reluctant to talk about problems, they were more afraid of offering creative ideas for improving products, processes, or performance. Researchers suggested that the primary reason behind employees' reticence was self-preservation. While it is understandable why some employees fear to bring up specific issues such as whistleblowing, the study found the innate protective instinct so compelling that it also often prevented employees from speaking up even when it was clear that the suggestion or opinion would have helped the organization. More specifically, researchers reported that the perceived risks of speaking up felt very personal and immediate to employees in their interviews. In contrast, the possible future benefit to the organization from sharing their ideas was uncertain.

Consequently, employees often instinctively played it safe by applying the adage, *"When in doubt, keep your mouth shut."* Employees shared with the researchers that in some cases, they feared speaking up because managers had been genuinely hostile about past suggestions. In other cases, managers' behavior was subtle, and employees were inhibited by body language, tone of voice, and other broad and often vague behaviors perceived by employees as retaliatory.

Organizational behavior researchers found that a culture of collective myths also proved chilling. For example, during their interviews, they heard stories of individuals in the organization who had said something in a public meeting and were suddenly taken off the project. The researchers also found that implicit, untested assumptions and perceptions also prevented employees from speaking out. In several situations, participants in the survey reported withholding information from a supervisor or manager because they believed (often without any evidence) that the manager felt personal ownership of the project, process, or issue in question and resented suggestions that implied a need for change. Employees also believed (again, without direct experience) that their manager would feel betrayed if constructive ideas for change were offered when more senior leaders were present at meetings.

Supreme Court Decision Creates a Duty to Act

Just as Georgia Power was beginning to understand the broad way employees defined retaliation, the courts had also started to interpret retaliation more broadly (although not as widely as Georgia Power employees described it). To establish a claim of retaliation, courts typically required that an employee show they engaged in a protected activity such as reporting discrimination and consequently suffered an adverse employment action such as being fired because of reporting their concern, which is an activity protected by state federal law. What immediately got the attention of Georgia Power's leaders, company attorneys, and outside legal counsel was that in *Burlington Northern & Santa Fe Railway Co. v. White*, the United States Supreme Court defined retaliation and adverse employment actions quite broadly.

In *Burlington Northern & Santa Fe Railway Co. v. White*, the Supreme Court held that to establish retaliation under Title VII, and a plaintiff must show that a reasonable employee would have found the challenged conduct "materially adverse," which means it "well might have dissuaded a reasonable worker from" making a report.

In other words, to show retaliation, a plaintiff must establish that the company's conduct would have discouraged a reasonable employee from reporting. For example, the Supreme Court concluded that potentially retaliatory behavior could include altering work schedules (even without reducing payment) or hiring private investigators to follow an employee if a reasonable employee would consider these actions retaliatory.

Although many of the slights and behaviors perceived by Georgia Power employees such as failure to be invited to a meeting or be copied on emails—did not measure up to the legal standard of retaliation, the company realized that Supreme Court's decision in the *Burlington Northern & Santa Fe Railway Co. v. White* case had significantly reduced the gap between the legal definition of retaliation and Georgia Power employees' perceptions of what constituted retaliation.

While many of Georgia Power's leaders embraced the company's efforts to mitigate the fear of retaliation, as with any cutting-edge corporate initiative, some had concerns. Some managers felt that identifying employees' behaviors as retaliatory and talking so extensively and openly about the problem might encourage employees to allege retaliation when they disagreed with a performance rating or disciplinary action.

As the company's D&I leader and the chief architect of this diversity and inclusion transformation project, I had a chance to speak directly to Mike Garrett, Georgia Power's CEO at the time. I asked him if he had any personal concerns about the negative connotation of the word "retaliation" and or concerns that the company might be opening the door for a flood of "meritless" employee claims of retaliation. His response to me was:

Shelton, the management team, discussed the issue; many people said we shouldn't use the word retaliation. They saw it as too negative. They wanted it placed under the open and trusting environment umbrella. Yes, this is about trust, but we also need to call what our employees call it—retaliation. In the short run, we may see an increase in claims of retaliation. That's OK. Because if we do our jobs the right way, we have nothing to fear, and ultimately, this will make us a better, stronger company.

Enterprise-wide Mandatory D&I Training

Based on the consulting firm's findings, a design team—comprised of the D&I coordinators, HR business consultants, hand-picked operation managers, workplace ethics coordinators, attorneys from the company's outside law firm, representatives from the company's Labor Relations Department, and external consultants—created a one-day training program that was mandatory for all the company's managers.

The company made a conscious decision not to focus the training on the legal definition of retaliation but instead directed that the training be designed to accomplish four specific objectives:

1. Increase managers' awareness and understanding of those behaviors that employees perceive as acts of retaliation.
2. Heighten managers' sensitivity to employees' fear of retaliation and identify alternate behaviors to eliminate retaliation instances.
3. Increase managers' awareness and understanding of both the nonlegal and legal aspects of retaliation.
4. Align managers' leadership behaviors with the company's values.

The company viewed the training as an opportunity to help bring about the desired culture change by assisting managers to become more comfortable with employees raising questions and delivering bad news. Senior company leaders worked hard to understand retaliation better and respond to this complex and challenging work environment issue. The training design team determined that to reduce retaliation and build trust, it was critical that the training also introduced three new leadership competencies that, if applied, would eventually build confidence and overcome the fear of retaliation. The three skills provided employees the "whys" behind decisions and actions, managing conflict more effectively, and giving or receiving performance feedback.

Six months after the external consultant reported its findings to the Georgia Power Management Council and Board of Directors, the company launched the *Creating a Trusting and Inclusive Culture: Retaliation Awareness and Skill Building Workshop* by conducting two pilot workshops. Senior leaders from both Southern Company (Georgia Power's parent company) and Georgia Power made up one pilot group. The other pilot group was comprised of a cross-section of Georgia Power officers, managers, and supervisors. The company's senior leaders attended the training program's pilot to ensure a collective understanding of the problem and learn how senior leadership might influence possible solutions.

The company decided to address the problem by starting at the top and focusing on what the company's leaders needed to do to reduce employees' perception of retaliation. Participants from the pilot workshop recommended four critical changes to the workshop:

1. Start the training with a "harder-hitting" introduction and present the ten behaviors that employees view as retaliatory at the beginning of the workshop.
2. Present the workshop's business case by emphasizing the connection between retaliation, trust, employee engagement, and organizational performance.
3. Provide managers with skills to address unfounded claims of retaliation by distinguishing between candid performance feedback and retribution.
4. Strengthen the workshop's skill-building parts by allowing participants to role play and interact with videotaped scenario discussions.

The feedback was used to revise the course, and the workshop was rolled out company-wide and became mandatory training for more than 1,100 company managers and supervisors. Utilizing a train-the-trainer methodology, the D&I department trained fifty high-potential managers to facilitate the workshop. These managers, in turn, taught the rest of their peers. The training began with a videotaped message from the company's president, which stated that combating the fear of retaliation is one of the top challenges leaders must address. The CEO emphasized his commitment to creating a trusting and inclusive culture and expectations for each company leader to commit. Senior executive support of this initiative was evidenced throughout the training.

The training utilized a workshop format that was highly experiential and personal. For example, employees were asked to share their own experiences of retaliation with each other. During the training, the facilitators focused on the ten behaviors that employees identified as creating a reprisal perception. The training incorporated videotaped scenarios utilizing professional actors but drawn from actual events at Georgia Power. After each vignette, the attendees separated into groups. They were asked to discuss what behaviors in the video might be perceived as retaliatory and what the supervisors might have done differently. The training also utilized live role-playing, with the facilitators acting out scenes, and participants were asked to provide feedback to the characters.

The company shared the results of its retaliation study and training with other interested companies. Georgia Power's diversity and inclusion department traveled to over twenty different companies to share the program.

Communication as a Platform for Change

Communication was also part of this culture change initiative. When talking to employees about retaliation, the company was careful to distinguish between legally actionable retaliation and the broader way in which employees might perceive retaliation.

Before, during, and after the training, the company's CEO communicated that the company was committed to creating a culture where employees were comfortable reporting concerns. For example, the CEO participated, along with other senior officers, in a closed-circuit television broadcast to all company employees. He emphasized the importance of reporting wrongdoing and the company's commitment to reducing the fear of retaliation. The broadcast was critical in reinforcing the message of the training, and the CEO thought it was important for all employees to know the focus of the training went beyond legal compliance and was directed at the more subtle behaviors that were not consistent with the company's values.

Another objective of the company's communication strategy was to raise awareness of its subtle actions that undermined employee engagement and reduced inclusion. It worked against the company's goal of creating a work environment where all employees were valued, respected, and productive. Specifically, the communication campaign was based on the belief that the faster the company heightened all employees' sensitivity to the fear of retaliation, the sooner it would achieve its desired culture.

What Gets Measure Gets Done

Research suggests it takes almost twenty-five years to change an organization's culture. The leadership at Georgia Power understood this when they implemented efforts to reduce employee fears of retaliation and accepted the conventional wisdom that only time would tell how much impact the training would have, moving the company closer to the desired culture.

However, two years after the retaliation awareness training launch, several signs pointed to the company's effective effort to reduce employee fear of retaliation. For example, one year after implementing the training, the percentage of employee concerns claiming retaliation decreased substantially. More than 65 percent of the employees who completed the company's Employee Engagement and Diversity Survey reported that the training increased their awareness and understanding and decreased their fear of retaliation. This was a substantial improvement from previous responses.

Think About This

Determined not to let the benefits of the training stay in the classroom, the company required every manager to create a development plan to improve their skills in the three areas: which were the focus of the training—communication and decision-making; conflict management; and performance feedback—after the training. The participants were also required to describe the specific ways they planned to improve their skills in the three areas noted above and share their development plan with *their* supervisors and employees. The development plans were also required to be incorporated into each manager's performance review.

Accountability for reducing employee fear of retaliation and demonstrating the behaviors taught in training started at the top, with the CEO and his direct report, and cascaded down through the management chain. Expectations were communicated to the company's managers through several vehicles, including 1:1 performance discussions.

The case study suggests that encouraging employees to speak out by reducing the fear of retaliation is not merely a matter of removing perceived or real barriers, such as a volatile leader or using discipline to inhibit bad behaviors. The problem cannot be solely addressed by putting formal systems in place, like telephone hotlines and suggestion boxes. Making employees feel safe enough to contribute fully and instilling a sense of obligation to offer suggestions for improvement requires a cultural change that helps the organization understand the likely costs (personal and immediate) versus the benefits (organizational and future) of employees speaking up.

Additionally, the case study demonstrates that leaders must explicitly invite and acknowledge employees' ideas for organizations to reduce their costs, even if they do not consistently implement them. The company's senior leaders must actively challenge the cultural myths and organizational norms that reinforce employee fears of speaking up. For example, managers should point out publicly that, contrary to common belief, employees should make suggestions openly and not feel as though they can only make personal recommendations because of fear of retaliation. The case study suggests that ideas are most helpful when openly discussed, and other employees can help develop them.

One of the case study's most compelling points is that employees might also be enticed to speak out and contribute more if they see some tangible benefit beyond personal acknowledgment for speaking up. For example, organizations should tailor their reward systems and recognition programs to share more directly in any cost savings or additional revenue generated by employees' ideas.

Georgia Power effectively held managers accountable by using its performance management process, affecting pay, promotion opportunities, and continued employment. It's important to note that Georgia Power's performance management process allowed managers to give and receive candid performance feedback to avoid creating a perception of retaliation and motivate them to act on the input. The company emphasized a strong focus on performance management as one of the primary methods for holding managers accountable for reducing employees' fears of retaliation in genuine and measurable ways.

CHAPTER 11

Authentic Leadership During a Time of Crisis

Introduction

This chapter is a bookend to the previous chapter. Implementing change requires strong leadership. However, even the most skilled leaders can be challenged during a time of crisis. Two leadership lessons are explained in the chapter. The first was that a CEO, who was well known for his systematic approach to problem-solving, acted quickly in response to a crisis. This correlates with the fact that the CEO decided not to wait until the legal strategy was finalized before implementing several important changes. The culture change plan was well-developed, included proper communication support and resources, and was correctly followed.

The second lesson is that the formerly hands-off CEO was very hands-on in the Georgia Power case study described in chapter ten. The CEO was reported to have been "annoying" in his aversion to detail. However, as we saw in chapter ten, the CEO held numerous high-level meetings when the time came to act, during which every detail of the culture change plan was developed and discussed.

We explore how the research of psychologists Irving Janis and Leon Mann to help explain the reasons for the CEO's atypical behavior.

Janis and Mann suggest that when a decision-maker (i.e., Georgia Power CEO) is faced with an emotional, consequential crisis, he or she depends upon hope and time. According to Janis and Mann, when the decision-maker sees realistic hope of finding a solution superior to all the risky options, that person follows a desirable pattern called "vigilance." Conversely, when the decision-maker loses hope of finding an acceptable option, he or she demonstrates either "defensive avoidance" or "hypervigilance." The symptoms of defensive avoidance are procrastination, passing the buck, and bolstering.

The research of Janis and Mann suggests that three decisional conflicts challenged Georgia Power's CEO during the racial discrimination lawsuit crisis. First, the CEO was a devout Christian who had always looked to settle differences without conflict, and he did not want to embarrass the company or its employees. The CEO's second challenge was charting a path that balanced a legal and cultural response to the crisis. Finally, the CEO was in the unenviable situation of being a white man born and raised in the South fighting against eight African American plaintiffs who were long-term employees. The CEO did not deny organizational norms that may have contributed to employee frustration and alienation. Instead, he adopted culture change efforts in addition to and while attempting to resolve the legal challenge.

We conclude by explaining several ways leaders can prevent decision-making disasters during a time of crisis. We lean heavily on the research conducted by Wooten and James, who specialized in crisis leadership. In addition to embedding preventive strategies in organizational standard operating policies and procedures, they recommend three additional for managing an organization crisis: (1)

learn to recognize the symptoms of bad decision-making, (2) identify the central no-win dilemma, and (3) learn to grasp the crisis firmly even when all options entail unpleasant personal consequences.

As an HR and diversity leader in the company, I had the privilege of talking to the CEO on numerous occasions and learning from his leadership style, rooted in his Christian faith and tested in the fires of crisis. The case study highlights an extraordinary success story about authentic leadership and speculates the valuable lessons other leaders need to learn to create and sustain tomorrow's workplace.

Apples and Trees

From his twenty-fourth-floor office in Georgia Power's black tower, CEO David Ratcliffe had a commanding view of downtown Atlanta. From there, he could see eye-to-eye with fellow corporate giants who helped shape the future of the city of Atlanta and the state of Georgia. But on a clear day, with a few questions to prompt his memory, Ratcliffe could also see back to Tifton, Georgia—his South Georgia hometown—where he had started his career with Georgia Power twenty-nine years earlier.

Even before he learned the business from the ground up, David Ratcliffe had already absorbed several valuable life lessons from his family and small-town upbringing in Tifton. Growing up, Ratcliffe's father was a scientist with the state's Coastal Plains Experiment Station, while his mother was a homemaker. He was raised in Tifton's town and absorbed and embraced the small-town values of church and home. In describing his upbringing, Ratcliffe once told me, *"I would consider myself a simple man with a strong Christian faith that drives my behavior. I try to understand what drives and motivates people and to learn from and emulate the good people who have gone before me."*

Ratcliffe's father had a degree in plant physiology and worked with the State Department of Agriculture, and Ratcliffe grew up working on a farm in South Georgia during the summer. That is where his interest in biology was born. While his father was a Phi Beta Kappa graduate with a master's degree from the University of Georgia, Ratcliffe didn't exactly burn up the academic halls at Valdosta State University. According to Ratcliffe, *"I had a lot of fun for my first two years, and then I decided I'd try to make good grades. Most of the other folks in biology were trying to get into veterinarian or medical school. I made good grades junior and senior years, but by that time, to get into medical school, I would have had to go back and start all over."*

Ratcliffe went on to receive a bachelor's degree in biology from Valdosta State University in 1970. However, he concedes that "If I had to do it all over again, I'd probably go to medical school. I have always been fascinated with what a wonderful machine the human body is." He later received a law degree from Woodrow Wilson College of Law in 1975 and became a Georgia Bar Association member.

He joined Georgia Power in 1971 when he asked a friend at a wedding if there were any jobs at the company. Ratcliffe joined the company team as a biologist and initially worked on the environmental side of the utility business. His first job was to make sure the company's power plants filed the necessary permits and complied with regulatory requirements. He shared with me that he felt lucky to have a job: *"I started with Georgia Power Company in 1971 when we were doing the first round of clean air and clean water projects around power plants. I grew up on the business's power plant operation side, asked many questions, and tried to learn as much as possible. I figured that a lot of biological and environmental issues were probably going to be challenging utilities in the years ahead. I believed that having grown up on that side of the business would give me a unique perspective."*

From that point on, Valdosta State University's memories were left in the dust as Ratcliffe quickly moved up the management ranks and gained valuable experience in all facets of the company. Along the way, he met and married his wife, Cecelia. Ratcliffe and his family hopscotched across the Southeast as Ratcliffe climbed the rungs on the Southern Company ladder. He served as Southern Company's vice president of fuel services and senior vice president of external affairs, president, and CEO of Mississippi Power before taking over the top job at Georgia Power Company.

Ratcliffe became president and CEO of Georgia Power in 1999. Under his leadership, the company continued to earn its reputation as the top producer for energy in the Southeast, defender of shareholder value, protector of a strong stock price, and contributor to the community—not bad for someone who did not even want to enter the corporate world.

Leadership Philosophy and Management Style

Ratcliffe's no-nonsense approach earned his management style such adjectives as "laid-back, family-oriented, and low-key. Ratcliffe—an unassuming executive known for cutting his grass at his Buckhead home—had faced many challenges while at the company's helm. However, members of the business community have nothing but praise for their leadership skills. One prominent Atlanta business leader who knew Ratcliffe described him as an engaging person who epitomizes Georgia Power's values: *"David focuses on the long-term while providing short-term results. He made the hard decisions but with a strong moral compass."*

A member of the company's board of directors described Ratcliffe as "ethical, compassionate, humble, extremely effective in engaging people . . . has a style that, while aggressive, is visionary yet practical. He is running a business that is thoroughly regulated, responsible to the environment, growing great people, and providing value to shareholders."

Ratcliffe told me in one of our many discussions that his leadership style is based on building relationships based on trust, openness, and accountability. *"I believe it's important to create an environment of honesty and feedback. I also think it is important always to maintain the highest levels of integrity, treat everyone like you want to be treated, value the differences of the people in your organization, encourage candor and feedback, be accountable, and never stop learning."*

Simply put, Ratcliffe had successfully run a business in one of the most competitive and fastest-growing regions in the country. And he had done it in a cost-effective yet sensitive and sound way. He had seen all types of challenges before. He acknowledged some similarities between its business environment in 2000 and what the company experienced when he first came to work at Georgia Power in March of

1971. For example, early in Ratcliffe's career, the company had navigated through a period of rapid growth, trying to meet new generation and transmission needs while complying with new environmental requirements. Consequently, rising costs created severe economic pressure, while the need for changes in the company's culture and work environment created significant employee backlash.

In February 2002, Ratcliffe was selected by the Georgia Minority Business Association as the Diversity CEO of the Year "because of his commitment to diversity at Georgia Power." According to Creed Pannell, publisher of the Atlanta Business Journal and host of the award luncheon, "the accomplishments Georgia Power has made through its diversity department under David Ratcliffe's leadership are extraordinary and should be applauded."

The Georgia Minority Business Association's primary goal is to allow business students, school officials, politicians, and business leaders to network. The organization's annual award program was designed to recognize outstanding business leaders for their contributions to their businesses, community, and accomplishments. Upon receiving the award, David Ratcliffe stated, *"I'm honored to accept this award on behalf of all Georgia Power employees who make our workplace one that values the diversity of our coworkers, customers, and communities. Our success depends on that."*

A Crisis Is a Terrible Thing to Waste

Ratcliffe shared with me that he considers the racial discrimination lawsuit against the company in 2000 the greatest business challenge he had ever had to face and feels he overcame it with "a great deal of help from some very knowledgeable people and a great deal of work in understanding the issues."

According to Ratcliffe, the most important business lesson he learned from the crisis was the value of honesty, integrity, and accountability in leadership. According to Ratcliffe, *"I do believe we face in corporate America a significant challenge to re-establish the confidence and credibility of the consuming public. Our responsibility to lead has never been more important than it is today. Almost every company has a code of ethics with high expectations. An ethical code won't work unless executives and employees are held accountable."*

I asked him why the class-action lawsuit, in particular, was so challenging for him to handle when he had been able to deal so effectively with so many other issues in a distinguished career. He replied:

> *I'm paranoid about making sure I'm accountable, and our leadership is accountable. If something doesn't smell right, people need to trust their instincts. In corporate America, too many times we get a whiff of things, we turn around and keep doing our job and don't react to smells. When things are wrong in corporate America, they don't get better with time. As in a football game, people need to act as referees by throwing down flags when they see something wrong.*

There are several independent reasons for believing the sincerity of Ratcliffe's statement. Widely regarded as a deeply religious man, he was known as a devoted and active member of his church and is seen as a congregation's lay leader. People in the company who know Ratcliffe best describe him as a person whose entire service notion is grounded in his faith. He approached his work at Georgia Power with an almost evangelical zeal.

Indeed, most of Ratcliffe's career shows a marked inclination toward maintaining harmony and teamwork. As a rising star in Southern Company, his low-key manner usually kept potentially explosive situations under control. As CEO, first of Mississippi Power, and later Georgia Power, Ratcliffe's success and reputation as an effective leader were based on his ability to build consensus and develop strong relationships. Ratcliffe's few criticisms centered on claims that sometimes he was too willing to appease opponents outside the company and too reluctant to take his CEO and president title out for a test drive and remind people inside the company who was in charge.

Ratcliffe vowed that he would change Georgia Power's perception from the "noose company" to one that welcomes diverse people, especially people of color. He responded to the firestorm caused by the racial discrimination class-action lawsuit by putting in place the structures and processes needed to change its culture to respected diversity and recognized the benefits of being more inclusive.

In the twenty-two months following the discrimination lawsuit, the company's nonlegal response to the crisis resulted in reviewing about sixty individual complaints raised by employees concerning compensation issues. The company subsequently made salary adjustments in about 30 percent of the cases. The company also improved employee access to job postings, conducted a comprehensive review of its pay structure, and provided diversity training for all employees. According to Ratcliffe, "From 2000 to 2004, we had a concerted effort to broaden the understanding of diversity. As you understand what it means, you understand how important it is to the company's success."

Ratcliffe also personally reached out to African American employees, including Cornelius Cooper, one of the lawsuit's original plaintiffs. However, Cooper declined to talk to Ratcliffe without his lawyer. Another African American employee did respond to Ratcliffe's s overture and told him a story of how the Ku Klux Klan attacked his boyhood home, burnt a cross in front of the family's house, and hung an effigy of a black man with a hangman's noose. David Ratcliffe acknowledged the pain, anger, and frustration with newfound empathy. He acknowledged publicly, "Now that I understand it, I have a sensitivity that I must have, and I understand why it's so offensive."

Ratcliffe's decision to change the culture at Georgia Power was unusual. In the C-suite club, whose members are exclusively privileged white men, preserving the status quo usually is far more important than bringing in new members who might be women or people of color. But there are rare exceptions, and the following words of David Ratcliffe confirmed that perhaps he is one of them:

Hugs are a way of rewarding employees who are willing to speak up. As part of that, executives must be able to admit to their mistakes openly. It is an important time in my judgment in corporate America. I do believe we are all a bit on trial here. What happened in the last nine months or so has shaken the confidence in corporate America's leadership. I'm not too fond of it that we are all painted with the same brush. Corporate America must admit its mistakes, fix them, and move on.

Implications for Crisis Leadership Theory

Four years after the initial Georgia Power lawsuit, James and Wooten published the seminal article *"Diversity Crisis: How Firms Manage Discrimination Lawsuits,"* which identified several strategies a company should employ for handling different types of class-action discrimination lawsuits, including race, sex, disability, religion, and sexual harassment. The authors focused on this specific threat because of the detrimental effects of class-action lawsuits on companies and the increasing diversity in organizations.

Wooten and James' *Discrimination Lawsuit Resolution Model* suggest that when allegations of discrimination attack an organization's reputation, the implications can be financial, strategic, and procedural. For example, they point out that a company will have substantial legal expenses, public relations difficulties, and possibly organizational restructuring because of such a legal crisis.

To further support their argument, James and Wooten point to Texaco, which in 1994 faced a discrimination lawsuit filed by six African American employees who claimed that white employees were hired or promoted at a higher rate. James and Wooten report that Texaco executives denied the allegations in response to these allegations, making the legal case linger for two years. However, the media noticed when the plaintiffs' attorneys released transcripts of executives denigrating African American employees. At the same time, federal prosecutors began a criminal investigation into whether executives had shredded evidence. Considering the public scrutiny, Texaco's CEO immediately shifted from denial rhetoric to a public apology. The company began working toward a resolution by setting aside funds for raises, restructuring human resources policies, and consulting African American leaders in the community.

Wooten and James looked at the Texaco case and seventy-six other companies reacting to a crisis precipitated by discrimination lawsuits. They identified factors that influence crisis response strategies and built a model of organizational responses to these crises. According to the Wooten and James *Discrimination Lawsuit Resolution Model*, most companies tend to behave defensively in threatening situations; for example, Texaco initially denied race discrimination accusations. However, Wooten and James Wooten discovered that because companies are often susceptible to pressure from stakeholders, this pressure can influence how companies ultimately respond.

Because of the publicity in the Texaco case, and its consequences, the company changed its reaction from defensiveness to accountability. Other behavioral responses by companies include retaliation, settlement, and change efforts. James and Wooten found that retaliation against the accusers is more common in sexual harassment lawsuits than in any other form of discrimination. In other words, companies were more likely to "blame the alleged victims" when the discrimination was based on sexual harassment and least likely to do so in cases of race discrimination.

In the few race cases in which a company initially retaliates, external pressure from civil rights groups and others eventually influences the company to change its response strategy from denial to acknowledgment and move toward a settlement. Moreover, when external stakeholders mobilize against the company and engage in public demonstrations, they often seek a financial resolution. It is more inclined to adopt changes to its human resources policies, procedures, and processes.

Wooten and James argue that stakeholder mobilization activity from African American interest groups or other civil rights groups and interested parties is most likely to accompany racial discrimination suits. Moreover, organizational and culture-change efforts in response to allegations are primarily initiated in race-based lawsuits, less so in sex-based lawsuits, and rarely in other forms of discrimination lawsuits. These cultural changes can include sweeping changes to organizational norms and human resource processes and policy change. Wooten and James identified four distinct paths of response to discrimination lawsuits:

1. Path 1 encompasses gender, religion, age, and disability discrimination lawsuits. Legal settlements typically resolve these cases.

2. Path 2 is most prevalent in sexual harassment lawsuits. These cases are characterized by retaliatory behavior directed toward the company's accusers and are followed by financial resolution.

3. Path 3 manifests mostly in racial discrimination cases. In these cases, the response is non-retaliatory and involves culture change efforts as well as settlement.

4. Path 4 is like the response in Path 2. The typical answer is that companies do not deny allegations and implement culture change efforts early in the crisis resolution process.

This seminal research conducted by James and Wooten found that, in general, defensive strategies that include denial rhetoric are common in responding to a crisis brought on by a discrimination lawsuit. However, as stakeholders and the public become involved in the process, the company loses some control of its outcome. When this happens, companies are more likely to adopt accommodative rhetoric and organizational change strategies. Finally, the longer a company delays resolution, the more time and resources are diverted from running the business.

Having discussed the theory, it is now possible to discuss Ratcliffe's crisis leadership behaviors in the context of the Wooten and James *Discrimination Lawsuit Resolution Model* and Georgia Power's responses to the crisis brought on by the race-based discrimination lawsuit.

First, Ratcliffe's leadership behaviors, which were the driving force behind Georgia Power's response, are both noteworthy in novelty and the company's ultimate resolution. Unlike the leaders of other companies involved in discrimination lawsuits, Ratcliffe did not deny organizational norms that may have contributed to employee frustration and alienation, nor did the company experience a threat from mobilized external stakeholders. However, under Ratcliffe's leadership, the company adopted culture-change efforts to resolve the lawsuit.

Based on Wooten and James' study, it is reasonable to conclude that Ratcliffe took this approach because previous legal actions had helped the company learn a more efficient and perhaps more effective way to resolve the 2000 class-action discrimination crisis. For example, Ratcliffe did not allow the company to get caught in the cycle of defensive routines described by Wooten and James or other behaviors that prevented them from resolving the crisis. Wooten and James suggest that such routines are dangerous because they can perpetuate a crisis and lead to questionable or unethical behaviors by the company, thereby adversely affecting its ability to resolve the crisis efficiently and effectively.

Secondly, the Georgia Power class-action racial discrimination lawsuit provides an interesting perspective for organizational theorists researching leadership behaviors during a crisis. Although the case highlighted the significance of the legal responsibility when the company confronted a race discrimination lawsuit, it also emphasizes that the law is not the only perspective the company considered when resolving the crisis. For example, Ratcliffe quickly involved external stakeholders and listened to their voices and counsel during the crisis. He intentionally separated the company's ethical responsibility to change its culture from the legal response to resolve the case in court.

Georgia Power implemented thirty-three diversity and inclusion initiatives to fundamentally correct or modify aspects of its cultural norms that contributed to racial discrimination perceptions and allegations. These initiatives included implementing policy, personnel, and structural changes that were not mandated in a legal settlement or forced on the company by a civil rights group, African American

BEYOND INCLUSION

interest groups, or other external stakeholders. Moreover, Ratcliffe's culture-change efforts reached out to prominent individuals in the metro Atlanta community who could help Georgia Power improve its diversity and inclusion practices. Specifically, within weeks of the lawsuit being filed, Ratcliffe created the Georgia Power Diversity Advisory Council (DAC) and solicited the council's advice on implementing the company's D&I initiatives.

In the wake of the racial discrimination suit, Ratcliffe and the DAC spent numerous hours putting in place processes, structures, and standards to change external perceptions of the company and transform the company's culture from a top-down, hierarchical, and white male-dominated culture to one that was more open, welcoming, and inclusive for all employees. Moreover, Ratcliffe asked the DAC to work directly with several teams of frontline employees to develop diversity management training, improve the way employees were selected for jobs, and create mentoring programs for women and people of color.

Ratcliffe further involved employees in the company's culture-change efforts by asking them to join employee councils and affinity groups chartered to help the company create a more inclusive work environment for all employees. Also, Ratcliffe recruited white males in middle management to support its diversity efforts.

Think About This

Unlike some other companies who faced class-action racial discrimination lawsuits during the same period, Georgia Power did not retaliate against the plaintiffs. Based on Wooten and James' *Discrimination Lawsuit Resolution Model,* Ratcliffe's leadership helped the discrimination lawsuit move more expeditiously toward a favorable resolution. Also, there were no stakeholder settlements because no external parties mobilized against the company. Discrimination Lawsuit Resolution Theory suggests that the absence of company retaliation against lawsuit plaintiffs and the lack of stakeholder mobilization against the company most likely attributed to a positive outcome for Georgia Power.

CHAPTER 12

Creating A Culture of Civility, Compassion, and Common Sense

Introduction

The key to managing tomorrow's workforce is communication! This chapter illustrates that in organizations, everything happens through communication and, more specifically, conversations. Whether it is a manager conveying performance expectations, an employee checking for understanding of an assignment, the organization recognizing someone for a significant accomplishment, or the CEO laying out a strategy for penetrating a new market, a dialogue is at the center of it. This is a given. It is also relevant to the discussion on diversity and inclusion because, in any conversation, there is an opportunity, but there is also a challenge. There is an opportunity to educate, engage, or influence employees. There is also an opportunity to offend, demotivate, and confuse employees. Often, the fear of offending people limits communication and can result in more harm than good.

An example of this might be a leader neglecting to give one of his or her direct reports constructive feedback for fear of offending. Let's add that race or gender might complicate the interpersonal dynamic in this scenario. Managers strongly believe they know that the employee is relevant to its performance effectiveness and, ultimately, their career mobility. But, because there is some level of discomfort or sense that this might be offensive, the feedback does not get shared.

Limited dialogue is also evident in organizations that value being politically correct. In these organizations, there are general norms about which topics to avoid. However, we can state with a high degree of certainty that many of these topics are on employees' minds, especially race, gender, religion, and social issues and events. Each year, there are so many events that have garnered national attention, such as the shooting of unarmed Black men, acts of domestic terrorism, a political election campaign, legalization of marijuana, gay marriages, etc. Our clients have shared that they are often troubled, excited, or personally impacted by these topics.

This chapter explores whether companies should provide a forum for employees to talk about these workplace issues. And, if so, should these conversations be facilitated? Should leaders be involved? Lastly, can CDOs play the bridge-builder role by helping disparate groups in the organization find common ground?

Compassion and Civility versus Correctness and Comfort

Most leaders are in their "zone," solving problems, leading organizations through challenging transitions and building highly marketable reputations doing so. However, having conversations about diversity, equity, and inclusion intimidates these same leaders. In many cases, these conversations extend beyond leaders' comfort zones. For some, these conversations are not on their radar as they are viewed as subordinate to the need to focus on the business. For others, no personal "WIFM" (what's in it for me) is felt to exist. While there may be some validity for these rationalizations, there are ample examples of how good organizations become great because diversity and inclusion are woven into the core business's fabric. Leaders can increase their value to their companies by inserting themselves into this formula for success. Still, it will involve a different set of behaviors than they might be used to, such as demonstrating vulnerability, being transparent, and discussing feelings. There are several approaches organizations can take to unlock barriers to dialogue:

- Create monthly forums.
- Encourage leaders to engage in candid conversations about race and ethnicity and personal biases.
- Incorporate skill-building around implicit bias and facilitating critical conversations within leadership training.
- Sponsor lunch and learns with roundtable discussions that enable employees to ask each other questions and share concerns and insights about specific topics.
- Encourage leaders to participate in roundtable forums with their peers to discuss common challenges and strategies within their respective organizations regarding diversity, equity, and inclusion.
- Invite outside speakers to discuss D&I topics.

Facilitating Courageous Conversation

Along with organizational initiated practices, leaders can also enhance their comfort, confidence, and competence to have a courageous conversation by devoting time and practice to three elements:

- **Self-awareness and self-reflection**—Gaining a better understanding of ourselves is the first step in enhancing relationships with others and increasing the ability to engage in meaningful conversations. Self-awareness requires managers to explore their contributions to the discussion. This awareness can be furthered by identifying and reflecting on personal filters or lens through which the world is viewed, stylistic preferences, and the impact of behaviors on others. Managers often judge themselves by their intentions. Employees often judge their managers by the effect their actions have on them. Effective interactions depend on bridging the gap between these two perceptions by anticipating where our intentions can be misinterpreted and following up to ensure behaviors were viewed as intended.
- **Curiosity**—Curiosity facilitates courageous conversations. It involves recognizing there are at least two sides to any story. Neither story paints a complete picture by itself. It also implies that employees want to understand the reasons behind their managers' actions and behaviors. "What makes them tick?" When managers are genuinely curious about the people on their team, they exhibit empathy, show vulnerability, and ask questions to learn—making room for "both/and" thinking. Listening with the intent to understand helps build a climate of openness, transparency, and inclusion. It helps to level power dynamics in interactions. Being curious in conversations and seeking understanding does not obligate the manager to

change their perspective or the action they intend to take. However, it may enable the manager to have more empathy for someone's experience or perspective.

- **Emotional intelligence**—Emotional intelligence is the ability to recognize, address, and manage one's emotions and others' emotions. It involves perceiving emotions and the ability to detect and accurately label emotions in facial expressions, words, and body language—including the ability to identify one's own emotions. It also requires understanding emotions, understanding what triggers our emotions, and appreciating complex relationships among different emotions. Lastly, it involves managing emotions and regulating emotions when having a courageous conversation, including negative ones, and managing them to achieve intended goals. With emotional intelligence, the question is not "Will strong feelings or emotions arise?" but making sure we handle them when they do arise by identifying and validating the emotions that are present, using knowledge of our own and others' feelings to be more empathetic, and using an understanding of emotions to suspend judgment and to engage others in the dialogue.

Understanding the Barriers to Courageous Conversations

According to Sue Derald Wing, the author of *Race Talk and the Conspiracy of Silence,* the primary reasons individuals avoid talking about race in multicultural settings, such as the workplace, stem from normative ground rules set by society and the company. Strategies for shifting the conversation require individuals to acknowledge personal biases and move beyond their comfort zones. Dr. Wing suggests that discussions about race must be preceded by:

- Understanding one's racial and cultural identity.
- Being open to admitting racial biases.
- Being open and comfortable in discussing topics of race and racism.
- Understanding the meaning of emotions.
- Validating and facilitating discussion of feelings.
- Controlling the process and not the content of the conversation on race.
- Unmasking the difficult dialogues through process observations and interventions.
- Avoiding awkward dialogue to be brewed in silence.
- Understanding differences in communication styles.
- Forewarning, planning, and purposefully instigating race talk.

Think About This

How do we have conversations about race and equity in the workplace? Employees come to work with various emotions, including fear, anxiety, anger, frustration, guilt, and confusion. It is no longer realistic to expect employees to leave those feelings at the door when they start work. If we are going to have an inclusive company, community, and country, we need to be willing and competent enough to have conversations that address diversity, racial inequities, inclusion, and social justice in the workplace. Today, more than ever, senior leaders, like you, must take steps to create safe spaces where people can share their feelings while being open and respectful, effectively build understanding and find common ground on diverse issues, and equip managers with the tools and resources to have healthy and productive conversations about race and equity.

What is the pathway to the next frontier? How do leaders achieve intercultural competence? In this chapter, we discussed a competency model that can serve as a foundation for moving forward. We suggest that organizations take the three specific pathways described in our model to increase their cross-cultural communication skills. These three pathways are client focus, courageous conversations, and cross-disciplinary collaborations. These pathways are relevant and essential to transforming an organization's culture and a critical step to reimagining the future of work, workers, and the workplace.

CHAPTER 13

The Future Workplace: The Role of the Chief Diversity Officer

Introduction

This chapter explores the role of the chief diversity officer (CDO) in shaping the reimagining of the future of work, workers, and the workplace.

Diversity and inclusion experts have consistently emphasized the importance of assigning accountability for guiding the organization's strategic diversity and inclusion efforts. According to these same practitioners, appointing a chief diversity officer (CDO) is crucial to ensuring an organization's diversity and inclusion strategy. This person can ensure that managers in the organization are trained to create inclusive work environments and lead diverse work teams. Moreover, chief diversity officers can advocate that the organization make managers' performance ratings and compensation dependent, in part, on their success in achieving diversity and inclusion goals.

A survey of diversity and inclusion professionals found that almost 70 percent of the Fortune 500 companies make it a common practice for the chief diversity officer to ensure diversity and inclusion goal accountability by integrating diversity goals into the performance appraisal criteria of senior executives in the organization. The chief diversity officer is also responsible for informing managers that success and a positive evaluation will include assessing how they contribute to the organization's diversity and inclusion strategy and emphasizing that diversity management is essential to attracting, developing, and retaining a qualified workforce.

The role of the chief diversity officer is considered vital to the organization because this individual can help the organization focus on diversity management to make the organization more inclusive, which contributes to business success. Diversity and inclusion practitioners argue that the chief diversity officer must advocate the business case that diversity and inclusion make good business sense, emphasizing that it enhances productivity, stimulates innovation, and helps expand services to meet the needs of a more diverse customer base.

This chapter examines how organizations structure or organize the diversity and inclusion function to advance or accelerate the company's diversity, equity, and inclusion efforts. The efficacy of the Chief Diversity Officer as a change agent is examined to see if they can be counted on to help their organization thrive in a post-pandemic business world.

Angels of Mercy or Barbarians at the Gate?

Diversity and inclusion experts argue that because it can take five to seven years to successfully implement diversity and inclusion initiatives in most organizations, the chief diversity officer must institutionalize initiatives by integrating them into organizations' strategic planning efforts. Moreover, diversity and inclusion professionals assert that effective oversight of the organization's diversity management requires eight specific competencies:

1. *Leading.* Gains agreement among senior leadership about the desire to move forward.

2. *Visioning.* Develops and champions a diversity vision. Develops programs and strategies to include a well-thought-out plan for specific managerial accountabilities.

3. *Diagnosing.* Analyzes the organization's readiness to move forward.

4. *Learning.* Facilitates efforts to increase awareness of the benefits of diversity. Performs diversity audits and conducts exit interviews. Encourages managers to research best practices.

5. *Changing.* Investigates ways to change organizational culture and structure. Conducts focus groups to identify barriers and develops plans to attract diverse employees. It helps leaders move away from simple compliance with equal employment opportunity guidelines and conducts cultural scans and assessments.

6. *Sustaining.* Drives leaders to find ways to better support diversity strategy. Promotes employee networks, support groups, or affinity groups and conducts compensation-equity analysis. Creates mentoring programs and designs career-development programs—advocates for alternative dispute resolution to review diversity-related issues.

7. *Maximizing.* Strengthens managers' ability to lead diverse work teams more effectively. Integrates diversity in critical human-

resource management systems such as performance management, selection, recruitment, succession planning, leadership development, and promotions. Introduces, adapts, or changes policies such as domestic partner benefits. Takes intentional steps to ensure the organization's workforce mirrors the demographic composition of the labor pool or population.

8. *Reinforcing.* Monitors the culture and work environment's early warning signs that indicate whether employees feel they are treated as unique individuals whose identities and abilities are respected and appreciated. Develops accountability measures to ensure the organizational change is in place in policies, systems, and processes. Designs early-warning detectors that signal if the organization is retreating from efforts to attract, retain, and develop employees with diverse backgrounds and qualifications.

The chief diversity officer is also responsible for integrating diversity management into an organization's strategic plan to foster a culture change that supports and values differences. Diversity-management practitioners point out that an organization must link diversity management to its overall strategic plan to ensure that diversity management initiatives are not considered extraneous. This could make them vulnerable to budget cuts.

Lastly, the business case in favor of hiring a chief diversity officer asserts that this individual could help foster a diverse and inclusive workplace that helps the organization reduce costs by reducing turnover, increasing employee retention across demographic groups, and improving employee morale. According to the Society for Human

Resource Management, the average diversity department has five employees. Aside from staff, the chief diversity officer may also have a budget for data collection and analysis, internal and external communications, and legal and compliance issues. Further, depending on the company, the chief diversity officer budget may include staff for diversity recruiting, talent development, supplier diversity, and supporting employee resource groups.

Chief diversity officers typically focus on the workforce and the work environment. Specific responsibilities often include increasing engagement and productivity, decreasing regrettable loss, improving the quality of the labor pool, reducing exposure to potential liabilities (lawsuits), and recruiting top talent. Organizations that had a chief diversity officer for five years or more primarily focused on diversity efforts on market penetration or growth and had budgeted for areas like marketing, sales development, emerging market development, global business development, and public relations. The most progressive organizations also use their diversity departments to understand how to foster and grow innovation.

Ain't Such a Thing as Superman

The Social Justice movement and subsequent social climate have impacted the diversity and inclusion efforts in the workplace in one way or another. It does, and we all know it. From the rhetorical bombardment of the presidential election cycle to post-inaugural developments, we are distracted. Some of us may be anxious and worried; some of us may be annoyed by those who feel anxious and just wish everyone would take it easy and give things a chance to settle down.

I have been a human resource professional for over two decades. My specialty is diversity and inclusion—precisely, helping people across the country and worldwide understand the inherent dignity of individuals and manage organizations better by getting the best from all people. In my professional opinion, I believe it is time that diversity and inclusion professionals help their organizations transpose our efforts from merely increasing the number of women and people of color in organizations to focusing on healthy and inclusive behaviors. Inside the company, inclusive practices change how people treat each other. Beyond the company, they change how products can be designed and interact with the outside world and even suppliers, customers, and communities' perspectives.

From city halls and charitable foundations, Fortune 500 companies to health systems and universities, diversity, equity, and inclusion are increasingly claimed as top priorities. The gap between what institutions commit to in their mission statements and how employees experience the workplace is often chasmal.

Many organizations hire a new staff member or executive to close the space between stated good intentions and reality. These leaders hold different titles: chief diversity officer, chief equity officer, dean, or vice president of diversity and inclusion. Throughout this chapter, I will refer to them as chief diversity officers or CDOs. Most of the people I know who hold these titles are women and people of color. I was one of them.

Nearly a decade ago, I met a black woman—I'll call her Sheila—at a diversity and inclusion (D&I) conference. We bonded over our surprise at the incredible whiteness of the conference panels. "If I must listen to another white woman talk about the glass ceiling, I might jump out a window." We spent the rest of the afternoon eating chicken nuggets and drinking lemonade at a Chick-fil-A restaurant, and it was time well-spent.

About six months after we met, Sheila called and told me that her organization had put her in charge of the task force responsible for helping the company become an "anti-racist" organization. I asked how things were going, and she replied, "It sucks. The trouble is that they don't want me to do my job." This is a complaint I hear repeatedly, and from the six CDOs I interviewed for this book, it's a complaint I have made myself.

Early in my tenure as a CDO, despite having been charged by the board of directors and the CEO to facilitate workplace conversations about topics like white privilege, unconscious bias, and racial inequities, I was told—often by those same executives—to "tone down the incendiary language." My CEO said some employees found the tone of the workshops "divisive." On one occasion, one senior executive told me that workshop participants complained of feeling "uncomfortable" with the workshop's content. On another occasion, I was given feedback that I was "biased toward white participants" after I attempted to engage all the workshop participants in a dialogue about how microaggressions and microinequities show up in the company's culture—a problem that the African American participants in the workshop amplified and reinforced frequently during the unconscious bias workshop. Several workshop participants shared that they knew a colleague "who left the organization in part because of what they saw as organizational biases."

I Was In The Right Place—
It Must Have Been The Wrong Time

Over and over in my role as CDO, I was told that I had chosen the "wrong time and place to bring up racial or gender biases" and that I needed to do a better job of "not making people feel uncomfortable." Since I already knew that the company employees desperately wanted the gender and racial biases to be addressed, I assumed my bosses essentially meant that I should focus my efforts on "making white people feel more comfortable." If I had to prioritize the comfort of white employees over the clearly expressed needs of the organization, if I had to avoid speaking in unambiguous terms about the very problems that I was charged with solving, if unconscious workshops were not the "right place" for open, honest dialogue about these issues—then what is the role of the company's chief diversity and inclusion officer?

"We want you to succeed," my bosses insisted. "Just meet people where they are." I had many difficult conversations with my bosses, and as time went on, I felt heard. Despite their initial resistance, they were willing to admit they might be wrong. Most of our senior leadership team cared enough about the work and enough about each other to address company culture problems and work toward change. I am proud to say that many of the companies I worked at are vastly different from those I was hired into. However, based on my research, I must wonder if this outcome is the exception rather than the rule. The more I spoke CDOs for this book, the more I realized there is a typical pattern.

A CDO—usually a woman or person of color—is enthusiastically hired by a company. The CDO feels empowered and excited to take on new challenges to create a diverse, equitable, and inclusive workplace. Then the CDO begins to experience and identify harmful workplace norms. Perhaps the CDO tries to point out inequities in the company culture or suggest possible solutions. That is when the "honeymoon period"—if there was one—ends.

A CDO that I interviewed—let's call him Charles—shared that during an interview process to fill a General Counsel position, the interview panel—all white—frequently described candidates of color as "lacking executive presence," "having raw talent," "lacking political savvy," or "needing polish." These terms were never used to describe white candidates. Charles suggested creating a rubric that spoke more specifically to what skills and competencies they were hiring to avoid stereotypes and harmful framing. "They looked at me as though I had "landed on the planet from Mars," Charles told me. "They were offended that I suggested they might be biased."

In other situations, a CDO might attempt to talk with a colleague about harmful actions or comments. I interviewed a CDO—a woman of color I'll call Magda, who worked for a quick-service restaurant industry—who heard a colleague repeating offensive stereotypes in a meeting. She shared with me that she tried to speak in a calm, measured voice and explain her remarks were harmful when she pulled her colleague aside after the meeting. Her colleague insisted that she had been misunderstood; when Magda pushed back, her colleague cried because she felt that she was being labeled a "racist."

I interviewed several CDOs who had written memos to their CEO and other company leaders, outlining repetitive microaggressions and clear expressions of bias. In her first one-on-one meeting with the CEO of a large bank in Chicago, a CDO, who I will call Helen, brought a list of harmful organizational cultural norms and practices—including the fact that people of color, particularly women, were frequently dismissed or ignored when they shared their experiences with gender bias. Among other examples, Helen recalled a young black female associate speaking passionately and with great vulnerability about growing up poor in Chicago and how hurtful it was that so many of its financial programs ignored "poor working-class people."

Helen said that she had to sit in meetings every day and listen to executives talk about long-term financial strategies. Her whole life, Helen told me, "I watched my mother work three jobs." Helen shared that she often argued that poor people couldn't wait for the "trickle-down benefits of long-term investments and that they needed investments in their community today." She revealed that her advice and recommendations were ignored, as fellow executives cited data about their funding programs. She shared with me that she often felt "helpless as she was forced to sit in the meeting after having taken the huge risk of speaking up in a room of more senior executives, listening to them recite cold hard facts and numbers." When Helen discussed this in her one-on-one meeting with the CEO, she was told the "bank made decisions based on data rather than emotion."

The unwillingness of white company leadership to listen to or believe their marginalized employees is another reason why so many CDOs are practically set up to fail. Stories about lived experiences—in the workplace, in the world—are data, too. That those stories are often told with emotion does not invalidate them.

Another pattern I noticed is that retaliation often follows denial. One of the CDOs I interviewed shared with me that on several occasions, he asked the senior leadership team to increase his budget so that he could hire an external consultant to help develop a strategy to address pay equity. Even when chief executives seemed somewhat receptive, he experienced some form of reprisal.

After Raheem—that's what I'll him— requested the budget increase with the "management council," he was disinvited from several meetings where important decisions about the organization's future were being made. He was told by the CEO, "you have too much on your plate, and there are other ways for you to give you input."

Hit the Road Jack

One CDO I'll call Su Yen, who has since left her job as CDO at a large technology company, proposed several measures to increase transparency and accountability for hiring people of color in senior roles. "The CEO went to all the other senior people on the leadership team to get their opinions about the process used to fill senior roles," Su Yen told me. "The CEO said that no one else on the team thought we needed to hire a minority executive search firm to the executive to fill these senior-level positions. He made me feel like I was crazy for raising the issue, even though it was my job to raise the issue. I think members of the management council felt pressured to agree with him. I felt like I was being undermined left and right [after that]. Finally, I quit. The CEO didn't want to change anything, so there was nothing more for me to do there."

This is not uncommon for many CDOs—especially women and people of color. They are hired as the company's chief culture officer and tasked with addressing bias, racism, and inequity within the company culture. They are often marginalized, ignored, undermined, and attacked for attempting to do so. They leave, or they are pushed out. The organization's leaders can say that they tried, that they are still trying, as the gap between what they commit to on their websites and how employees experience the workplace continues to widen.

Research on the impact of diversity and inclusion on business performance has found that diverse organizations were up to 35 percent more likely to outperform their less diverse competitors. In organizations where diversity and inclusion are treated as real priorities, CDOs are hired and expected to help create and sustain a diverse, equitable, and inclusive workplace with limited resources. If this is truly a company's aim, hiring a CDO is insufficient. Diversity, equity, and inclusion must be part of everyone's job; have a place among everyone's top priorities; and be incorporated into how the organization hires, promotes, makes decisions, and approaches all its objectives.

Think About This

CDOs are often brought in to respond to an existing problem, clean up an organization's image, or publicly signal a commitment to diversity, equity, and inclusion that may not exist. In too many cases, changing a company's culture is placed entirely on the CDO's shoulders. When efforts fail, the CDO becomes the scapegoat. The organization's leaders can say they tried, that they are still trying; they can rest secure in the belief they have the best intentions. They might choose to hire another CDO or place the burden of change on some HR leader. Then the pattern begins all over again, as the gap between what companies commit to on their websites and how employees experience the workplace continues to widen.

Because of the pandemic, several organizations experienced seismic change and reinvention. Still, they failed to keep pace with that growth by putting the internal policies and structures that would prevent disparate treatment toward individual employees—especially women. These failures stem from a toxic combination of ignorance of senior leaders, the inability to see the impact of rapid growth, and the internal dysfunction that ensued. In some cases, I believe the problem could also be attributed to intentional, company-level systemic bias.

Following the coal justice movement, the truth is inescapable: from the top-down, companies have failed as organizations to create safe and inclusive workplaces where all people, especially women, feel valued and respected. I believe that cultural elements within most organizations and dysfunction and mismanagement have allowed unhealthy behaviors to flourish unchecked. This includes a detrimental "boy's club" culture fostered for decades, and inappropriate behavior permeated throughout numerous organizations in the country.

It happened on our—diversity professionals'—watch, and ultimately, we let far too many people down. I believe I speak for most diversity professionals when I say we understand that this impacted current and former employees at numerous organizations. We regret our inability to prevent and extinguish discrimination, harassment, retaliation, and other unhealthy—not to mention illegal—behaviors in our respective companies and society in general.

After George Floyd's death in the summer of 2020, we have seen numerous organizations act regarding multiple instances of unacceptable behavior. Several of these high-profile cases resulted in the termination of prominent corporate leaders. Unfortunately, various organizations are currently investigating allegations of sexual harassment that are being brought to their attention.

As a diversity professional, I had to answer many questions from friends and colleagues. The question I was asked the most often was, "Are we safe?" Women asked me, "Are we safe?" LGBTQ people asked me, "Are we safe?"

It's winter in America, and it seems everyone in the country needs some assurance of their safety and well-being. We thought that the presidential election campaign talk has continued after the election and now emboldens unhealthy behaviors.

We, diversity professionals, can no longer be a part of the problem—particularly if, as change agents, we want to investigate and address the many injustices in our companies, communities, and the country. No matter your gender, race, ethnicity, or sexual orientation, we need to do a better job listening to and amplifying the stories and doubling down on our efforts to make our companies a place where all employees are valued, respected, and productive.

Although things are better than they once were at some of the companies I worked for, the work is far from over—indeed, it will never be over. Diversity, equity, and inclusion require ongoing, daily practice and commitment from all employees, especially those at the top.

Many company leaders who hire a CDO fail to understand or internalize—that they can't see that they are part of the problem. They and only they have the power to remove the barriers to creating a diverse, equitable, and inclusive workplace. An excellent place to start is changing their behavior, challenging their own biases, listening, and doing the work—even when it is not easy, convenient, or comfortable. And while CEOs and senior leaders persist in their denial and dodge their responsibility, employees in their companies continue to pay a professional and emotional toll that is far too high.

CHAPTER 14

Inclusion through Justice and Equity

Introduction

We conclude this journey by discussing the challenges ahead as we reimagine the future of work, workers, and the workplace. We describe realistic short-term and long-term goals and the challenges organizational leaders face in achieving desired business goals while attempting to put the pandemic in their rearview mirror.

Throughout the history of business, employees have had to adapt to managers, and managers had to adapt to organizations. That world—and those rules—are over! Because of the COVID-19 global pandemic, things will be reversed with managers and organizations adapting to employees in the future. This means that to succeed and thrive, organizations must rethink and reimagine everything they know about work. The demographics of employees are changing, and so are employee expectations, values, attitudes, perspectives, and work styles. Previous organizational behavior and culture-change models must be replaced with leadership styles aligned with the future of work, workers, and the workplace. Leaders must also revise their traditional organizational structure, rewrite people policies to empower employees, reinvent work to remain competitive, and reset the culture and work environment to adjust to a rapidly changing world. The best way to truly prepare your organization for the global transformations underway—and their impacts—is to think "beyond inclusion" by reimagining the company, reinventing work and workers, revising people policies and processes, and resetting the culture and work environment.

Client Case Study

Why don't more leaders and organizations make inclusion a priority? I believe it is because they don't know what they don't know. There is a gap in their authentic awareness. Some leaders think that diversity is enough, but to activate the promise of diversity, creativity, and innovation, leaders must become more than just open to others. They must become skilled and competent at inclusion. At the foundation of that competence is emotional intelligence.

How does a person move from being an exclusive, culturally incompetent leader to be an inclusive, culturally competent leader? As I stated previously, it starts with emotional intelligence: leaders must begin to see not only how and why we see the world the way they do but what they might be missing. After discovering their blind spots, leaders must find seamless, relevant, applicable ways to embed cross-cultural agility into their leadership styles and the company's culture.

One of my clients, a small technology company, is an example of a company working hard to embody diversity and bring inclusion into the organization. But it wasn't always easy. An embarrassing incident in which a board member posted some unfavorable remarks on Twitter about #BlackLivesMatter provoked a backlash from employees, suppliers, and customers.

Instead of merely seeing this as a public relations incident requiring damage control, the CEO saw the experience as a wake-up call and a soul-searching journey of self-examination about who the company is and who the company thought it was. The incident provoked the CEO to ask, "What else are we missing? What conscious or unconscious biases are holding us back from activating and achieving our goals?"

The company established an external Diversity Advisory Council of prominent community members and senior company leaders. The company also hired several consultants, including minority-owned reputation management and multicultural marketing firm. The company also hired my firm, Icarus Consulting, to help advance and accelerate the company's diversity, equity, and inclusion efforts. The Diversity Advisory Council provided oversight of the work that included surveys, focus groups, and leadership assessments. We interviewed company leaders to assess their commitment to diversity and inclusion. Leaders and employees attended bias training to help them integrate learning into their personal and daily work lives. The overall goal of their efforts was to become more diverse and lead more inclusively.

The company hired its first chief diversity officer (CDO). Within months, the CDO changed the internal policies, which helped create a more inclusive work environment. The CDO facilitated employee town halls that focused on issues of diversity and inclusion. In the months that followed, the company started to decrease employee complaints about inappropriate remarks. Employees reported that "they felt valued, respected, and [took] pride in the company's new direction and were glad to a part of it."

The company's intentional effort to include employees' unique perspectives sparked productivity and creativity, eventually leading to better product development, including a new software application customized for some of their customers' most competitive markets.

The CEO has been a critical leader in championing diversity and inclusion at the company, helping to implement its strategies and integrate them into daily operations. I interviewed the CEO, and he revealed that he intentionally looked for opportunities to "spend time with employees who were different from him and discuss similarities and differences." In a moment of vulnerability, he revealed that his personal goal was to move beyond tolerance to mutual respect. I asked him to provide a concrete example of what he had done to move from tolerance to a more profound respect level. The CEO explained there was a time he would schedule a meeting on Good Friday, one of the holiest Christian days, and he would excuse the absence of Christian teammates: "That's tolerance." He explained that he no longer schedules meetings on Good Friday or other Christian holy days. "It's not much, but I'm trying to live and work with a deeper level of understanding and showing mutual respect."

Moving from Organizational Comfort to Cultural Competence

In her book *Inclusion: Diversity in the Workplace and the Will to Change,* Jennifer Brown, an expert in workplace solutions and diversity and inclusion, makes a clear and critical distinction between diversity and inclusion for leaders. According to Brown, diversity is the mix, and inclusion is making the mix work. Brown suggests that it is inclusion that is the crucial transformative challenge for twenty-first-century leaders. Brown makes a compelling case for inclusion as a business strategy, saying that if leaders want to attract and retain top talent, they must foster work environments in which employees thrive.

I strongly agree with Jennifer Brown and believe that inclusion unleashes talent and unpacks the power of teams, making them more collaborative and creative. It is inclusion that optimizes and engages a multicultural workforce and accelerates innovation. As a result, two things happen. First, employees become more engaged, collaborative, productive, and innovative. Second, organizations expand existing markets, open new ones, and develop new products based on a deeper understanding of customers, cultures, and unmet niches.

Brown suggests that inclusive leadership requires a deep understanding of how each of us is similar and dissimilar. Again, I agree with my good friend Jennifer Brown and add that calling out differences unleashes the true creative contributions of diverse perspectives that play off each other and lead to better work relationships, more significant innovation, and profitability that benefits individuals and teams and organizations. Inclusive leaders leverage the differences in their team to make the team stronger. According to Jennifer Brown, we all have our unique differences. Every person has unique characteristics that define and influence why they walk, talk, think, believe, and act the way they do.

Leaders must also become cross-culturally agile. At the heart of this, cultural agility is emotional intelligence. This requires leaders to embrace and celebrate individual differences. Leaders need to understand in a profound, visceral, business-grounded way how to activate their teams' diversity. Culturally incompetent managers seek control through uniformity. Authentic, culturally competent leaders create the future by being open and including the new, different, and unusual.

Contributing to the Triple Bottom Line: Financial, Social, Environmental

When diversity and inclusion practitioners are trying to show the value or build the business case for diversity, they talk about direct and indirect ways in which diversity and inclusion contribute to organizations' bottom lines. While the bottom line typically refers to revenues or increased business share, an expanded definition of it—the triple bottom line—includes the financial, social, and environmental impact and appears to have greater relevance across industry sectors. A couple of examples of how diversity and inclusion efforts contribute to the bottom line include:

- The organization's ability to attract more business from external, diverse groups (e.g., professional associations, fraternities, etc.), leading to increases in revenue generation
- Enhanced health-care service delivery to diverse communities

Changing Demographics and Customer Expectations

Knowing your clients helps organizations in every industry because it enables companies to improve service delivery and enhance customer satisfaction and retention. Companies recognize that reaching this understanding is not a one-time endeavor. Clients' needs may evolve and change over time or because new generations of customers may surface where needs and expectations are different.

Understanding customers and prospective customers enable organizations to move into new markets, and in today's economy and business landscape, the potential is global. Companies competing for business internationally recognize the importance of customizing services and products to their target markets. The depth of research that goes into this exercise is immense, and research suggests that the profits organizations stand to gain are phenomenal.

Research suggests that consumer purchasing power and global consumer spending are shifting from baby boomers who are trimming the fat on their purchases to GenX and Millennials who are in the prime of their spending power and the least impacted by any downturns in the economy. This shift appears to have affected the way organizations are staying in touch with the market. Retail and consumer goods companies are:

- Ensuring that product offerings in emerging markets are explicitly tailored for consumers' lives, needs, and pocketbooks.
- Reassessing techniques for market analysis to assess which consumer and behavior shifts are permanent and which are not.
- Focusing on accurate rather than perceived value.

In looking at U.S. urban centers, and where purchasing power is expected to be the most robust, nine groups of urban consumers are projected to generate three-quarters of urban consumption growth from 2020 to 2030, and three groups alone generate about half of that growth:

- Retiring and elderly (sixty-plus years) in the most extensive metro areas: This group will grow by more than one-third, from 164 million in 2020 to 222 million in 2030. They will generate 51 percent of urban consumption growth and 19 percent of urban consumption growth.

- Working-age consumers (fifteen to fifty-nine years) in the top five largest states (California, New York, Texas, Florida, Pennsylvania: Their number will expand by 20 percent—an additional 100 million people. Their per capita consumption is expected to more than double. By 2030, they will spend 12 cents of every $1 of urban use.

- Working-age consumers (fifteen to fifty-nine years) in the top five southern states (i.e., Florida, Virginia, Georgia, North Carolina, Tennessee, South Carolina): The already-large numbers and per capita consumption of this group will grow modestly by 7 percent and 24 percent, respectively, from 2020 to 2030. Many younger consumers are under income pressure and are cost-conscious in their spending.

We can borrow from the intelligence that is done to tap into global markets and leverage this domestically. The U.S. has many vibrant cultures and subgroups that contribute to our overall economy. There are plenty of opportunities in the U.S.'s largest urban areas to increase market share.

U.S. customers vary by industry. For academia, it is the tuition-paying students. In manufacturing, it extends to other businesses. In health care, it includes patients. For example, understanding the client or patient in health care is especially important in disease prevention and treatment. It enables health care providers to mitigate the risk of providing irrelevant or inappropriate services. Not all industries absorb as much trouble, yet it is still essential for all sectors to understand the needs of the different demographic groups receiving or impacted by the company's offerings.

Preparing Workers to Reenter the New Workplace

In Feb 2021, I spoke at the National Association of African Americans in Human Resources (NAAAHR) national conference on *"Inclusion by Disruption."* During the question and answer, a woman asked me, "How can I get a good job with a criminal record?" She went on to state (with a lot of courage and conviction, I might add), "I was serving time for robbery and theft. While in prison, I completed rehabilitation, and after my release, I earned my degree. I have stayed out of trouble and built a life for myself. However, I cannot get a job that pays more than the minimum wage."

This woman's past, like so many others, was an obstacle to working in several jobs. In the future, I believe it should be one of the primary responsibilities of diversity and inclusion practitioners to encourage companies and entire industries to take a reform-minded approach to meet their organization's talent needs and better meeting the needs of the communities and customers they serve.

Part of our national identity is grounded in the idea that America is a place where people can start anew. The woman who had the courage to share her story exemplifies how individuals, their families, their communities, and our society benefit when we practice forgiveness and extend redemption to those who sincerely repent past mistakes. The dividends are both spiritual and tangible.

But too often, hiring practices lack that "quality of mercy"; otherwise, qualified applicants are rejected based on past convictions for low-level criminal activity. Policymakers and business leaders need to begin rethinking these punitive hiring practices. They need to start asking, "How can we better respond to the needs of potential employees who have criminal records and who need a fresh start?" I believe it is about time that D&I leaders play a leading role in helping their organization craft Second Chance Policies and Initiatives.

It appears this reform line of thinking is gaining momentum at every level of government, judging by support for the First Step Act that was signed into law in 2018. This comprehensive criminal justice reform law offers an innovative approach in areas like sentencing and rehabilitation to reduce recidivism. Though it only applies to federal offenses, it is a step in the right direction, and I hope businesses follow Washington's lead.

I fully realize that in specific jobs, there are sensitivities. For instance, it would be difficult to make a case for a job applicant with a past financial crime that would undermine customer trust, like embezzlement, money laundering, or identity theft. However, when companies consider potential hires, they should evaluate whether an applicant warrants an exemption if they pose no financial, safety, or security risk to the company, employees, or customers.

D&I leaders, working in concert with their HR teammates, should examine ways to streamline the process and reduce applicants' burdens. This streamlining could include delegating responsibility for reviewing these requests for waivers and exemptions to the vice president of talent acquisition instead of requiring the case to be reviewed by a legal, compliance, or ethics committee.

Organizations could also narrowly define their current prohibitions without increasing risk for the company. Recent studies tell us about seventy-seven million people have some criminal record. Many are not violent or career criminals, but people who made a mistake early in life have since paid their debt to society. These individuals could be a significant economic resource, yet they face hiring barriers that leave them unemployed or underemployed. The value of the lost output of people with criminal records who have difficulty finding employment has been estimated at almost $100 billion. This represents a significant drain on our economy. Opening a path forward for more of these people will reduce recidivism and poverty while strengthening families and communities.

Forgiveness is less about changing the past than it is about changing the future. Welcoming these individuals back into the community's mainstream could be a significant competitive advantage for companies and industries, particularly in today's tight labor market. The company, communities, and the country will benefit because it will mean new opportunities for millions of people, putting them on the path toward a stable, productive place in society. Most of all, it is the right thing to do, and in keeping with values of diversity, equity, and inclusion.

This is an important opportunity for the field of diversity and inclusion. We've taken a significant step in 2018 with the First Step Act. The private sector should look for ways to expand career opportunities for those who have paid their debt. D&I leaders can play a vital role in leading the way forward.

Developing Sustainable D&I Strategies

When asked about D&I, a common sentiment shared by leaders when asked about D&I is that they look forward to the day when they no longer must think about it, and it has become interwoven into the fabric as a part of how their organizations operate. To make this a reality, it will take deliberate and strategic effort to ensure alignment between overarching company goals and strategies and D&I objectives. We've helped several of our clients accomplish this by taking an integrated approach across units, levels, and functional areas within the organization. One practice included taking content from training classes and creating sound bites used during staff meetings.

Enhancing Talent Management Capability and Capacity

The war for talent is still alive and well. The labor market is more informed and better educated than before the pandemic, and job seekers are being courted by companies worldwide. Recognizing this, companies strive to be viewed as an employer of choice. Brand equity is a critical component in attracting top talent. Research suggests that job candidates, particularly Millennials, want to work for companies where diversity and inclusion are ingrained into the culture. Our clients tell us that their organizations have attracted top, diverse talent because of positive perceptions of their multicultural, inclusive cultures.

Increasing Trust by Reducing Bias

"Aha" has become a common mantra during leadership training on implicit bias. Through candid discussions, these light bulb moments create awareness that institutional practices and individual behaviors are linked to beliefs and thoughts camping out below consciousness. Leaders recognize how powerful their unconscious bias is in shaping their interactions with people on their team. For example, awareness of one's bias that women should not play a key role in the company may shine a light on the fact that women's selection and promotion into mission-critical positions may only occur rhetorically. Experiencing these "aha" moments for leaders can better understand the systemic impact that unconscious biases have in the workplace and lead to more buy-in when D&I strategies are proposed that challenge barrier to full inclusion of women and people of color.

Optimizing High Impact Business and Employee Resource Groups

Many large corporations have observed the evolution of their employee resource groups (ERGs). Once viewed strictly as social clubs whose purpose was to benefit their membership by providing a haven for networking, mentoring, and venting, these groups have expanded their scope of impact within organizations. Also referred to as business resource groups (BRGs), these teams provide perspectives on new product or service development and represent the organization's talent attraction efforts and business development efforts. Dozens of companies are now considering increasing ERGs or BRGs because of their proven value and impact.

Enhancing and Expanding the Company's Brand

D&I activities often enable organizations to connect face-to-face with the community. Sponsorship of fundraising events within diverse communities, participation in conferences like the National Society of Hispanic MBAs, National Black MBA Association, and others provide external stakeholders a chance to experience and interact with the company. The dividend is expanded brand awareness for companies, which translates into increased external interest, making it easier to attract and retain top talent.

Developing Realistic Metrics with Teeth

What gets measured gets done. While this might be viewed as a given for functional areas like sales, marketing, operations, and finance, it has been an uphill battle for D&I. Establishing metrics and tracking the success of D&I initiatives has been given inconsistent superficial attention in many companies. Too often, leaders have viewed D&I as an expendable activity. Suppose the adage "what gets measured gets done" is true. In that case, D&I leaders need to get busy establishing baseline metrics, developing D&I scorecards and dashboards, and including D&I KPIs in the company's regular performance reports.

My company, Icarus Consulting, has developed a D&I scorecard that helps organizations track their status and progress. Our clients use our scorecard with success, as indicated by their managers using it to track recruitment and retention performance. We encourage D&I practitioners to collaborate in building a repository of external intelligence that includes D&I benchmarks, best practices, and other data-driven tools and processes to benefit companies that desperately need them.

Enlisting the Board in Reimagining the Company

Another impactful driver of progress and change in the success storyline is specific board members' roles. There are potent anecdotes and stories of how board members have stimulated new thinking within the organizations they serve and how this has led to paradigm shifts and measurable progress on the D&I front. One such story is reflected in an interview we conducted with one of our clients' board chair. He shared how he had changed the way the company measured its spending with diverse suppliers. He also boasted of eliminating the "zero-sum" strategies for attracting, engaging, developing, and retaining diverse talent and suppliers.

Some Final Thoughts

In the summer of 2020, for eight minutes and forty-six seconds, George Floyd was pinned down with a knee on his neck and unable to breathe. In Minnesota, where George Floyd was killed, the rate of unarmed Black people killed is four times higher than it is for Whites. While far from being its only manifestation, this is what racism looks like. It seems we barely have time to grieve one death before another is captured on cellphone video, and we may never learn about countless other invisible atrocities.

Protests continue to erupt across the country, demanding justice and an end to police brutality in response to the killings of black people, who human decency and the rule of law have failed. There is a long, tragic history of this failure, which both saddens and outrages. The Jim Crow era, Tulsa Race Massacre, and thousands of lynchings exemplify the unpunished reign of lawlessness, terror, and death unleashed on Black people. Dealing honestly and effectively with racism remains America's unfinished business.

While protest has proven to be a critical driver of change, it's not the only one. Diversity, equity, and inclusion professionals have been a force for change, education, and opportunity in America for over four decades. Our companies, communities, and the country have been deeply affected by multiple crises, but the D&I community is more determined than ever to drive the needed changes. At Icarus Consulting, we extend our sincere condolences to the families of those impacted by racial violence, but we owe these martyrs more. As Dr. King's words remind us, "Injustice anywhere is a threat to justice everywhere." The entire D&I profession must redouble its efforts to forge a more humane and just society.

The entire D&I community must join with the martyrs' families to call for national legislation to end racial violence and increase police accountability. I look forward to partnering with other D&I thought leaders to create forums and programs focused on anti-racism awareness, racial equity, equal opportunity, and social justice. We call on all business and academic partners, civic, faith, and philanthropic leaders, as well as other organizations and people of goodwill, to join with the D&I community in committing to the difficult, long-term work of improving racial equity and ensuring greater accountability for equity and justice.

It may be unrealistic to think about a "solution" to racism, but let's work diligently and urgently to assess and reform the current situation. Diversity, equity, and inclusion must become realities in America. Whether we allow these values to drain our companies, communities, and country or serve as a dynamic catalyst to prosperity is both a choice and a challenge. I believe that diversity, equity, and inclusion are some of the country's greatest assets and are the best hope for the future. It is a lighthouse that will give us the insights and perspectives needed to navigate the storm of simmering tensions—and find creative solutions for achieving a more inclusive America. I have faith in this country and all its diversity—although sometimes it makes me *wanna holla* and throw up both my hands.

APPENDIX A

MY TOP FIVE FAVORITE BOOKS ON DIVERSITY, EQUITY, AND INCLUSION

Diversity, Inc.: The Failed Promise of a Billion-Dollar Business

In Diversity, Inc., award-winning journalist Pamela Newkirk shines a bright light on the diversity industry, asking the tough questions about what has been effective and why progress has been so slow. Newkirk highlights the rare success stories, sharing valuable lessons about how other industries can match those gains. But as she argues, despite decades of handwringing, costly initiatives, and uncomfortable conversations, organizations have fallen far short of their goals apart from a few exceptions. *Diversity, Inc.* incisively shows the vast gap between the rhetoric of inclusivity and real achievements. If we are to deliver on the promise of true equality, we need to abandon ineffective, costly measures and commit ourselves to combat enduring racial attitudes.

White Fragility: Why It's So Hard for White People to Talk About Racism

In this vital, necessary, and beautiful book, antiracist educator Robin DiAngelo deftly illuminates the phenomenon of white fragility and allows us to understand racism as a practice not restricted to bad people. Referring to the defensive moves that white people make when challenged racially, white fragility is characterized by emotions such as anger, fear, and guilt, and behaviors including argumentation and silence. These behaviors, in turn, function to reinstate white racial equilibrium and prevent any meaningful cross-racial dialogue. In this in-depth exploration, DiAngelo examines how white fragility develops, how it protects racial inequality, and what we can do to engage more constructively.

The Memo: What Women of Color Need to Know to Secure a Seat at the Table

Lean In for women of color: Minda Harts provides a no-BS look at the odds stacked against women of color in professional settings, from the wage gap to biases and microaggressions, with actionable takeaways. *The Memo* is the much-needed career advice guide for women of color specifically, finally ending the one-size-fits-all approach of business books that lump together women across races and overlook the unique barriers to success for women of color. In a charismatic and relatable voice, Minda Harts brings her entrepreneurial experience as CEO of The Memo to the page and her past career life as a fundraising consultant to top colleges across the country. With wit and candor, Harts begins by acknowledging the "ugly truths" that keep women of color from getting the proverbial seat at the table in corporate America: microaggressions, systemic racism, white privilege, etc. Harts validates that women aren't making up the discrimination they feel, even if it isn't always overt. From there, she gives a straight talk on addressing these issues head-on and provides a roadmap to help women of color and their allies make real change to the system. With chapters on network building, office politics, money, and negotiation, *The Memo* covers all the basics of any good business book. But through the author's lens, it offers support and long-overdue advice, particularly for women of color.

So You Want to Talk About Race

Widespread reporting on aspects of white supremacy—from police brutality to the mass incarceration of Black Americans, has put a media spotlight on racism in our society. Still, it is a difficult subject to talk about. How do you tell your roommate her jokes are racist? Why did your sister-in-law take umbrage when you asked to touch her hair—and how do you make it right? How do you explain white privilege to your white, privileged friend? *In So You Want to Talk About Race*, Ijeoma Oluo guides readers of all races through subjects ranging from intersectionality and affirmative action to "model minorities" to make the seemingly impossible possible: honest conversations about race and racism and how they infect almost every aspect of American life.

Talking to Strangers: What We Should Know about the People We Don't Know

Michael Gladwell argues that something is very wrong with the tools and strategies we use to make sense of people we don't know. And because we don't know how to talk to strangers, we invite conflict and misunderstanding in ways that profoundly affect our lives and our world. In the audiobook version of *Talking to Strangers*, you'll hear the voices of people he interviewed—scientists, criminologists, military psychologists. Court transcripts are brought to life with re-enactments. You hear the contentious arrest of Sandra Bland by the side of the road in Texas. As Gladwell revisits Bernie Madoff's deceptions, Amanda Knox's trial, and the suicide of Sylvia Plath, you hear directly from many of the players in these real-life tragedies.

APPENDIX B

JUSTICE, EQUITY, DIVERSITY, AND INCLUSION (JEDI) DEFINITIONS

ableism—Negative attitudes and prejudice toward an individual based on physical, mental, or physical and mental disabilities.[1]

accessibility—Refers to the design of products, devices, services, or environments for people with disabilities. The accessible design concept ensures direct/unassisted access and indirect access, meaning compatibility with a person's assistive technology (computer screen readers).[2] See also *universal design*.

accommodation—See reasonable accommodation.

acculturation—The process of addressing cultural differences, cultural change, and adaptation between groups. Acculturation is the process of learning and incorporating the language, values, beliefs, and behaviors that make up a distinct culture. This concept is not to be confused with assimilation, where an individual or group may give up certain aspects of their culture to adapt to that of the prevailing culture.[2]

affirmative action—Any action taken or required to correct the effects of past discrimination, to eliminate present discrimination, or to prevent discrimination in the future.[3]

affirmative action plan—The written document through which management ensures that all persons have equal opportunities in recruitment, selection, appointment, promotion, training, discipline, and related employment areas. The plan is tailored to the employer's workforce and the skills available in the labor force. It prescribes specific actions, goals, timetables, and responsibilities and describes resources to meet identified needs. The plan is a comprehensive, results-oriented program designed to achieve equal employment opportunity rather than merely to ensure nondiscrimination.[2]

agender—A person who is internally ungendered or does not have a felt sense of gender identity.[4]

ageism—Discrimination against individuals because of their age, often based on stereotypes[4].

aggressive (ag)—A term used to describe a female-bodied and female-identified person who prefers presenting as masculine. This term is mostly used in urban communities of color.[5]

agnosticism—In the popular sense, an agnostic is someone who neither believes nor disbelieves in God, whereas an atheist denies in God. However, in strict importance, agnosticism believes that human reason is incapable of providing sufficient rational grounds to justify either the belief that God exists or the belief that God does not exist. Insofar as one holds that our beliefs are rational only if they are sufficiently supported by human reason, the person who accepts the philosophical position of agnosticism will have neither the belief that God exists nor the belief that God does not exist is rational.[6]

alien—Any person not a citizen or national of the United States.[7]

alien (illegal)—An alien who has entered the United States illegally and is deportable if apprehended, or an alien who entered the United States legally but has fallen *out of status* and is deportable. Also known as an *undocumented alien*.[8]

alien (resident)—See *permanent resident*.

ally—Someone who makes the commitment and effort to recognize their privilege (based on gender, class, race, sexual identity, etc.) and works in solidarity with oppressed groups in the struggle for justice.[9]

American Indian (Native American) or Alaska Native—A person having origin in North America's original peoples and maintains cultural identification through tribal affiliation or community recognition.[9]

Americans with Disabilities Act (ADA)—Enacted in 1990, the ADA is a civil rights law that prohibits discrimination against individuals with disabilities in all public living areas, including jobs, schools, transportation, and all public and private places that are open to the public. The purpose of the law is to make sure that people with disabilities have the same rights and opportunities. The ADA is divided into five titles (or sections) related to different areas of public life—

employment, state and local government, public accommodations, telecommunications, and miscellaneous provisions.[10]

androgynous—Someone who reflects an appearance that is both masculine and feminine, or who appears to be neither or both a male and female.[11]

anti-oppression—Recognizing and deconstructing the systemic, institutional, and personal forms of disempowerment used by certain groups over others, actively challenging the different types of oppression.[11]

anti-Semitism—Refers to prejudice or discrimination against Jews as individuals and as a group. Anti-Semitism is based on stereotypes and myths that target Jews as people, their religious practices and beliefs, and the Jewish State of Israel.[12]

Asian or Pacific Islander—A person having origin in any of the original peoples of the Far East, Southeast Asia, the Indian Subcontinent, or the Pacific Islands. This area includes China, Japan, Korea, the Philippine Islands, and Samoa.

asexual—Refers to a person who does not experience sexual attraction or has little interest in sexual activity.[13]

assimilation—The process whereby a group gradually adopts the characteristics of another culture.[14]

atheism—A lack of belief in gods and supernatural beings.[15]

bias—A tendency to believe that some people, ideas, and so on are better than others that usually results in treating some people unfairly.[16]

bicultural—A bicultural person could function effectively and appropriately and select appropriate behaviors, values, and attitudes within two cultures.[17]

bicurious—A curiosity about having sexual relations with someone of the same gender/sex.[18]

bi-gendered (1)—A person whose gender identity is a combination of male/man and female/woman.[19]

bi-gendered (2)—Like bisexual. It can be used to describe people who identify with two or more genders (multigender). Do not confuse this term with Two-Spirit, associated explicitly with Native American and First Nations cultures.[20]

bigot—An obstinate and intolerant believer in a religion, political theory, and so on.[20]

bigotry—Intolerant prejudice that glorifies one's group and denigrates members of other groups.[21]

biological sex—Refers to a person's biological status and is typically categorized as male, female, or intersex. There are many indicators of biological sex, including sex chromosomes, gonads, internal reproductive organs, and external genitalia.[22]

biphobia—The irrational fear and intolerance of people who are bisexual.[23]

biphobia (internalized)—When a person who is bisexual is uncomfortable or not accepting of his/her sexual orientation, the person has been taught by society and possibly his/her community that being bisexual is unacceptable, immoral, does not exist, or is a phase.[24]

bisexual (1)—Also *bi*. Having emotional, romantic, or sexual attractions to both men and women,[25] but not necessarily simultaneously or equally.[26]

bisexual (2)—This term is used differently by different people. It can be used to mean attraction to two genders, attraction to men and women specifically, attraction to all genders, or attraction regardless of gender.[27]

blind—A term most frequently used to describe severe vision loss. Either *blind* or *low vision* are acceptable terms to describe all degrees of vision loss.[28]

bullying—Intimidating, exclusionary, threatening, or hostile behavior against an individual.[28]

butch—An overtly/stereotypically masculine or masculine-acting woman. It can be used to denote an individual or the dominant role in a lesbian relationship.[29]

camp—A form of humor in which one makes fun of one's oppression by exaggerating stereotypes that the oppressor projects onto the oppressed. Camp makes fun of stereotypes and laughs at the sting of oppression.[30]

Chicano/a—A term adopted by some Mexican Americans to demonstrate pride in their heritage, born out of the national Chicano Movement that was politically aligned with the civil rights movement to end racial oppression and Mexican Americans' social inequalities. Chicano pertains to the experience of Mexican-descended individuals living in the U.S., but not all Mexican Americans identify as Chicano.[30]

cisgender—Replaces the terms *non-transgender* or *bio man/bio woman* to refer to individuals who have a match between the sex they were assigned at birth, their bodies, and their gender identity.[31]

cissexism—The set of attitudes and behaviors which value and normalize cisgender people while keeping transgender and gender-nonconforming people invisible or treating them as inferior or deviant.[32]

civil rights—Personal rights guaranteed and protected by the Constitution, e.g., freedom of speech and press and freedom from discrimination (The National Multicultural Institute).

Civil Rights Act of 1964—The Act outlawed discrimination based on race, color, religion, sex, or national origin, required equal access to public places and employment, and enforced schools' desegregation and the right to vote. It did not end discrimination, but it did open the door to progress further.[33]

civil union—A relationship between a couple legally recognized by a governmental authority with many of the rights and responsibilities of marriage. See also *marriage* and *domestic partnership*.[34]

classism—Any attitude or institutional practice that subordinates people due to income, occupation, education, or economic condition.[35]

closeted—The opposite of being *out*, being closeted means that one's sexual orientation is concealed or presumed to be heterosexual.[36]

collusion—When people act to perpetuate oppression or prevent others from working to eliminate oppression.[37]

colonialism—Colonization can be defined as invasion, dispossession, and subjugation of a people. The invasion need not be military; it can begin or continue as a geographical intrusion in the form of agricultural, urban, or industrial encroachments. The result of such incursion is the dispossession of vast amounts of lands from the original inhabitants. This is often legalized after the fact. The long-term result of such massive dispossession is institutionalized inequality. The colonizer/colonized relationship is, by nature, an unequal one that benefits the colonizer at the expense of the colonized.[38]

colorblind—Term used to describe the personal, group, and institutional policies or practices that do not consider race or ethnicity as a determining factor. The term "colorblind" deemphasizes or ignores race and ethnicity as a large part of one's identity.[38]

"coming out" (1)—Shorthand for *coming out of the closet*. The phrase refers to several aspects of lesbian, gay, and bisexual persons' experiences: self-awareness of same-sex attractions, the telling of one or a few people about these attractions, widespread disclosure of same-sex attractions, and identification with the lesbian, gay and bisexual community.[39]

"coming out" (2)—The process of becoming aware of one's queer sexual orientation, one's Two-Spirit or trans identity, accepting it, and telling others about it. LGBT+ people may come out about gender and sexuality and often come out repeatedly to new people. This is an ongoing process that may not include everybody in all aspects of one's life. Coming out usually occurs in stages and is a nonlinear process. An individual may be "out" in only some situations or to certain family members or associates and not others. Some may never come out to anyone besides themselves.[40]

communism—A political theory from Karl Marx advocated class war and led to a society in which all property is publicly owned. Each person works and is paid according to their abilities and needs.[41]

Critical Race Theory—The Critical Race Theory movement considers many of the same issues that conventional civil rights and ethnic studies take up but places them in a broader perspective that includes economics, history, and even feelings and the unconscious. Unlike traditional civil rights, which embrace incrementalism and step-by-step progress, critical race theory questions the very foundations of the liberal order, including equality theory, legal reasoning, enlightenment rationalism, and constitutional law principles.[42]

cross-cultural—Refers to cultures around the world. There is no universally agreed-upon distinction between diversity management and cross-cultural work. However, "cross-cultural" sometimes refers only to country or regional cultures rather than a broader definition of culture.[42]

cross-dresser—People who cross-dress wear clothing traditionally or stereotypically worn by another gender in their culture. They vary in how completely they cross-dress, from one article of clothing to fully cross-dressing. Those who cross-dress are usually comfortable with their assigned sex and do not wish to change it. Cross-dressing is a form of gender expression and is not necessarily tied to sexual activity or sexual orientation.[43]

culture—The shared patterns of behaviors and interactions, implicit constructs, and affective understanding are learned through socialization. These shared patterns identify the members of a culture group while also distinguishing those of another group.[44]

cultural appropriation—Theft of cultural elements—including symbols, art, language, customs, etc.—for one's use, commodification, or profit, often without understanding, acknowledgment, or respect for its value in the original culture. Results from the assumption of a dominant (i.e., white) culture's right to take other cultural elements.[45]

cultural assimilation—An individual, family, or group gives up certain aspects of its culture to adapt to the dominant culture; a process of learning that leads to the ability to effectively respond to the challenges and opportunities posed by the presence of social cultural diversity in a defined social system; knowledge, awareness and interpersonal skills that allow individuals to increase their understanding, sensitivity, appreciation and responsiveness to cultural differences and the interactions resulting from them. Acquiring cultural competency varies among different groups and involves ongoing relational process tending to inclusion and trust-building; a process of learning that leads to the ability to effectively respond to the challenges and opportunities posed by the presence of social-cultural diversity in a defined social system.[45]

cultural competence—A set of congruent behaviors, attitudes, and policies that come together in a system, agency, or among professionals to enable that system, agency, or those professions to work effectively in cross-cultural situations. The word *culture* is used because it implies the integrated human behavior pattern that includes thoughts, communications, actions, customs, beliefs, values, and companies of a racial, ethnic, religious, or social group. The word *competence* is used because it implies having the capacity to function effectively.

Five essential elements contribute to a system's, institution's, or agency's ability to become more culturally competent, which include:

- Valuing diversity
- Having the capacity for cultural self-assessment
- Being conscious of the dynamics inherent when cultures interact
- Having institutionalized cultural knowledge
- Having developed adaptations to service delivery reflecting an understanding of cultural diversity

These five elements should be manifested at every organization level, including policymaking, administrative, and practice. Further, these elements should be reflected in the organization's attitudes, structures, policies, and services.[46,47]

cultural conditioning—The unconscious process by which we are socialized to adopt our own group's way of thinking.[48]

cultural essentialism—The practice of categorizing groups of people within a culture or from other cultures according to essential qualities[49]

cultural humility—The ability to maintain an interpersonal stance other-oriented (or open to the other) about cultural identity aspects most important to the person. Cultural humility focuses on taking responsibility for our interactions with others rather than achieving a state of knowledge or awareness. The approach of cultural humility goes beyond the concept of cultural competence to encourage individuals to identify and acknowledge their own biases. Cultural humility admits that it is impossible to be adequately knowledgeable about cultures other than one's own.[50] Principles that guide the cultural humility approach:

- Lifelong learning and critical self-reflection
- Recognizing and mitigating/challenging power imbalances
- Institutional accountability to model the principles[51]

cultural pluralism—Recognition of the contribution of each group to a common civilization. It encourages the maintenance and development of different lifestyles, languages, and convictions. It is a commitment to deal cooperatively with common concerns. It strives to create conditions of harmony and respect within a culturally diverse society.[52]

culture—A social system of meaning and custom developed by a group of people to assure its adaptation and survival. These groups are distinguished by a set of unspoken rules that shape values, beliefs, habits, patterns of thinking, behaviors, and styles of communication.[53]

deaf culture—Describes the social beliefs, behaviors, art, literary traditions, history, values, and shared companies of communities that are affected by deafness and which use sign languages as the main means of communication.[54]

demi-sexual—A person who does not experience sexual attraction unless they form an emotional connection with the partner. It's more commonly seen in but by no means confined to romantic relationships. The term demi-sexual comes from the orientation being "halfway between" sexual and asexual.[55]

denial—Refusal to acknowledge the societal privileges that are granted or denied based on an individual's ethnicity or other groupings.[56]

diaspora—The voluntary or involuntary movement of peoples from their homelands into new regions; these are people who live outside their natal (or imagined natal) territories and recognize that their traditional homelands are reflected deeply in the languages they speak, religions they adopt, and the cultures they produce.[57,58]

different consequences—Outcomes are applied to different groups exhibiting identical behaviors, yet one group's behavior is valued, and the other is devalued.[57]

differential validation—Validation of tests at different score levels for different classes of people. This is not equivalent to lowering standards for one or more groups to favor them over others. Differential validation occurs only where one class's lower test scores predict a level of job performance equivalent to that predicted by the higher scores of another class.[57]

disability—A functional limitation that affects an individual's ability to perform certain functions.[59]

disability (ADA)—A person who has a physical or mental impairment that substantially limits one or more major life activities. This includes people who record such an impairment, even if they do not currently have a disability. It also includes individuals who do not have a disability but are regarded as having a disability. The ADA also makes it unlawful to discriminate against a person based on that person's association with a person with a disability.[60]

discrimination—Behavior that treats people unequally because of their group memberships. Discriminatory behavior, ranging from slights to hate crimes, often begins with negative stereotypes and prejudices.[61]

discrimination (legal)—In constitutional law, discrimination is the grant by a statute of privileges to a class arbitrarily designated from a sizable number of persons, where no reasonable distinction exists between the favored and disfavored classes. Federal laws, supplemented by court decisions, prohibit discrimination in employment, housing, voting rights, education, and public facilities access. They also proscribe discrimination based on race, age, sex, nationality, disability, or religion. Also, state and local laws can prohibit discrimination in these areas and others not covered by federal laws.[62]

diversity—Diversity includes how people differ, and it encompasses all the different characteristics that make one individual or group different from another. A broad definition includes not only race, ethnicity, and gender—the groups that most often come to mind when the term *diversity* is used—but also age, national origin, religion, disability, sexual orientation, socioeconomic status, education, marital status, language, and physical appearance. It also involves different ideas, perspectives, and values.[63]

diversity climate—The degree to which an organization implements fair human resource policies and socially integrates underrepresented employees. Diversity climate is a function of individual-level factors involving the extent of prejudice and stereotyping in organizations, group-intergroup factors referring to the degree of conflict between various groups within an organization, and organizational-level factors regarding such domains as organizational culture. Diversity climate is also the degree that underrepresented personnel is integrated into higher-level positions and within an organization's social networks and whether institutional bias prevails in an organization's human resource systems such as recruiting, hiring, training, developing, promoting, and compensating employees.[63]

diversity communication—The process of providing information to employees and managers regarding diversity management strategy and progress. Activities include conveying information via employee newsletters, closed-circuit television, employee focus groups, town-hall meetings, organization websites, and social media. [63]

diversity competency—A process of learning that leads to an ability to effectively respond to the challenges and opportunities posed by the presence of social-cultural diversity in a defined social system. [63]

diversity management—A strategically driven process whose emphasis is on building skills, making quality decisions that bring out the best in every employee, and assessing organizational mixtures and tensions because of changing workforce and customer demographics. [63]

diversity management initiatives—Proactive and intentional actions to get the best from the mix of employees, customers, suppliers, and other stakeholders to achieve organizational objectives. Actions often include efforts to improve human resource processes and enhance organizational culture, such as how the organization recruits, hires, trains, mentors, promotes, develops, and integrates employees. [63]

diversity management training—Intentional actions to educate a culturally diverse workforce and sensitize employees and managers to differences in the organization, such as gender, race, and generation, to maximize all employees' potential productivity. Numerous organizations with these goals in mind have developed training programs such as Managing Diversity, Valuing Differences, and Leading Diverse Work Teams. [63]

BEYOND INCLUSION

diversity metrics—The process of quantitatively and qualitatively measuring the impact of the organization's diversity strategy.[63]

diversity practitioner or professional—Individual responsible for managing the diversity management initiatives or the chief diversity officer in an organization. This person has expertise in diversity management but may or may not be a full-time diversity professional.[63]

domestic partner—In many states, domestic partnerships create a legal relationship for the couple that grants them rights equal to those granted in marriage. In others, domestic partnerships are no more than a cohabitation agreement with couples receiving fewer rights than married couples.[64] See also *civil union* and *marriage*.

dominant culture—The most potent cultural grouping. For example, in most parts of the United States, the dominant culture comprises white, English-speaking, middle- to upper-income Christians.[64]

drag/drag queen or king—Individuals who dress as the opposite sex for entertaining others at bars, clubs, or other events.[65]

dysphoria—A profound state of unease or dissatisfaction. Dysphoria may accompany depression, anxiety, or agitation. It can also mean someone that is not comfortable in their current body, particularly in cases of gender dysphoria.[66]

duty to accommodate—The obligation of an employer, service provider, or union to take steps to eliminate disadvantage to employees, prospective employees, or clients resulting from a rule, practice, or physical barrier that has or may harm individuals or groups protected under state or federal law.[66]

emigration—The act of leaving one's own country to settle permanently in another, moving abroad. See also *immigration*.[67]

empowerment—When target group members refuse to accept the dominant ideology and their subordinate status and take actions to redistribute social power more equitably.[68]

environmental equity—Measures the amelioration of the myriad inequities and disproportionate impacts that groups in society have faced, especially in environmental protection and access to nature and the environmental goods that aren't equally shared culturally.[68]

equal access—Absence of barriers to admittance, such as those motivated by cultural or racial discrimination, to society's companies. This includes access to services, programs, and employment. An outreach program is often needed to inform people that the program is available.[68]

equal employment opportunity—The process of administering human resource activities to ensure equal access in all phases of the employment process. Employment decisions are based solely on applicants' merit and fitness. They include employees related to specific jobs, regardless of race, color, religion, sex, age, national origin, handicap, marital status, or criminal record. (EEO) Title VII of the Civil Rights Act of 1964 prohibits discrimination in any aspect of employment based on an individual's race, color, religion, sex, or national origin.[68]

Equal Employment Opportunity Commission (EEOC)—The federal government agency mandated to enforce Title VII of the Civil Rights Act of 1964, as amended. The commission has five members, each appointed to a five-year term by the United States president with Congress's advice and consent. The federal Equal Employment Opportunity Commission has the power to bring suits, subpoena witnesses, issue guidelines that have the force of law, render decisions, provide legal assistance to complainants, and so on about fair employment.[68]

equal pay—As required by the Equal Pay Act of 1963 for employers subject to the Fair Labor Standards Act, businesses must provide equal pay for men and women performing the same or substantially similar jobs in the same establishment. For example, in a department store, a female salesperson in the ladies' shoe department must receive pay equal to that of a male salesperson.[68]

equity—The proactive reinforcement of policies, practices, attitudes, and actions that produce equitable power, access, opportunities, treatment, impacts, and outcomes for all.[69]

equity (campus context)—The creation of opportunities for historically underrepresented populations to have equal access to and participate in educational programs that can close the achievement gaps in student success and completion.[70]

ethnicity—A dynamic set of historically derived and traditional ideas and practices that (1) allows people to identify or to be identified with groupings of people based on presumed (and usually claimed) commonalities including language, history, nation or region of origin, customs, ways of being, religion, names, physical appearance, and genealogy or ancestry; (2) can be a source of meaning, action, and identity; and (3) confers a sense of belonging, pride, and motivation.[71]

ESL—(E)nglish as a (S)econd (L)anguage; a term used to describe language learning programs in the United States for individuals for whom English is not their first or native language. [71]

essentialism—The practice of categorizing an entire group based on assumptions about what constitutes the "essence" of that group. Essentialism prevents individuals from remaining open to individual differences within groups. [71]

ethnic—An adjective used to describe groups that share a common language, race, customs, lifestyle, social view, or religion. Everyone belongs to an ethnic group. The term is often confused with nonwhite. "Ethnic," however, refers to those traits that originate from ethnic, linguistic, and cultural ties with a specific group. [71]

ethnicity—A social construct that divides people into smaller social groups based on values, behavioral patterns, language, political and economic interests, history, and ancestral geographical base. [71]

ethnocentrism—The belief that one group is right and must be protected and defended. The negative aspect involves a blatant assertion of personal and cultural superiority. Characterized by, or based on, the attitude that one's group is superior. Ethnocentric habitual disposition is to judge foreign peoples or groups by the standards or practices of one's own culture or ethnic group. The method of using an ethnic group as a frame of reference, the basis of judgment, or standard criteria from which to view the world. Ethnocentrism favors one ethnic group's cultural norms and excludes the realities and experiences of other ethnic groups.[72]

eurocentrism—Reflecting a tendency to interpret the world in terms of Western, and mainly European, values, and experiences. The practice of using European culture as a frame of reference or standard criteria from which to view the world. Eurocentrism favors European cultural norms and excludes other cultural groups' realities and experiences (The National Multicultural Institute).[72]

FTM/F2M—Abbreviation for a female-to-male transgender or transsexual person.[73]

feminism—Theory and practice that advocates for educational and occupational equity between men and women; undermines traditional cultural practices that support the subjugation of women by men and the devaluation of women's contributions to society. [73]

femme—A woman whose sexual identification is lesbian who is notably or stereotypically feminine in appearance and manner.[74]

gay—A man whose primary romantic, emotional, physical, and sexual attractions are to other men. This term can also be used to apply to lesbians, bisexuals, and on some occasions, be used as an umbrella term for all LGBT+ people.[75]

gender—Refers to the socially constructed roles, behaviors, activities, and attributes that a given society considers appropriate for the different sexes. While aspects of biological sex are similar across different cultures, aspects of gender may differ.[76]

genderism—The system of belief that there are only two genders (men and women) and that gender is inherently tied to one's sex assigned at birth. It holds cisgender people as superior to transgender people and punishes or excludes those who don't conform to society's expectations of gender.[77]

genderqueer—A term used by some people who identify their gender as falling outside the male and female binary constructs. They may define their gender as falling somewhere on a continuum between male and female, or they may define it as wholly different from these terms. They may also request that pronouns be used to refer to them that are neither masculine nor feminine, such as *zie* instead of *he* or *she* or *hir* instead of *his* or *her* (see pronoun chart at the end). Some genderqueer people do not identify as transgender.[78]

gender binary system—A system of oppression that requires everyone to be raised, either male or female, masculine or feminine. It eliminates the possibility for other gender expressions and gives power to people whose genders do not break gender norms at the expense of transgender and intersex people.[79]

gender characteristics—Gender characteristics can change over time and are different between cultures. Words that refer to gender include "man," "woman," "transgender," "masculine," "feminine," and "genderqueer." Gender also refers to one's sense of self as masculine or feminine, regardless of external genitalia. Gender is often conflated with sex; however, this is inaccurate because "sex" refers to bodies, and "gender" refers to personality characteristics. [79]

gender-confirming surgery—Medical surgeries are used to modify one's body to be more congruent with one's gender identity. See also *sex reassignment surgery*.[80]

gender cues—What human beings use to attempt to discern the gender/sex of another person.[81]

gender diversity—Refers to the extent to which a person's gender identity, role, or expression differs from the cultural norms prescribed for people of a sex.[82]

gender dysphoria—Refers to the discomfort or distress that is associated with a discrepancy between a person's gender identity and that person's sex assigned at birth (and the associated gender role and primary and secondary sex characteristics).[83]

gender expression—Refers to how a person communicates gender identity to others through behavior, clothing, hairstyles, voice, or body characteristics.[84]

gender fluid—A person whose gender identification and presentation shifts, whether within or outside of societal, gender-based expectations.[85]

gender identity—Refers to a person's internal sense of being male, female, or something else.[86]

gender-neutral/gender-inclusive—Inclusive language to describe relationships (*spouse* and *partner* instead of *husband/boyfriend* and *wife/girlfriend*), spaces (gender-neutral/inclusive restrooms are for use by all genders), pronouns (*they* and *ze* are gender-neutral/inclusive pronouns), among other things.[87]

gender nonconforming—An adjective and umbrella term to describe individuals whose gender expression, gender identity, or gender role differs from gender norms associated with their assigned sex.[88]

gender normative—A person who, by nature or by choice, conforms to gender-based societal expectations. Also referred to as *genderstraight*.[89]

gender role—Refers to a pattern of appearance, personality, and behavior that, in each culture, is associated with being a boy/man/male or a girl/woman/female. A person's gender role may or may not conform to what is expected based on a person's sex assigned at birth. Gender role may also refer to the social role one lives in (e.g., as a woman, a man, or another gender), with some role characteristics conforming and others not conforming to what is associated with girls/women or boys/men in each culture and time.[90]

gender variant—A synonym for *gender diverse* and *gender nonconforming*; *gender diverse* and *gender nonconforming* are preferred to *gender variant* because variance implies a standard normativity of gender.[91]

generalization—A conclusion based on insufficient or biased evidence. A rush to a conclusion before having all the relevant facts.[92]

glass ceiling—Barriers, either real or perceived, that affect the promotion or hiring of protected group members.[93]

global environmental racism—Race is a potent factor in sorting people into their physical environment and explaining social inequality, political exploitation, social isolation, and quality of life. Racism influences land use, industrial facility siting, housing patterns, infrastructure development, and who gets what, when, where, and how much. Environmental racism refers to any policy, practice, or directive that differentially affects or disadvantages (whether intended or unintended) individuals, groups, or communities based on race or color.[93]

harassment—Unwelcome, intimidating, exclusionary, threatening, or hostile behavior against an individual based on a category protected.[93]

hate crime (FBI)—A criminal offense against a person or property motivated in whole or in part by an offender's bias against a race, religion, disability, sexual orientation, ethnicity, gender, or gender identity.[94]

hate crime (Virginia) –

    i. A criminal act committed against a person or property with the specific intent of instilling fear or intimidation in the individual against whom the act is perpetrated because of race, religion, or ethnic origin or that is committed for restraining that person from exercising his or her rights under the Constitution or laws of this Commonwealth or the United States,

ii. any illegal act directed against any persons or their property because of their race, religion, or national origin and

iii. all other incidents, as determined by law enforcement authorities, intended to intimidate, or harass any individual or group because of race, religion, or national origin.[95]

hermaphrodite—An out-of-date and offensive term for an intersex person.[96]

heteronormativity—The societal assumption and norm that all people are heterosexual. The basic civil rights and social privileges that a heterosexual person automatically receives are systematically denied to gay, lesbian, or bisexual persons simply because of their sexual orientation.[97]

heterosexism—The belief or assumption that everyone is or should be heterosexual; the idea that being heterosexual is normal, natural, and healthy, and all other people are somehow unnatural, abnormal, and unhealthy.[98]

heterosexual—A male whose sexual orientation is toward females or a female whose sexual orientation is toward males. Also referred to as *straight*.[99]

hidden bias—See *implicit bias*.

Hispanic—A person, regardless of race, who is of Spanish culture or origin. This includes persons from Mexico, Central or South America, Puerto Rico, the Dominican Republic, and Cuba. The U.S. Census Bureau defines Hispanic as people who classify themselves in Spanish, Hispanic, or Latino categories, including Mexican, Mexican American, Chicano, Puerto Rican, and Cuban.[71]

homophobia—The fear of homosexuality and homosexual people and all things associated with homosexuality.[100]

homophobia (internalized)—When a lesbian or gay person is uncomfortable or not accepting of his/her sexual orientation.[101]

homosexual—A male whose sexual orientation is toward men or a female whose sexual orientation is toward females. Homosexual males typically prefer the term *gay*, and homosexual females typically prefer the term *lesbian*.[102]

human rights—Freedoms that all people enjoy, simply because they are human. Human rights are supposed to apply equally to all people regardless of characteristics such as age, race, or gender. The Universal Declaration of Human Rights extends these rights to all people around the world. The basic rights and freedoms to which all humans are entitled, often held to include the right to life and liberty, freedom of thought and expression, and equality before the law.[103]

identity sphere—The idea that gender identities and expressions do not fit on a linear scale, but rather on a sphere that allows room for all expression without weighting any one expression better than the rest.[103]

illegal alien—See *alien (illegal)*.

immigrant—An alien who has been granted the right by U.S. Citizenship and Immigration Services to reside permanently in the United States and to work without restrictions in the United States. Also known as a *lawful permanent resident*.[104]

immigration—The action of coming to live permanently in a foreign country. See also *emigration*.[105]

implicit bias—Also known as unconscious or hidden bias, implicit biases are negative associations that people unknowingly hold. They are expressed automatically, without conscious awareness. Many studies have indicated that implicit biases affect individuals' attitudes and actions, thus creating real-world implications, even though individuals may not be aware that those biases exist within themselves. Notably, implicit biases have been shown to trump individuals' stated commitments to equality and fairness, thereby producing behaviors that diverge from the explicit attitudes that many people profess. The Implicit Association Test (IAT) is often used to measure implicit biases regarding race, gender, sexual orientation, age, religion, and other topics.[106]

inclusion—Authentically bringing traditionally excluded individuals and/or groups into processes, activities, and decisions/policymaking in a way that shares power.[107]

inclusion (campus context)—Defined as the active, intentional, and ongoing engagement with diversity—in the curriculum, in the curriculum, and in communities (intellectual, social, cultural, geographical) with which individuals might connect—in ways that increase awareness, content knowledge, implicit sophistication and empathic understanding of the complex ways individuals interact within systems and companies.[108]

inclusive excellence—Comprehensive effort to link diversity and quality. It is about transitioning diversity and inclusion from isolated initiatives to a catalyst for educational excellence. The four elements of inclusive excellence are:

- Focus on student intellectual and social development
- Purposeful development and utilization of organizational resources to enhance student learning
- Attention to cultural differences learners bring to the educational experience, enhancing the enterprise
- A welcoming community that engages all its diversity in the service of student and organizational learning[109]

inclusive language—Words or phrases that include all potential audiences from any identity group. Inclusive language does not assume or connote the absence of any group. An example of gender-inclusive language is using "police officers" instead of "policemen." [109]

inclusive leadership—The ability of managers (regardless of their human dimension of diversity) to get all the individual and organizational mixes of an organization working better together for higher business and social outcomes. [109]

identity group—A group, culture, or community with which an individual identifies or shares a sense of belonging. Individual agency is crucial for identity development; no person should be pressured to identify with any existing group but should instead have the freedom to self-identify on their terms.[109]

indigenous—Originating from a culture with ancient ties to the land in which a group resides.[110]

indigeneity—Indigenous populations are composed of the existing descendants of the peoples who inhabited the present territory of a country wholly or partially at the time when persons of a different culture or ethnic origin arrived there from other parts of the world, overcame them by conquest, settlement, or other means, and reduced them to a nondominant or colonial condition. They are people who today live more in conformity with their particular social, economic, and cultural customs and traditions than with the companies of the country of which they now form part, under a state structure which incorporates mainly national, social, and cultural characteristics of other segments of the population which are predominant.[110]

individual racism—Learned behavior taught through socialization, manifested in attitudes, beliefs, and behaviors. The beliefs, attitudes, and actions of individuals that support or perpetuate racism; can occur at both a conscious and unconscious level and can be active or passive. Examples include telling a racist joke, using a racial epithet, or believing in whites' inherent superiority. [110]

institutional racism—Conscious or unconscious exercise of notions of racial superiority by social companies through policies, practices, procedures, organizational culture, and organizational values. Refers specifically to how institutional policies and practices create different outcomes for different racial groups. The institutional policies may never mention any racial group. Still, their effect is to create advantages for whites and oppression and disadvantage for people from groups classified as people of color. An example includes city sanitation department policies that concentrate trash transfer stations and other environmental hazards disproportionately in communities of color.[110]

intent vs. impact—This distinction is an integral part of inclusive environments; the intent is what a person is meant to do, and impact is its effect on someone else. Regardless of intent, it is imperative to recognize how behaviors, language, actions, etc., affect or influence other people. An examination of what was said or done and how it was received is the focus, not necessarily intended.[110]

internalized racism—Occurs in a racist system when a racial group oppressed by racism supports the supremacy and dominance of the dominating group by maintaining or participating in the set of attitudes, behaviors, social structures, and ideologies that undergird the dominating group's power. [110]

intergender—A person whose gender identity is between genders or a combination of genders.[111]

intersectionality—A feminist sociological theory, intersectionality is the interconnected nature of social categorizations such as race, class, and gender as they apply to a given individual or group, regarded as creating overlapping and interdependent systems of discrimination or disadvantage.[112]

intersex—Various conditions that lead to atypical development of physical sex characteristics are collectively referred to as intersex conditions. These conditions can involve abnormalities of the external genitals, internal reproductive organs, sex chromosomes, or sex-related hormones.[113]

invisible minority—A group whose minority status is not always immediately visible, such as some disabled people and LGBT+ people. This lack of visibility may make organizing for rights difficult.[114]

isms—A way of describing any attitude, action, or institutional structure that subordinates (oppresses) a person or group because of their target group, color (racism), gender (sexism), economic status (classism), older age (ageism), religion (e.g., anti-Semitism), sexual orientation (heterosexism), language/immigrant status (xenophobia), etc.[115]

Kinsey scale—Moving away from the dichotomy of heterosexual or homosexual, Dr. Alfred Kinsey and his colleagues developed the Heterosexual-Homosexual Rating Scale, a seven-point scale ranging from 0 to 6. The scale runs from exclusively heterosexual (0) to equally heterosexual and homosexual (3) to exclusively homosexual (6).[116]

Latino/a—Individual living in the United States originating from or having a heritage relating to Latin America. [71]

LGBTQ (QIA)—Acronym for "Lesbian Gay Bisexual Transgender Queer (Questioning Intersex Allies)." The movement's description expanded from gay and lesbian to LGBTQ, and some include questioning, intersex, allies, same-gender-loving, asexual, pansexual, and polyamorous.[119]

LGBT, LGBTQ, LGBTQA, LGBTQAI, LGBTQQAI, TBLG—These acronyms refer to lesbian, gay, bisexual, transgender, queer, ally, intersex, and questioning.[119]

lesbian—A woman whose sexual orientation is toward other women.[117]

lesbian baiting—The heterosexist notion that any woman who prefers the company of a woman or who does not have a male partner is a lesbian.[118]

lipstick lesbian—Usually refers to a lesbian with a feminine gender expression.[120]

male lesbian—A male-bodied person who identifies as a lesbian. This differs from a heterosexual male in that a male lesbian is primarily attracted to other lesbians, bisexual, or queer-identified people. May sometimes identify as gender diverse or as a female/woman.[121]

marginalization—The placement of minority groups and cultures outside mainstream society. All that varies from the norm of the dominant culture is devalued and, at times, perceived as deviant and regressive.[110]

marriage—A legal status that is given to a couple by a state government. Regardless of where the marriage is issued and subject to a few exceptions, it should be recognized by every state and nation around the world. Marriage is desirable because it has several individual rights, protections, and obligations at both the state and federal levels for both spouses. Marriage for same-sex couples became legal in 2015, meaning that it is now an option for most couples.[122]

metrosexual—First used in 1994 by British journalist Mark Simpson, who coined the term to refer to an urban, heterosexual male with a strong aesthetic sense who spends a great deal of time and money on his appearance and lifestyle.[123]

microaggression—Brief and commonplace verbal, behavioral, and environmental indignities, whether intentional or unintentional, communicate hostile, derogatory, or negative racial, gender, sexual orientation, or religious slights and insults to the target person or group.[124]

migrant worker—A worker who moves from place to place to do seasonal work.[125]

minority group—A subordinate group whose members have significantly less control or power over their lives than members of a dominant or majority group. A group that experiences a narrowing of opportunities (success, education, wealth, etc.) is disproportionately low compared to their numbers in society.[126]

MSM—Men who engage in same-sex behavior but who may not

necessarily self-identify as gay or bisexual.[127]

MTF/M2F—Abbreviation for male-to-female transgender or transsexual person.[128]

multicultural—Of or about more than one culture. [110]

multiculturalism—Multiculturalism is an acknowledgment that, as people, we are culturally diverse and multifaceted, and a process through which the sharing and transforming of cultural experiences allow us to rearticulate and redefine new spaces, possibilities, and positions for ourselves and others. There are many different—and sometimes conflicting—ideas around the highly contested term of "multiculturalism." While more mainstream discourses around diversity and multiculturalism have become abundant, such definitions—particularly when historical and asocial in their grounding—tend to miss parts of the picture and may thus unproductively disguise, and even reproduce (perhaps unintentionally), forms of injustice and oppression still prevalent in our society. Acknowledging and respecting the various cultures, religions, races, ethnicities, attitudes, and opinions within an environment. The theory and practice promote the peaceful coexistence of all identities and people. [110]

multicultural education—A long-term life commitment and dynamic process; it is for all people, it is inclusive, and it is the beginning of self-respect and respect for other cultures. It is building awareness, respect, interest, and appreciation of the cultures of various racial, ethnic, and social groups and a willingness to create policies, programming, and practices that encourage the expression, exchange of information, and inclusion of different cultural perspectives. [110]

myth—An ill-founded belief, usually based on limited experience, which is given uncritical acceptance by members of a group, especially in support of existing or traditional practices and companies.[129]

native—A person born in a specified place or associated with a place by birth, whether subsequently resident there or not.[130]

nativism—An irrational prejudice against immigrants and in favor of the native-born members of a culture. It is often associated with racism in that the targets of nativism typically belong to a different ethnic group than the perpetrators.[131]

naturalization—Naturalization is the process by which U.S. citizenship is granted to a foreign citizen or national after he or she fulfills the requirements established by Congress in the Immigration and Nationality Act.[132]

neo-colonization—Term for current policies adopted by international and Western "First World" nations and organizations that exert regulation, power, and control over "Third World" nations disguised as humanitarian help or aid. These policies are distinct but related to the "original" period of colonization of Africa, Asia, and the Americas by European nations. [132]

nonwhite—A protected group or protected classes that have been historically underrepresented in organizations or who have been oppressed or ignored in society, whether legislation exists to protect these groups. For equal-employment opportunity official reporting purposes, and for purposes of the workforce analysis required in Revised Executive Order No. 4, the term "nonwhite" includes blacks, Hispanics, Alaska Natives or American Indians, and Asian or Pacific Islanders. [132]

nonwhite recruitment—Special recruitment efforts undertaken to assure that qualified protected class members are well represented in the applicant pools for positions from or in which they have been excluded or substantially underutilized. Such efforts may include contacting organizations and media with known protected-class constituencies. Open job posting and advertising and equal-opportunity employer statements necessary in many situations are nondiscrimination matters rather than affirmative action recruitment.[132]

norm—An ideal standard binding upon the members of a group and serving to guide, control, or regulate power and acceptable behavior.[132]

organizational climate—A measure (real or perceived) of the organization's work environment related to professional interpersonal interactions. Climate refers to individual and group experiences in an organization and the quality and extent of the interaction between those various groups and individuals. Diversity and inclusion efforts are not complete unless they also address climate. In a healthy environment, individuals and groups generally feel welcomed, respected, and valued by the organization. A healthy environment is grounded in respect for others, nurtured by dialogue between those of differing perspectives, and is evidenced by a pattern of civil interactions among community members. Not all aspects of a healthy climate necessarily feel positive—indeed, uncomfortable, or challenging situations can lead to increased awareness, understanding, and appreciation. Tension, while not always positive, can be healthy when handled appropriately. [132] Conversely, individuals or groups often feel isolated, marginalized, and even unsafe. [132]

organizational culture—A set of values within an organization that becomes practices. The rules of "how things get done here" can be both spoken and unspoken. An organization's values are often based on the company founders' values.[132]

organizational preference or tradition—Refers to the thinking or practices that are sometimes confused with requirements. An example of a corporate preference is a company almost always hires employees with degrees from certain schools or universities, even though other schools offer comparable degrees.[132]

oppression (institutionalized)—Systematic mistreatment of people within a social identity group supported and enforced by the society and its institution, solely based on its membership in the social identity group.[133]

oppression (internalized)—The way members of an oppressed group come to internalize the oppressive attitudes of others toward themselves and those like them.[134]

others—Typically used to identify separation between and among groups. It has been used in social sciences to understand how societies and groups exclude *others* they want to subordinate or do not fit into their society.[135]

outing—To *out* someone is to declare their sexual orientation publicly without their permission.[136]

overt racism—Racism that is frank and open, including graffiti, intimidation, or physical violence, legitimates negative racial stereotypes. Racial and ethnic slurs or so-called jokes are other examples of apparent racial discrimination. People often ignore racism because they do not know how to deal with it.[154]

Pan-Africanism—Describes the theory relating to the desire to educate all African diaspora peoples of their common plight and connections. Some theorists promote linking all African countries across the continent through a provincial government, language, ideology, or belief.[71]

pangender—A person whose gender identity is comprised of all or many gender expressions.[137]

pansexual (1)—A term most used outside academia as a sexual identity (and sexual orientation) term like *bisexuality*, but more inclusive of trans people. It also shows an awareness of the implied gender binary in the term *bisexual*.[138]

pansexual (2) An individual attracted to and may form sexual and romantic relationships with men, women, and people who identify outside of the gender binary. "Omnisexual" is another term that can be used. The idea that pansexuality is more inclusive of trans people suggests that trans men are not men and trans women are not women and exist outside of the realms of attraction for bisexual people who are attracted to men and women.[139]

people-/person-first language—A way of describing disability involves putting the word *person* or *people* before the word *disability* or the name of a disability, rather than placing the disability first and using it as an adjective. Some examples of people-first language might include saying "person with a disability," "woman with cerebral palsy," and "man with an intellectual disability." The purpose of people-first language is to promote the idea that someone's disability label is just a disability label, not the individual's defining characteristic.[140]

people of color—A term defined by race or color only, not citizenship, place of birth, religion, language, or cultural background. The term applies to black, aboriginal, Chinese, South Asian, Southeast Asian, Filipino, Latin American Canadian, and others. These terms are generally regarded as positive identities as opposed to "nonwhites," "women and people of color," "visible women and people of color," or "ethnics." Also known as "racially visible people."[71,154]

person of color—This is not a term that refers to the real biological or scientific distinction between people, but the collective experience of being targeted and oppressed by racism. While each oppressed group is affected by racism differently, and each group maintains its own unique identity and culture, there is also the recognition that racism can unite oppressed people in a collective of resistance. For this reason, many individuals who identify as members of racially oppressed groups also claim the political identity of being people of color. This in no way diminishes their specific cultural or racial identity; instead, it is an affirmation of the multiple layers of every individual's identity. This term also refrains from the subordinate connotation of triggering labels like "nonwhite" and "minority."[71, 154]

person with a disability—A person who has a physical or mental impairment that substantially limits one or more of such person's major life activities, has a record of such impairment, or is regarded as having such an impairment. Also called "physically challenged person." See "physically challenged person" for further definitions as to the meaning of disability.[59,60]

permanent resident—Any person not a citizen of the United States residing in the U.S. under legally recognized and lawfully recorded permanent residence as an immigrant. Also known as a *permanent resident alien, resident alien permit holder,* and *green cardholder.*[141]

physically challenged person—A person who has a physical or mental impairment that substantially limits one or more of such person's major life activities, has a record of such impairment, or is regarded as having such an impairment. Also known as "person with a disability."

The following are general definitions as to the meaning of disability: "physical or mental impairment" means (1) any physiological disorder or condition, cosmetic disfigurement, or anatomical loss affecting one or more of the following body systems: neurological, musculoskeletal, particular sense organs, respiratory (including speech organs), cardiovascular, reproductive, digestive, genitourinary, hemic and lymphatic, skin and endocrine; or (2) any mental or psychological disorder such as mental retardation, organic brain syndrome, emotional or mental illness and specific learning disabilities. The term "physical or mental impairment" includes, but is not limited to, such diseases and conditions as orthopedic, visual, speech, and hearing impairments, cerebral palsy, epilepsy, muscular dystrophy, multiple sclerosis, cancer, heart disease, diabetes, mental retardation, emotional illness, drug addiction, and alcoholism.

"Major life activities" means functions such as caring for oneself, performing manual tasks, walking, seeing, hearing, speaking, breathing, learning, and working.

"Has a record of such impairment" means has a history of a mental or physical impairment that substantially limits one or more life activities.

"Is regarded as having an impairment" means: (1) has a physical or mental impairment that does not substantially limit major life activities, but an agency treats that as constituting such a limitation; (2) has a physical or mental impairment that substantially limits major life activities only because of the attitudes of others toward such impairment; or (3) has none of the impairments defined above but is treated by an agency as having such an impairment.

"Substantially limits" refers to the degree to which the impairment affects employability. A disabled individual who is likely to have trouble securing, retaining, or advancing in employment will be considered substantially limited. [59,60]

pluralism—A situation in which people of different social classes, religions, races, etc., are together in a society but continue to have their different traditions and interests.[142]

polyamory—The practice of having multiple open, honest love relationships.[143]

power—Access to resources, position, status, wealth, or personal strength of character that gives a person, a group, or a system the ability to influence others. Power can be used to affect others positively or negatively.[142]

prejudice—An opinion, prejudgment, or attitude about a group or its members. Prejudice can be positive but usually refers to a negative attitude. Prejudices are often accompanied by ignorance, fear, or hatred. Prejudices are formed by a complex psychological process that begins with attachment to a close circle of acquaintances or an *in-group* such as a family. Prejudice is often aimed at *out-groups*.[144]

privilege—A special right, advantage, or immunity granted or available only to a person or group of people.

privilege (heterosexual)—Those benefits derived automatically by being heterosexual are denied to people of other sexual orientations. Also, the benefits that individuals receive because of claiming heterosexual identity or denying their own sexual identity.[145]

privilege (white)—This refers to the unquestioned and unearned set of advantages, entitlements, benefits, and choices bestowed on people solely because they are white. Generally, white people who experience such privilege do so without being conscious of it.[146]

protected classes—Groups identified in Executive Order No. 6 (nonwhites, women, disabled persons, and Vietnam-era veterans) are specially protected against employment discrimination.[71]

queer—An umbrella term that individuals may use to describe a sexual orientation, gender identity, or gender expression that does not conform to dominant societal norms.[147]

questioning—An identity label for a person who is exploring their sexual orientation or gender identity and is in a state of a moratorium in terms of identity formation.[148]

quotas—In employment law, court-ordered or court-approved hiring and promoting specified numbers or ratios of nonwhites or women in positions from which a court has found they have been excluded because of unlawful discrimination. Quotas are not the same as goals and timetables (The National Multicultural Institute).

race—A dynamic set of historically derived and traditional ideas and practices that (1) sorts people into ethnic groups according to perceived physical and behavioral human characteristics; (2) associates differential value, power, and privilege with these characteristics and establishes a social status ranking among the different groups; and (3) emerges (a) when groups are perceived to pose a threat (political, economic or cultural) to each other's world view or way of life; and (b) to justify the denigration and exploitation (past, current, or future) of, and prejudice toward, other groups.[149]

race relations—Interaction between diverse racial groups within one community. [149]

racial/ethnic groups—The four racial/ethnic groups protected by federal equal employment opportunity laws are blacks, Hispanics, Asians or Pacific Islanders, and American Indians or Alaska Natives. Racial/ethnic groups are defined by the federal government as follows:

- **white** (not of Hispanic origin): Persons having roots in Europe's original peoples, North Africa, or the Middle East
- **black** (not of Hispanic origin): Persons having roots in any of Africa's black racial groups
- **Hispanic**: Persons of Mexican, Puerto Rican, Cuban, Central or South American, or other Spanish culture or origin, regardless of race
- **Asian or Pacific Islander**: Persons having origins in any of the original peoples of the Far East, Southeast Asia, the Indian Subcontinent, or the Pacific Islands—this area includes, for example, China, Japan, Korea, the Philippine Islands, and Samoa
- **American Indian or Alaska Native**: Persons having origins in North America's original peoples and maintaining cultural identification through tribal affiliation or community recognition[149]

racial and ethnic identity—An individual's awareness and experience being a member of a racial and ethnic group; the racial and ethnic categories that an individual chooses to describe him or herself based on biological heritage, physical appearance, cultural affiliation, and early socialization, and personal experience.[150]

racial equity—The condition that would be achieved if one's racial identity no longer influenced how one fares. Racial equity is one part of racial justice and must be addressed at the root causes and not just the manifestations. This includes eliminating policies, practices, attitudes, and cultural messages that reinforce differential outcomes by race or fail to eliminate them.[150]

Racial Identity Development Theory—A theory that discusses how people in various racial groups and multiracial identities form their self-concept. It also describes some typical phases in remaking that identity based on learning and awareness of systems of privilege and structural racism, cultural and historical meanings attached to racial categories, and factors operating in the larger socio-historical level (e.g., globalization, technology, immigration, and increasing multiracial population).[151]

racial reconciliation—Reconciliation involves three ideas. First, it recognizes that America's racism is systemic and institutionalized, with far-reaching effects on political engagement and economic opportunities for women and people of color. Second, reconciliation is engendered by empowering local communities through relationship-building and truth-telling. Lastly, justice is the essential component of the social process—justice that is best termed as restorative rather than retributive while still maintaining its strong punitive character.[152]

racially visible people—A term defined by race or color only, not citizenship, place of birth, religion, language, or cultural background. The term applies to black, aboriginal, Chinese, South Asian, Southeast Asian, Filipino, and Latin American Canadians. These terms are generally regarded as positive identities as opposed to "nonwhites," "women and people of color," "visible women and people of color," or "ethnics." Also known as "people of color." [152]

racism (cultural)—Refers to representations, messages, and stories conveying that behaviors and values associated with white people or *whiteness* are automatically better or more normal than those related to other racially defined groups. [153,154]

racism (environmental)—Refers to racial discrimination in environmental policy-making and the enforcement of regulations and laws: the deliberate targeting of communities of color for toxic waste facilities, the official sanctioning of the life-threatening presence of poisons and pollutants in communities, and the history of excluding people of color from the leadership of the environmental movement. [153,154]

racism (individual)—The belief that all race members possess characteristics or abilities specific to that race, especially to distinguish it as inferior or superior to another race or races. [155]

racism (institutional)—Refers specifically to how institutional policies and practices create different outcomes for different racial groups. [156]

racism (internalized)—Internalized racism is the person consciously or subconsciously accepting the dominant society's racist views, stereotypes, and biases toward one's ethnic group. It gives rise to patterns of thinking, feeling, and behaving that result in discriminating, minimizing, criticizing, finding fault, invalidating, and hating oneself while simultaneously valuing the dominant culture.[157]

racism (structural)—The macrolevel systems, social forces, companies, ideology, and processes that interact with one another generate and reinforce inequities among racial and ethnic groups.[158]

radicalism—The belief or actions of people who advocate thorough or complete political or social reform.[159]

reasonable accommodation—Any modification or adjustment to a job or the work environment that will enable a qualified applicant or employee with a disability to participate in the application process or perform essential job functions. Reasonable accommodation also includes adjustments to assure that a qualified individual with a disability has rights and privileges in employment equal to employees without disabilities.[160]

refugee—Generally, any person outside his or her country of nationality who is unable or unwilling to return to that country because of persecution or a well-founded fear of persecution based on the person's race, religion, nationality, membership in a social group, or political opinion.[161]

resident alien—See *alien (resident)*.

reparations—States have a legal duty to acknowledge and address widespread or systematic human rights violations when the state caused the violations or did not seriously try to prevent them. Reparations initiatives seek to address the harms caused by these violations.[162]

representation—The results of intentional efforts to achieve a balanced workforce. It refers to an area of emphasis in diversity management where the goal is to ensure that people are hired based on their qualifications, thereby making the various business units, departments, teams, and functions equitable regarding the various dimensions of diversity and/or making those dimensions mirror the labor market or customer base.[71]

reverse discrimination—Unfair treatment of members of a dominant or majority group (Society of Human Resources Management); according to the National Multicultural Institute, this term is often used by opponents of affirmative action who believe that these policies are causing members of traditionally dominant groups to be discriminated against. The Supreme Court considers it illegal to consider race and other demographic categories in hiring and other employment-related decisions.[71]

right—A resource or position that everyone has equal access or availability to regardless of their social group memberships.[163]

safe space—A place where anyone can relax and be fully self-expressed, without fear of being made to feel uncomfortable, unwelcome, or unsafe because of biological sex, race/ethnicity, sexual orientation, gender identity or expression, cultural background, age, or physical or mental ability; a place where the rules guard each person's self-respect and dignity and strongly encourage everyone to respect others.[164]

same-gender-loving—A term sometimes used by members of the African American/Black community to express an alternative sexual orientation without relying on terms and symbols of European descent.[165]

selective perception—A subconscious process of noticing a specific behavior by one group while not noticing or dismissing the same behavior on the part of another group (The National Multicultural Institute).[165]

sex—System of classification based on biological and physical differences, such as primary and secondary sexual characteristics. Differentiated from *gender*, which is based on the social construction and expectations of the category's "men" and "women."[167,168,169]

sex assignment—The initial categorization of an infant as male or female.[167]

sexism—A system of beliefs or attitudes which relegates women to limited roles and/or options because of their sex.[166]

sexual harassment—Interference, intimidation, or other offensive behavior from one work associate to another and based in part on the gender of the workers involved. The intent is to exert power over another.[166]

sexual identity—How a person identifies physically: female, male, in between, beyond, or neither.[168]

sexual orientation—Refers to an individual's enduring physical, romantic, and/or emotional attraction to another person.[169]

sexual reassignment surgery—A term used by some medical professionals to refer to a group of surgical options that alter a person's sex. Also known as *gender-confirming surgery*.[168]

sizeism—The mistreatment of or discrimination against people based upon their perceived (or self-perceived) body size or shape.[170]

social class—The hierarchical order of a society based on social rank indicators such as income, occupation, education, ownership of property, family, religion, and political relationships.[171]

social power—Access to resources that enhance chances of getting what one needs or influencing others to lead a safe, productive, and fulfilling life.[171]

socialism—A political and economic theory of social organization that advocates that the means of production distribution and exchange should be owned or regulated by the community.[171]

social justice—Social justice includes a vision of a society where the distribution of resources is equitable, and all members are physically and psychologically safe and secure. Social justice involves social actors who have a sense of agency and social responsibility toward and with others and society.[172]

stealth (1)—This term refers to when a person *chooses to be secretive* in the public sphere about their gender history, either after transitioning or while successfully passing. Also referred to as *going stealth* or *living in stealth mode*.[173]

stealth (2)—The phrase "chooses to be secretive" can be read as derogative here. The GLAAD page on gender language explains that "while some transgender people may use these terms among themselves, it is not appropriate to repeat them in mainstream media unless it's in a direct quote. The terms refer to a transgender person's ability to go through daily life without others, assuming they are transgender. However, the terms themselves are problematic because "passing" implies "passing as something you're not," while "stealth" connotes deceit. When transgender people live as their authentic selves and are not perceived as transgender by others, that does not make them deceptive or misleading.[174]

stereotype—A false belief, image, or distorted truth about a person or group—a generalization that allows for little or no individual differences or social variation. Stereotypes are based on images in mass media or reputations passed on by parents, peers, and other society members. Stereotypes can be positive or negative.[175]

stereotyping—An extension of prejudice by labeling others based solely on their membership in a group and then labeling others like them in one general characteristic, as if they have the same characteristic; also, false generalizations of a group of people that result in an unconscious or conscious categorization of members of that group. Stereotypes may be based upon misconceptions about ethnic, linguistic, geographical, religious, physical, or mental attributes, race, age, marital status, and gender. Stereotyping tends to lump together members of a group and think of them as types rather than individuals. All group members are falsely assumed to be alike, with exceptions being ignored or their existence denied. It is to generalize when we have an unpleasant experience with an individual belonging to a group. The resulting feelings of aversion and hostility, which may or may not be justified, are sometimes irrationally generalized to include all members of that group.[175]

structural racism/racialization—Refers to the system of social structures that produce cumulative, durable, race-based inequality. It is also a method of analysis used to examine how historical legacies, individuals, structures, and companies work interactively to distribute material and symbolic advantages and disadvantages along racial lines.[154,176]

systemic discrimination—A general condition, practice, or approach that applies equally to the majority but negatively affects opportunities or results for specific groups of people.[154]

tolerance—Acceptance and open-mindedness to different practices, attitudes, and cultures; does not necessarily mean agreement with the differences.[154,176]

transgender—An umbrella term for persons whose gender identity, gender expression, or behavior does not conform to that typically associated with the sex they were assigned at birth. *Trans* is sometimes used as shorthand for *transgender*. Not everyone whose appearance or behavior is gender-nonconforming will identify as a transgender person.[177]

transition—A complicated, multistep process that can take years as transgender people align their anatomy with their sexual identity and/or gender expression with their gender identity.[178]

transman/trans guy—An identity label sometimes adopted by female-to-male transsexuals to signify that they are men while still affirming their history as females.[179]

transphobia—Fear or hatred of transgender people.[180]

transphobia (internalized)—When a person who is transgender is uncomfortable or not accepting of his/her own gender identity.[181]

transsexual—A term that refers to people whose gender identity is different from their assigned sex. Often, transsexual people alter or wish to alter their bodies through hormones, surgery, and other means to make their bodies as harmonious as possible with their gender identities.[182]

transvestite (1)—Individuals who regularly or occasionally wear the clothing socially assigned to a gender not their own but are usually comfortable with their anatomy and do not wish to change it (i.e., they are not transsexuals). *Cross-dresser* is the preferred term for men who enjoy or prefer women's clothing and social roles.[183]

transvestite (2)—This term has different connotations for different generations that might want to be explained, as Bowling Green State University does in their glossary. They define the term as "[a]n older term, synonymous with the more politically correct term cross-dresser, which refers to individuals who have an internal drive to wear clothing associated with a gender other than the one they were assigned at birth. Transvestite has fallen out of favor due to its psychiatric, clinical, and fetishistic connotations."[184]

unconscious bias—See *implicit bias.*

underrepresented—Refers to groups denied access that has suffered past institutional discrimination in the United States, including African Americans, Asian Americans, Hispanics or Chicanos/Latinos, and Native Americans. This is revealed by an imbalance in the representation of different groups in common pursuits such as education, jobs, housing, and so on, resulting in marginalization for some groups and individuals and not for others relative to the number of population members involved. Other groups in the United States have been marginalized and are currently underrepresented. These groups may include but are not limited to other ethnicities; adult learners; veterans; people with disabilities; lesbian, gay, bisexual, and transgender individuals; people from different religious groups; and people from different economic backgrounds.[185]

underserved populations—Groups disadvantaged because of structural or societal obstacles and disparities.[185]

underutilization—The condition of having fewer protected group members in a job classification than would be reasonably expected by their availability in the labor force.[185]

United States Commission on Civil Rights—An independent, bipartisan agency established by Congress in 1957 and directed to: (1) investigate complaints alleging that citizens are being deprived of their right to vote by reason of their race, color, religion, sex, age, handicap or national origin, or by reason of fraudulent practices; (2) study and collect information concerning legal developments constituting discrimination or a denial of equal protection of the laws under the Constitution because of race, color, religion, sex, age, handicap or national origin, or in the administration of justice; (3) appraise federal laws and policies with respect to discrimination or denial of equal protection of the laws because of race, color, religion, sex, age, handicap or national origin, or in the administration of justice; (4) serve as a national clearinghouse for information in respect to discrimination or denial of equal protection of the laws because of race, color, religion, sex, age, handicap or national origin; and (5) submit reports, findings, and recommendations to the president and Congress. [185]

unisex—Clothing, behaviors, thoughts, feelings, relationships, etc., which are considered appropriate for members of any gender/sex.[186]

universal design—The process of creating products that are usable by people with the widest possible range of abilities, operating within the widest possible range of situations; whereas *accessibility* primarily refers to design for people with disabilities.[187]

values—General guiding principles that govern all activities, how people should behave, and the principles that should guide behavior.[42]

valuing diversity—The recognition that it is not only ethical and fair to make one's organization accessible to all people but that their differences in identity, perspective, background, and style are, in fact, valuable qualities and human resources that can significantly enrich and strengthen the organization and its capacity to achieve excellence.[42]

visually impaired—A phrase used to describe people who can only see little. They understand better with technical aids such as magnifiers, telescopes, special glasses, and computers with unique features such as large print.[59,60]

white fragility—Discomfort and defensiveness of a white person when confronted by information on racial inequality and injustice.[188]

white privilege—refers to the unquestioned and unearned set of advantages, entitlements, benefits, and choices bestowed on people solely because they are white. White people who experience such privilege may or may not be conscious of it (The National Multicultural Institute).[188]

white supremacy—An historically-based, institutionally perpetuated system of exploitation and oppression of continents, nations, and peoples of color by white peoples and countries of the European continent for maintaining and defending a system of wealth, power, and privilege.[188]

workforce diversity—Refers to ways people in a workforce are like and different from one another. In addition to the characteristics protected by law, other similarities and differences commonly cited include background, education, language skills, personality, sexual orientation, and work role.[42]

workforce profile—An organizational snapshot illustrating the dispersion of race, national origin, gender, and disability groups within specified employment categories.[42]

xenophobia—A culturally based fear of outsiders. It has often been associated with the hostile reception given to those who immigrate to societies and communities. It could result from a genuine fear of strangers, or it could be based on competition for jobs, ethnic, racial, or religious prejudice.[189]

ze—Gender-neutral pronouns that can be used instead of he/she.[190]

zir—Gender-neutral pronouns that can be used instead of his/her.[191]

APPENDIX C
NOTES

1. Fierros, E. G. (2006). One Size Does Not Fit All: A Response to Institutionalizing Inequity. Disability Studies Quarterly, 26(2). Retrieved from http://www.dsq-sds.org/article/view/683/860.

2. Henry, S. L., Abou-Zahra, S., and Brewer, J. (2014). The role of accessibility in a universal web. In Proceedings of the 11th Web for All Conference (W4A '14). ACM: New York. doi#10.1145/2596695.2596719.

3. Santa Fe College Office of Diversity. Terms associated with diversity: affirmative action. Retrieved from http://www.sfcollege.edu/diversity/?section=defining_diversity.

4. University of California-Berkeley Gender Equity Center. (2013). Definition of terms: agender. Retrieved from http://geneq.berkeley.edu/lgbt_resources_definiton_of_terms#agender.

5. University of California-Berkeley Gender Equity Center. (2013). Definition of terms: aggressive. Retrieved from http://geneq.berkeley.edu/lgbt_resources_definiton_of_terms#aggressive.

6. Rowe, W. L. (1998). Agnosticism. In E. Craig Routledge Encyclopedia of Philosophy. Routledge: New York.

7. U.S. Citizenship and Immigration Services. (2015). Glossary:

alien. Retrieved from https://www.uscis.gov/tools/glossary.

8. Internal Revenue Service. (2016). Immigration terms and definitions involving aliens: illegal alien. Retrieved from https://www.irs.gov/Individuals/International-Taxpayers/Immigration-Terms-and-Definitions-Involving-Aliens.

9. OpenSource Leadership Strategies. The dynamic system of power, privilege, and oppression (PDF). Retrieved from http://www.opensourceleadership.com/documents/DO%20Definitions.pdf.

10. ADA National Network. What is the Americans with Disabilities Act (ADA)? Retrieved from https://adata.org/learn-about-ada.

11. Movimiento Estudiantil Chican@ de Aztlán. (2003). Glossary of terms relating to sexuality and gender (PDF). Retrieved from http://www.nationalmecha.org/documents/GS_Terms.pdf.

12. Anti-Defamation League. (2013). A brief history of anti-Semitism (PDF). Retrieved from http://www.adl.org/assets/pdf/education-outreach/Brief-History-on-Anti-Semitism-A.pdf.

13. American Psychological Association - Divisions 16 and 44. (2015). Key terms and concepts in understanding gender diversity and sexual orientation among students [Pamphlet]. Retrieved from http://www.apa.org/pi/lgbt/programs/safe-supportive/lgbt/key-terms.pdf.

14. Santa Fe College Office of Diversity. Terms associated with diversity: assimilation. Retrieved from http://www.sfcollege.edu/diversity/?section=defining_diversity.

15. American Atheists. What is atheism? (n.d.). Retrieved from

https://atheists.org/activism/resources/what-is-atheism.

16. Bias [Def. simple]. (n.d.). In Merriam Webster Online, Retrieved February 19, 2016, from http://www.merriam-webster.com/dictionary/bias.

17. Santa Fe College Office of Diversity. Terms associated with diversity: bicultural. Retrieved from http://www.sfcollege.edu/diversity/?section=defining_diversity.

18. Green, E. R., & Peterson, E. N. [LGBT Resource Center at UC Riverside]. (2006). LGBTQI terminology (PDF). Retrieved from http://www.lgbt.ucla.edu/documents/LGBTTerminology.pdf.

19. Green, E. R., & Peterson, E. N. [LGBT Resource Center at UC Riverside]. (2006). LGBTQI terminology (PDF). Retrieved from http://www.lgbt.ucla.edu/documents/LGBTTerminology.pdf.

20. Trans Student Educational Resource. Retrieved from http://www.transstudent.org/definitions/

21. Racial Equity Resource Guide. (n.d.). Glossary. Retrieved from http://www.racialequityresourceguide.org/about/glossary.

22. American Psychological Association. (2012). Guidelines for psychological practice with lesbian, gay, and bisexual clients. American Psychologist, 67(1), 10-42. doi: 10.1037/a0024659.

23. Movimiento Estudiantil Chican@ de Aztlán. (2003). Glossary of terms relating to sexuality and gender (PDF). Retrieved from http://www.nationalmecha.org/documents/GS_Terms.pdf.

24. Ball State University. (n.d.). Safe zone training (PDF). Retrieved from https://cms.bsu.edu/media/WWW/Departmental Content/CounselingCenter/PDFs/SafeZone-

Participant%20Manual%20-%20Full%20Version%20-May%202012.pdf.

25. American Psychological Association. (2008). Answers to your questions: For a better understanding of sexual orientation and homosexuality. Washington, DC: Retrieved from www.apa.org/topics/sorientation.pdf.

26. Movimiento Estudiantil Chican@ de Aztlán. (2003). Glossary of terms relating to sexuality and gender (PDF). Retrieved from http://www.nationalmecha.org/documents/GS_Terms.pdf.

27. The attached resource provides many definitions for bisexuality from different sources. https://robynochs.com/2015/10/11/the-definition-of-bisexuality-according-to-bi/

28. ABILITY magazines. (n.d.). Guidelines to terminology. Retrieved from http://www.abilitymagazine.com/terminology.html.

29. Butch (n.d.). In LGBTQ Lexicon Online, Retrieved March 23, 2016, from http://lgbtqlexicon.net/butch/.

30. Southern Illinois University-Edwardsville: Safe Zone. (n.d.). LGBT terminology. Retrieved from https://www.siue.edu/lgbt/definitions.shtml.

31. American Psychological Association - Divisions 16 and 44. (2015). Key terms and concepts in understanding gender diversity and sexual orientation among students [Pamphlet]. Retrieved from http://www.apa.org/pi/lgbt/programs/safe-supportive/lgbt/key-terms.pdf.

32. Grollman, E. A. (2012). What is transphobia? And what is cissexism? Retrieved from http://kinseyconfidential.org/transphobia/.

33. National Park Service. (n.d.). Civil Rights Act of 1964. Retrieved from http://www.nps.gov/subjects/civilrights/1964-civil- rights-act.htm.

34. Southern Illinois University-Edwardsville: Safe Zone. (n.d.). LGBT terminology. Retrieved from https://www.siue.edu/lgbt/definitions.shtml.

35. Santa Fe College Office of Diversity. Terms associated with diversity: classism. Retrieved from http://www.sfcollege.edu/diversity/?section=defining_diversity.

36. University of Alaska-Southeast. (n.d.). LGBTIQ terminology and definitions (PDF). Retrieved from http://www.uas.alaska.edu/juneau/activities/safezone/docs/lgbtiq_terminology.pdf.

37. Adams, M., Bell, L. A., & Griffin, P. (1997). Teaching for diversity and social justice: A sourcebook. New York, NY: Routledge.

38. LaRocque, E. (n.d.). Colonization and racism. Retrieved from http://www3.nfb.ca/enclasse/doclens/visau/index.php?mode=theme&language=english&theme=30662&film=16933&excerpt=612109&submode=about&expmode=2.

39. American Psychological Association. (2008). Sexual orientation & homosexuality: Answers to your questions for a better understanding. Retrieved from http://www.apa.org/topics/lgbt/orientation.aspx.

40. Qmunity. Retrieved from http://qmunity.ca/wp-content/uploads/2015/03/Queer_Terminology_Web_Version Sept_2013 Cover_and_pages_.pdf

41. Dobbs, D. (2000). Communism. The Journal of Politics, 62(2), 491-510.

42. Delgado, R. & Stefancic, J. (2001). Critical Race Theory: An introduction. New York: New York University Press.

43. American Psychological Association. (2011). Answers to your questions about transgender people, gender identity, and gender expression. Retrieved from http://www.apa.org/topics/lgbt/transgender.aspx.

44. University of Minnesota Center for Advanced Research on Language Acquisition. (n.d.). What is culture? Retrieved from http://carla.umn.edu/culture/definitions.html.

45. Colours of Resistance. (n.d.). Cultural appropriation. Retrieved from http://www.coloursofresistance.org/definitions/cultural-appropriation/.

46. National Center for Cultural Competence, Georgetown University, Center for Child and Human Development. (n.d.). Curricula enhancement module series: Definitions of cultural competence. Retrieved from http://nccccurricula.info/culturalcompetence.html.

47. Cross, T., Bazron, B., Dennis, K., & Isaacs, M. (1989). Towards a culturally competent system of care, Volume 1. Washington, D.C.: Georgetown University Child Development Center, CASSP Technical Assistance Center.

48. Santa Fe College Office of Diversity. Terms associated with diversity: cultural conditioning. Retrieved from http://www.sfcollege.edu/diversity/?section=defining_diversity.

49. Matthes, E. H. (2016). Cultural Appropriation Without Cultural

Essentialism? Social Theory & Practice, 42(2), 343-366.

50. Levi, A. (2009). The ethics of nursing student international clinical experiences. Journal of Obstetric, Gynecologic, and Neonatal Nursing, 38(1), 94-99.

51. Tervalon, M. & Murray-Garcia, J. (1998). Cultural humility versus cultural competence: a critical distinction in defining physician training outcomes in multicultural education. Journal of Health Care for the Poor and Underserved, 9(2), 117-125.

52. Institute for Democratic Renewal and Project Change Anti-Racism Initiative. (n.d.). 15 tools for creating healthy, productive interracial/multiracial communities: A community builder's tool kit (PDF). Retrieved from http://www.racialequitytools.org/resourcefiles/idr.pdf.

53. Institute for Democratic Renewal and Project Change Anti-Racism Initiative. (n.d.). 15 tools for creating healthy, productive interracial/multiracial communities: A community builder's tool kit (PDF). Retrieved from http://www.racialequitytools.org/resourcefiles/idr.pdf.

54. Santa Fe College Office of Diversity. Terms associated with diversity: deaf culture. Retrieved from http://www.sfcollege.edu/diversity/?section=defining_diversity.

55. Yule, M.A., Brotto L.A., Gorzalka B.B. (2017). Human Asexuality: What Do We Know About a Lack of Sexual Attraction? Current Sexual Health Reports. Volume 9, Issue 1, pp 50–56

56. Institute for Democratic Renewal and Project Change Anti-Racism Initiative. (n.d.). 15 tools for creating healthy, productive

interracial/multiracial communities: A community builder's tool kit (PDF). Retrieved from http://www.racialequitytools.org/resourcefiles/idr.pdf.

57. Diaspora: Definitional Differences. (2002, March 03). Retrieved April 11, 2016, from http://www.postcolonialweb.org/diasporas/ashcroft.html

58. Ashcroft, B., Garet, G., and Tiffin, H. (1998). Key concepts in post-colonial studies. London and New York: Routledge.

59. ABILITY magazines. (n.d.). Guidelines to terminology. Retrieved from http://www.abilitymagazine.com/terminology.html.

60. ADA National Network. (n.d.). What is the definition of disability under the ADA? Retrieved from https://adata.org/faq/what- definition-disability-under-ada.

61. Southern Poverty Law Center. (n.d.). Test yourself for hidden bias. Retrieved from http://www.tolerance.org/activity/test-yourself-hidden-bias.

62. Discrimination (n.d.). In the Free Dictionary Online, Retrieved March 24, 2016, from http://legal-dictionary.thefreedictionary.com/discrimination.

63. University of California-Berkeley Center for Equity, Inclusion, and Diversity. (n.d.). Glossary of terms. Retrieved from http://diversity.berkeley.edu/glossary-terms.

64. Akhbari, K. (2015). The ultimate guide to gay marriage laws. Retrieved from http://www.legalmatch.com/law-library/article/ultimate-guide-to-gay-marriage-laws.html.

65. American Psychological Association. (2011). Answers to your

questions about transgender people, gender identity, and gender expression. Retrieved from http://www.apa.org/topics/lgbt/transgender.aspx.

66. Cole, C.M., O'Boyle, M., Emory, L.E., et al. (1997). Comorbidity of Gender Dysphoria and Other Major Psychiatric Diagnoses. Archives of Sex Behavior Vol. 26 Issue. 1 13-26.

67. Emigration (n.d.). In Oxford Dictionaries Online, Retrieved February 19, 2016, from http://www.oxforddictionaries.com/us/definition/american_english/emigration.

68. Adams, M., Bell, L. A., and Griffin, P. (1997). Teaching for diversity and social justice: A sourcebook. New York, NY: Routledge.

69. Applied Research Center. (2009). Catalytic Change: Lessons learned from the racial justice grantmaking assessment (PDF). Retrieved from http://racialequity.org/docs/Racial_justice_assessment_loresFINAL.pdf.

70. Association of American Colleges and Universities. (n.d.). Making excellence inclusive. Retrieved from http://www.aacu.org/making-excellence-inclusive.

71. Markus, H.R. (2008). Pride, prejudice, and ambivalence: Toward a unified theory of race and ethnicity. American Psychologist, 63(8), pp. 651-70.

72. Santa Fe College Office of Diversity. Terms associated with diversity: ethnocentrism. Retrieved from http://www.sfcollege.edu/diversity/?section=defining_diversity.

73. University of California-Berkeley Gender Equity Center. (2013). Definition of terms: FTM/F2M. Retrieved from http://geneq.berkeley.edu/lgbt_resources_definiton_of_terms#ftm.

74. Walker J.J, Golub S.A, Bimbi D. S & Parsons J.T. (2012) Butch Bottom–Femme Top? An Exploration of Lesbian Stereotypes. Journal of Lesbian Studies. 90-107.

75. Southern Illinois University-Edwardsville: Safe Zone. (n.d.). LGBT terminology. Retrieved from https://www.siue.edu/lgbt/definitions.shtml.

76. American Psychological Association. (2011). Answers to your questions about transgender people, gender identity, and gender expression. Retrieved from http://www.apa.org/topics/lgbt/transgender.aspx.

77. University of California-Berkeley Gender Equity Center. (2013). Definition of terms: genderism. Retrieved from http://geneq.berkeley.edu/lgbt_resources_definiton_of_terms#genderism.

78. American Psychological Association. (2011). Answers to your questions about transgender people, gender identity, and gender expression. Retrieved from http://www.apa.org/topics/lgbt/transgender.aspx.

79. Movimiento Estudiantil Chican@ de Aztlán. (2003). Glossary of terms relating to sexuality and gender (PDF). Retrieved from http://www.nationalmecha.org/documents/GS_Terms.pdf.

80. Green, E. R., & Peterson, E. N. [LGBT Resource Center at UC Riverside]. (2003-2004). LGBTQI terminology (PDF). Retrieved

from http://www.lgbt.ucla.edu/documents/LGBTTerminology.pdf.

81. Green, E. R., & Peterson, E. N. [LGBT Resource Center at UC Riverside]. (2006). LGBTQI terminology (PDF). Retrieved from http://www.lgbt.ucla.edu/documents/LGBTTerminology.pdf.

82. American Psychological Association - Divisions 16 and 44. (2015). Key terms and concepts in understanding gender diversity and sexual orientation among students [Pamphlet]. Retrieved from http://www.apa.org/pi/lgbt/programs/safe-supportive/lgbt/key-terms.pdf.

83. American Psychological Association - Divisions 16 and 44. (2015). Key terms and concepts in understanding gender diversity and sexual orientation among students [Pamphlet]. Retrieved from http://www.apa.org/pi/lgbt/programs/safe-supportive/lgbt/key-terms.pdf.

84. American Psychological Association. (2011). Answers to your questions about transgender people, gender identity, and gender expression. Retrieved from http://www.apa.org/topics/lgbt/transgender.aspx.

85. University of California-Berkeley Gender Equity Center. (2013). Definition of terms: gender fluid. Retrieved from http://geneq.berkeley.edu/lgbt_resources_definiton_of_terms#genderfluid.

86. American Psychological Association. (2011). Answers to your questions about transgender people, gender identity, and gender expression. Retrieved from http://www.apa.org/topics/lgbt/transgender.aspx.

87. University of California-Berkeley Gender Equity Center. (2013). Definition of terms: gender-neutral. Retrieved from http://geneq.berkeley.edu/lgbt_resources_definiton_of_terms#gender_neutral.

88. American Psychological Association - Divisions 16 and 44. (2015). Key terms and concepts in understanding gender diversity and sexual orientation among students [Pamphlet]. Retrieved from http://www.apa.org/pi/lgbt/programs/safe-supportive/lgbt/key-terms.pdf.

89. Green, E. R., & Peterson, E. N. [LGBT Resource Center at UC Riverside]. (2006). LGBTQI terminology (PDF). Retrieved from http://www.lgbt.ucla.edu/documents/LGBTTerminology.pdf.

90. American Psychological Association - Divisions 16 and 44. (2015). Key terms and concepts in understanding gender diversity and sexual orientation among students [Pamphlet]. Retrieved from http://www.apa.org/pi/lgbt/programs/safe-supportive/lgbt/key-terms.pdf.

91. University of California-Berkeley Gender Equity Center. (2013). Definition of terms: gender variant. Retrieved from http://geneq.berkeley.edu/lgbt_resources_definiton_of_terms#gender_variant.

92. Purdue Online Writing Lab. (2013). Using rhetorical strategies for persuasion. Retrieved from https://owl.english.purdue.edu/owl/resource/588/04/.

93. Movimiento Estudiantil Chican@ de Aztlán. (2003). Glossary of terms relating to sexuality and gender (PDF). Retrieved from http://www.nationalmecha.org/documents/GS_Terms.pdf.

94. Federal Bureau of Investigation. (n.d.). Hate crimes: Overview. Retrieved from https://www.fbi.gov/about- us/investigate/civil rights/hate_crimes/overview.

95. VA Code § 52-8.5 (2015).

96. Green, E. R., & Peterson, E. N. [LGBT Resource Center at UC Riverside]. (2006). LGBTQI terminology (PDF). Retrieved from http://www.lgbt.ucla.edu/documents/LGBTTerminology.pdf.

97. Southern Illinois University-Edwardsville: Safe Zone. (n.d.). LGBT terminology. Retrieved from https://www.siue.edu/lgbt/definitions.shtml.

98. Ball State University. (n.d.). Safe zone training (PDF). Retrieved from https://cms.bsu.edu/media/WWW/Departmental Content/CounselingCenter/PDFs/SafeZone-Participant%20Manual%20-%20Full%20Version%20-May%202012.pdf.

99. Ball State University. (n.d.). Safe zone training (PDF). Retrieved from https://cms.bsu.edu/-/media/WWW/Departmenta lContent/CounselingCenter/PDFs/SafeZone-Participant%20Manual%20-%20Full%20Version%20-May%202012.pdf.

100. University of Alaska-Southeast. (n.d.). LGBTIQ terminology and definitions (PDF). Retrieved from http://www.uas.alaska.edu/juneau/activities/safezone/docs/lgbtiq_terminology.pdf.

101. Ball State University. (n.d.). Safe zone training (PDF). Retrieved from https://cms.bsu.edu/-/media/WWW/DepartmentalContent/CounselingCenter/PDFs/Safe

Zone-Participant%20Manual%20-%20Full%20Version%20-May%202012.pdf.

102. Ball State University. (n.d.). Safe zone training (PDF). Retrieved from https://cms.bsu.edu/media/WWW/Departmental Content/CounselingCenter/PDFs/SafeZone-Participant%20Manual%20-%20Full%20Version%20-May%202012.pdf.

103. Green, E. R., & Peterson, E. N. [LGBT Resource Center at UC Riverside]. (2006). LGBTQI terminology (PDF). Retrieved from http://www.lgbt.ucla.edu/documents/LGBTTerminology.pdf.

104. Internal Revenue Service. (2016). Immigration terms and definitions involving aliens: immigrant. Retrieved from https://www.irs.gov/Individuals/International-Taxpayers/Immigration-Terms-and-Definitions-Involving-Aliens.

105. Immigration [Def. 1]. (n.d.). In Oxford Dictionaries Online, Retrieved March 23, 2016, from http://www.oxforddictionaries.com/us/definition/american_english/immigration.

106. Staats, C. (2013). State of the science implicit bias review (PDF). Retrieved from http://kirwaninstitute.osu.edu/docs/SOTS- Implicit_Bias.pdf.

107. MP Associates and Center for Assessment and Policy Development. (2013). www.racialequitytools.org glossary (PDF). Retrieved from http://www.racialequitytools.org/images/uploads/RET_Glossar

y913L.pdf.

108. Association of American Colleges and Universities. (n.d.). Making excellence inclusive. Retrieved from http://www.aacu.org/making-excellence-inclusive.

109. Williams, D. A., Berger, J. B., & McClendon, S. A. (2005). Toward a model of inclusive excellence and change in post-secondary companies. Washington, DC: Association of American Colleges and Universities.

110. Sandberg McGuinne, J. (November 24, 2014). Official definitions of indigeneity. [Blog post]. Retrieved from https://johansandbergmcguinne.wordpress.com/official-definitions-of-indigeneity/.

111. Green, E. R., & Peterson, E. N. [LGBT Resource Center at UC Riverside]. (2006). LGBTQI terminology (PDF). Retrieved from http://www.lgbt.ucla.edu/documents/LGBTTerminology.pdf.

112. Intersectionality. (n.d.). In Oxford Dictionaries Online, Retrieved March 23, 2016, from http://www.oxforddictionaries.com/us/definition/american_english/intersectionality.

113. American Psychological Association. (2011). Answers to your questions about individuals with intersex conditions. Retrieved from http://www.apa.org/topics/lgbt/intersex.aspx.

114. University of California-Berkeley Gender Equity Center. (2013). Definition of terms: invisible minority. Retrieved from http://geneq.berkeley.edu/lgbt_resources_definiton_of_terms#invisible_minority.

115. Institute for Democratic Renewal and Project Change Anti-Racism Initiative. (n.d.). 15 tools for creating healthy, productive interracial/multiracial communities: A community builder's tool kit (PDF). Retrieved from http://www.racialequitytools.org/resourcefiles/idr.pdf.

116. Grollman, E. A. (2012). The Kinsey Scale: Its purpose and significance. Retrieved from http://kinseyconfidential.org/kinsey- scale-purpose-significance/.

117. Ball State University. (n.d.). Safe zone training (PDF). Retrieved from https://cms.bsu.edu/media/WWW/Departmental Content/CounselingCenter/PDFs/SafeZone-Participant%20Manual%20-%20Full%20Version%20-May%202012.pdf.

118. Green, E. R., & Peterson, E. N. [LGBT Resource Center at UC Riverside]. (2006). LGBTQI terminology (PDF). Retrieved from http://www.lgbt.ucla.edu/documents/LGBTTerminology.pdf.

119. Southern Illinois University-Edwardsville: Safe Zone. (n.d.). LGBT terminology. Retrieved from https://www.siue.edu/lgbt/definitions.shtml.

120. Green, E. R., & Peterson, E. N. [LGBT Resource Center at UC Riverside]. (2006). LGBTQI terminology (PDF). Retrieved from http://www.lgbt.ucla.edu/documents/LGBTTerminology.pdf.

121. Green, E. R., & Peterson, E. N. [LGBT Resource Center at UC Riverside]. (2006). LGBTQI terminology (PDF). Retrieved

from http://www.lgbt.ucla.edu/documents/LGBTTerminology.pdf.

122. Watts, A. (2015, October 20). Marriage compared to civil unions. Retrieved from http://www.legalmatch.com/law-library/article/marriage-compared-to-civil-unions.html.

123. Green, E. R., & Peterson, E. N. [LGBT Resource Center at UC Riverside]. (2006). LGBTQI terminology (PDF). Retrieved from http://www.lgbt.ucla.edu/documents/LGBTTerminology.pdf.

124. Sue, D.W. (2010). Microaggressions in everyday life: Race, gender, and sexual orientation. Hoboken, NJ: Wiley.

125. Migrant workers [Def. 1.1]. (n.d.). In Oxford Dictionaries Online, Retrieved March 23, 2016, from http://www.oxforddictionaries.com/us/definition/american_english/migrant?q=migrant+worker#migrant 5.

126. Schaefer, R. T. (1993). Racial and ethnic groups. Dayton, OH: University of Dayton.

127. University of California-Berkeley Gender Equity Center. (2013). Definition of terms: MSM. Retrieved from http://geneq.berkeley.edu/lgbt_resources_definiton_of_terms#msm.

128. University of California-Berkeley Gender Equity Center. (2013). Definition of terms: MTF/M2F. Retrieved from http://geneq.berkeley.edu/lgbt_resources_definiton_of_terms#mtf.

129. Santa Fe College Office of Diversity. Terms associated with diversity: myth. Retrieved from

http://www.sfcollege.edu/diversity/?section=defining_diversity.

130. Native [Def. 1]. (n.d.). In Oxford Dictionaries Online, Retrieved February 19, 2016, from http://www.oxforddictionaries.com/us/definition/american_english/native.

131. Nativism - Civil Liberty Glossary Definition. (n.d.). Retrieved April 06, 2016, from http://civilliberty.about.com/od/immigrantsrights/g/Nativism-Definition.htm.

132. U.S. Citizenship and Immigration Services. (2015). Glossary: naturalization. Retrieved from https://www.uscis.gov/us-citizenship/citizenship-through-naturalization.

133. Cheney, C., LaFrance, J., & Quinteros, T. (2006). Institutionalized oppression definitions (PDF). Retrieved from https://www.pcc.edu/resources/illumination/documents/institutionalized-oppression-definitions.pdf.

134. Internalized oppression. (n.d.). Retrieved April 06, 2016, from http://psychology.wikia.com/wiki/Internalized_oppression.

135. Southern Illinois University-Edwardsville: Safe Zone. (n.d.). LGBT terminology. Retrieved from https://www.siue.edu/lgbt/definitions.shtml.

136. University of Alaska-Southeast. (n.d.). LGBTIQ terminology and definitions (PDF). Retrieved from http://www.uas.alaska.edu/juneau/activities/safezone/docs/lgbtiq_terminology.pdf.

137. University of California-Berkeley Gender Equity Center. (2013). Definition of terms: pangender. Retrieved from

http://geneq.berkeley.edu/lgbt_resources_definiton_of_terms#pangender.

138. American Psychological Association - Divisions 16 and 44. (2015). Key terms and concepts in understanding gender diversity and sexual orientation among students [Pamphlet]. Retrieved from http://www.apa.org/pi/lgbt/programs/safe-supportive/lgbt/key-terms.pdf.

139. Qmunity - http://qmunity.ca/wp-content/uploads/2015/03/Queer_Terminology_Web_Version Sept_2013 Cover_and_pages_.pdf

140. An Introductory Guide to Disability Language and Empowerment. (n.d.). Retrieved April 06, 2016, from http://sudcc.syr.edu/LanguageGuide/.

141. U.S. Citizenship and Immigration Services. (2015). Glossary: lawful permanent resident. Retrieved from https://www.uscis.gov/tools/glossary.

142. Pluralism [Def. simple]. (n.d.). In Merriam Webster Online, Retrieved February 19, 2016, from http://www.merriam-webster.com/dictionary/pluralism.

143. University of California-Berkeley Gender Equity Center. (2013). Definition of terms: polyamory. Retrieved from http://geneq.berkeley.edu/lgbt_resources_definiton_of_terms#polyamory.

144. Southern Poverty Law Center. (n.d.). Test yourself for hidden bias. Retrieved from http://www.tolerance.org/activity/test-yourself-hidden-bias.

145. Green, E. R., & Peterson, E. N. [LGBT Resource Center at UC

Riverside]. (2006). LGBTQI terminology (PDF). Retrieved from http://www.lgbt.ucla.edu/documents/LGBTTerminology.pdf.

146. McIntosh, P. (1988). White privilege and male privilege: A personal account of coming to see correspondences through work in women's studies. Working paper, Wellesley College Center for Research on Women, Wellesley, MA.

147. American Psychological Association - Divisions 16 and 44. (2015). Key terms and concepts in understanding gender diversity and sexual orientation among students [Pamphlet]. Retrieved from http://www.apa.org/pi/lgbt/programs/safe-supportive/lgbt/key-terms.pdf.

148. American Psychological Association - Divisions 16 and 44. (2015). Key terms and concepts in understanding gender diversity and sexual orientation among students [Pamphlet]. Retrieved from http://www.apa.org/pi/lgbt/programs/safe-supportive/lgbt/key-terms.pdf.

149. Markus, H. R. (2008). Pride, prejudice, and ambivalence: Toward a unified theory of race and ethnicity. American Psychologist, 63(8), pp. 651-70.

150. Adams, M., Bell, L. A., & Griffin, P. (1997). Teaching for diversity and social justice: A sourcebook. New York, NY: Routledge.

151. MP Associates and Center for Assessment and Policy Development. (2013). www.racialequitytools.org glossary (PDF). Retrieved from http://www.racialequitytools.org/images/uploads/RET_Glossar

y913L.pdf.

152. Position Paper on Reconciliation. (2007). Retrieved April 06, 2016, from http://winterinstitute.org/about-us/position-paper/.

153. MP Associates and Center for Assessment and Policy Development. (2013). www.racialequitytools.org glossary (PDF). Retrieved from http://www.racialequitytools.org/images/uploads/RET_Glossary913L.pdf.

154. Home - Colours of Resistance Archive. (n.d.). Retrieved April 06, 2016, from http://www.coloursofresistance.org/definitions/environmental-racism/.

155. Racism [Def. 1.1]. (n.d.). In Oxford Dictionaries Online, Retrieved February 19, 2016, from http://www.oxforddictionaries.com/us/definition/american_english/racism.

156. Racial Equity Resource Guide. (n.d.). Glossary. Retrieved from http://www.racialequityresourceguide.org/about/glossary.

157. Lipsky, S. (1987). Internalized racism. Seattle, WA: Rational Island. Retrieved from http://www.div17.org/TAAR/media/topics/internalized-racism.php.

158. Powell, j. a. (2008). Structural racism: Building upon the insights of John Calmore. North Carolina Law Review. 2008; 86(3): pp. 791–816.

159. Journal for Study of Radicalism, 2006 (Vol. 1, no. 1) - Fall 2011 (Vol. 5, no. 2)

160. U.S. Equal Employment Opportunity Commission/U.S. Department of Justice/Civil Rights Division. (2001). Americans with Disabilities Act: Questions and answers. Retrieved from http://www.ada.gov/qandaeng.htm.

161. U.S. Citizenship and Immigration Services. (2015). Glossary: refugee. Retrieved from https://www.uscis.gov/tools/glossary.

162. International Center for Transitional Justice. Reparations. Retrieved from https://www.ictj.org/our-work/transitional-justice- issues/reparations.

163. National Conference for Community and Justice—St. Louis Region. Unpublished. Accessed via Racial Equity Resource Guide. (n.d.). Glossary. Retrieved from http://www.racialequityresourceguide.org/about/glossary.

164. Southern Illinois University-Edwardsville: Safe Zone. (n.d.). LGBT terminology. Retrieved from https://www.siue.edu/lgbt/definitions.shtml.

165. Green, E. R., & Peterson, E. N. [LGBT Resource Center at UC Riverside]. (2006). LGBTQI terminology (PDF). Retrieved from http://www.lgbt.ucla.edu/documents/LGBTTerminology.pdf.

166. Santa Fe College Office of Diversity. Terms associated with diversity: sexism. Retrieved from http://www.sfcollege.edu/diversity/?section=defining_diversity.

167. American Psychological Association - Divisions 16 and 44. (2015). Key terms and concepts in understanding gender diversity and sexual orientation among students [Pamphlet]. Retrieved from http://www.apa.org/pi/lgbt/programs/safe-

supportive/lgbt/key-terms.pdf.

168. Green, E. R., & Peterson, E. N. [LGBT Resource Center at UC Riverside]. (2006). LGBTQI terminology (PDF). Retrieved from http://www.lgbt.ucla.edu/documents/LGBTTerminology.pdf.

169 American Psychological Association. (2011). Answers to your questions about transgender people, gender identity, and gender expression. Retrieved from http://www.apa.org/topics/lgbt/transgender.aspx.

170. Sizeism (n.d.). In Oxford Dictionaries Online, Retrieved April 6, 2016, from http://www.oxforddictionaries.com/us/definition/american_english/sizeism.

171. Szalai, E., & Szalai, Erzsâebet. (2005). Socialism: An analysis of its past and future (1st ed.). Budapest; New York: Central European University Press.

172. Adams, M., Bell, L. A., & Griffin, P. (1997). Teaching for diversity and social justice: A sourcebook. New York, NY: Routledge.

173. Green, E. R., & Peterson, E. N. [LGBT Resource Center at UC Riverside]. (2003-2004). LGBTQI terminology (PDF). Retrieved from http://www.lgbt.ucla.edu/documents/LGBTTerminology.pdf.

174. "GLAAD Media Reference Guide - Transgender." GLAAD, April 19. 2017, www.glaad.org/reference/transgender.

175. Southern Poverty Law Center. (n.d.). Test yourself for hidden bias. Retrieved from http://www.tolerance.org/activity/test-

yourself-hidden-bias.

176. Shakti Butler, www.world-trust.org

177. American Psychological Association. (2011). Answers to your questions about transgender people, gender identity, and gender expression. Retrieved from http://www.apa.org/topics/lgbt/transgender.aspx.

178. University of California-Berkeley Gender Equity Center. (2013). Definition of terms: transition. Retrieved from http://geneq.berkeley.edu/lgbt_resources_definiton_of_terms#transition.

179. University of California-Berkeley Gender Equity Center. (2013). Definition of terms: transman. Retrieved from http://geneq.berkeley.edu/lgbt_resources_definiton_of_terms#transman.

180. University of California-Berkeley Gender Equity Center. (2013). Definition of terms: transphobia. Retrieved from http://geneq.berkeley.edu/lgbt_resources_definiton_of_terms#transphobia.

181. Ball State University. (n.d.). Safe zone training (PDF). Retrieved from https://cms.bsu.edu/-/media/WWW/DepartmentalContent/CounselingCenter/PDFs/SafeZone-Participant%20Manual%20-%20Full%20Version%20- May%202012.pdf.

182. American Psychological Association. (2011). Answers to your questions about transgender people, gender identity, and gender expression. Retrieved from http://www.apa.org/topics/lgbt/transgender.aspx.

183. University of California-Berkeley Gender Equity Center. (2013). Definition of terms: transvestite. Retrieved from http://geneq.berkeley.edu/lgbt_resources_definiton_of_terms#transvestite.

184. Bowling Green State University - https://www.bgsu.edu/content/dam/BGSU/multicultural-affairs/documents/queer- glossary.pdf

185. Santa Fe College Office of Diversity. Terms associated with diversity: underutilization. Retrieved from http://www.sfcollege.edu/diversity/?section=defining_diversity.

186. Southern Illinois University-Edwardsville: Safe Zone. (n.d.). LGBT terminology. Retrieved from https://www.siue.edu/lgbt/definitions.shtml.

187. Henry, S. L., Abou-Zahra, S., and Brewer, J. (2014). The role of accessibility in a universal web. In Proceedings of the 11th Web for All Conference (W4A '14). ACM: New York. doi#10.1145/2596695.2596719.

188. MP Associates and Center for Assessment and Policy Development. (2013). www.racialequitytools.org glossary (PDF). Retrieved from http://www.racialequitytools.org/images/uploads/RET_Glossary913L.pdf.

189. Crossman, A. (2016). Xenophobia. In About Education Online, Retrieved April 11, 2016, from http://sociology.about.com/od/X_Index/g/Xenophobia.htm.

190. University of California-Berkeley Gender Equity Center. (2013). Definition of terms: ze/hir/hirs. Retrieved from

http://geneq.berkeley.edu/lgbt_resources_definiton_of_terms#ze.

191. University of California-Berkeley Gender Equity Center. (2013). Definition of terms:

192. University of California-Berkeley Gender Equity Center. (2013). Definition of terms: ze/zir/hirs. Retrieved from http://geneq.berkeley.edu/lgbt_resources_definiton_of_terms#zir.

APPENDIX D
REFERENCES

Adams, C. "Affinity Groups Bring Employees Together to Reach Company Goals." *The Citizen*, February 2005.

Adams, C. "Audit Shows Improvement In Job Selection Process." *The Citizen*, February 24, 2003.

Adams, C. "First Phase of Workplace Ethics Rolls Out." *The Citizen*, October 19, 2001.

Atlanta Inquirer. "*David Ratcliffe Diversity CEO Of The Year Award.*" High Beam Research, http://www.highbeam.com/doc/1pl-79132897.html.

Atlanta Inquirer. (2001, August 4). "Georgia Power Hires Manager for New Ethics Department." *Atlanta Inquirer*, August 4, 2001.

Atlanta Journal-Constitution. "Georgia Power: Appoints Diversity Executive In The Face of Lawsuit." *Atlanta Journal-Constitution*, August 18, 2000.

Atlanta Tribune Magazine. "Being the Best." September 2008.

Babcock, P. "Diversity Accountability Requires More Than Numbers." SHRM Online, http:www.shrm.org/hrdisciplines/diversity/articles/pages/more than numbers. aspx.

Barber, J. "Training Recognizes Importance of Supervisor-Employee Relationship." *The Citizen*, July 29, 2002.

Barber, J. "Company Completed First Year With New Ethics Process." *The Citizen*, March 10, 2003.

Barber, J. "Council Makes Employees Part of the Solution." *The Citizen*, March 2005.

Barber, J. "What's In It For Me: Culture Change Initiatives Aim To Answer The Question For Every Employee." *The Citizen*, May 2007.

Bates, R. "New Course For Employees Focuses on Sexual Harassment, Discrimination." *The Citizen*, April 7, 2003.

Benson, J. "Training Aims To Change Behaviors and Build Trust." *The Citizen*, November 2007.

Benson, J. "Employees Take Charge of Their Careers: Supervisors Create Opportunities." *The Citizen*, January 2008.

Blackmon, D. A., and N. Harris. "Racial Bind: Black Utility Workers In Georgia Sees Nooses As Sign of Harassment." *Wall Street Journal*, April 2, 2001.

Browning, L. "Peer Review New Avenue For Employee Concerns."

The Citizen, September 7, 2001.

Bucher, R. and P. Bucher, P. Diversity Consciousness: Opening Our Minds to People, Cultures, and Opportunities. New York: Prentice-Hall, 2003.

Buono, A. F., and K. Kerber. "Rethinking Organizational Change: Reframing The Challenge Of Change Management." *Organizational Development Journal, 23* (3), (2005): 23-38.

Cagle, T. (2005, August 15). "Southern Company: Then and Now." *Southern Company Highlights*, August 15, 2005.

Carrell, M. R., T. Honeycutt, and E.E. Mann. "Defining Workforce Diversity Programs and Practices in Organizations: A Longitudinal Study." *Labor Law Journal, 57* (1), (2006):5-49.

Citizen Now. "*David Ratcliffe Receives Diversity CEO of the Year Award.*" Southern Company Today, http://sotoday.southernco.com/gpc/ratcliffe_diversityaward.shtml.

Citizen Online. "Diversity Advisory Council Transformed Into External Oversight Group." *Citizen Online*, November 3, 2005.

Class Action Watch. (2002, January). "Judge Refuses to Extend Class-Action To Race Discrimination Lawsuit." *Class Action Watch*, January, (2002).

Clayton, C. B. "The Brutus Syndrom: Is Your Bottom Line Being

Bullied." *The Spartacus Analytics Group*, January 2005.

Cole, Y. "Three White Guys Who Get It." *DiversityInc*, Apri, 2005.

Cornelius Cooper, Michael Edwards, Sarah Jean Harris v. Southern Company, Georgia Power Company, and Southern Company Services, Inc., File No. 2000CV26045 (Superior Court of Fulton County July 27, 2000).

Cornelius Cooper, Michael Edwards, et al. v. Southern Company, Georgia Power, et al., 02-12230 (United States Court of Appeals For The Eleventh Circuit November 10, 2004).

Cox, T., Jr. Creating the Multicultural Organization: A Strategy for Capturing the Power of Diversity, (1st ed.). San Francisco: Jossey-Bass, 2002.

Cox, T. H., and B. Blake. "Managing Cultural Diversity: Implications for Organizational

Competitiveness." *Academy of Management Executive*, vol. 5, no. 3, (1991): 45–56.

Cross, E.Y., and M.B. White, M.B. (Eds.). The Diversity Factor: Capturing the Competitive Advantage of a Changing Workforce. Chicago: Irwin Professional Publishers, 1996.

Dansky, K., and R. Weech-Maldonado. (2003). "Organizational Strategy and Diversity Management: Sensitive Diversity Orientation as a Moderating Influence." *Health Care Management Review,* 28 (3), (2003): 243-253.

DiversityBusiness.com. "Georgia Power Has New Diversity Executives In Place. *DiversityBusiness.com News,* May 22. 2003

Dwyer, S., O.C. Richard, and K. Chadwick. *Gender Diversity in Management And*

Firm Performance: The Influence of Growth Orientation and Organizational Culture. *Journal of Business Research*, vol. 56, no. 12, (2003): 1009–1019.

Edmondson, A., and J.R Detert. "Why Employees Are Afraid To Speak." *Harvard Business Review*, May 2007.

Frederick, L. (2003, December 15). "Ratcliffe to Take of Southern, Succeeded by Mississippi Power's Mike Garrett." *The Citizen on* December 15, 2003.

Frederick, L. "New Year Ushers in a New President: Meet Mike Garrett." *The Citizen*, January 2004.

Frederick, L. "Ratcliffe Reign Yields Triumphs, Crises, and Challenges." *The Citizen*, April 2004.

Frederick, L. "Workplace Ethics Cases Decrease." *The Citizen*, April 2005.

Friedman, S. "Learning To Make More Effective Decision: Changing Beliefs As A Prelude To Action." *The Learning Organization, 11* (2), (2004) 110-128.

Garrett, M. "Assessing the Impact of Managing Differently." *The Citizen*, June 2004.

Gilbert, J. A., and J.M. Ivancevich. "Valuing Diversity: A Tale of Two Organizations." *Academy of Management Executive*, vol. 14, no. 1, (2000): 93–105.

Giley, S. A. "Does Your Company Pass The Test?" *Atlanta Tribune: The Magazine*, September 2007.

Golembiewski, R. T. *Managing Diversity in Organizations*, Tuscaloosa, London:University of Alabama Press, 1995.

Goode, S.J. Representative Bureaucracy: "African-American Mayors and Employees in Municipal Government." Tuscaloosa, AL: University of Alabama, 2000.

Goode, S. J., and J.N. Baldwin, J. N. "Predictors of African-American Representation in Municipal Government." *Review of Public Personnel Administration*, vol. 25, no. 1, (2005): 29–55.

Good, S.J. "Diversity Managers: Angels of Mercy or Barbarians at the Gate." Bloomington, IL iUniverse: 2014

Hastings, R. R. (2009, January). "*Should Diversity Pay the Price in an*

Unstable Economy?" SHRM Online, http://www.shrm.com.

Hastings, R. "SHRM 2007 State of Workplace Diversity Management Report: A Call To Action." *SHRM,* http://www.shrm.org/diversity/library_published/nonIOC/CMS_024713.asp . Society for Human Resource Management.

Hayles, R. and A.M. Russell. The Diversity Directive: Why Some Initiatives Fail and What to Do About It. New York: McGraw-Hill, 1996.

Hollon, J. (2008, February 26). "The Diversity Dilemma." *Workforce, February 26, 2008.*

Hopkins, W.E. *Ethical Dimensions of Diversity.* Thousand Oaks, CA: Sage, 1997.

HRM Guide.com. (2008, March 4). "Few Organizations Define Diversity." *HRM Guide.com, March 4, 2008.*

Ingram, et al., v. The Coca-Cola Company, 1-98-CV-3679 (RWS) (United States District Court Northern District Of Georgia December 1, 2006).

Iwata, Kay. The Power of Diversity: 5 Essential Competencies for Leading a Diverse Workforce. Petaluma, CA: Global Insights, 2004.

Jackson, S.E., and M.N. Ruderman. *Diversity in Work Teams: Research Paradigms for a Changing Workplace,* 5th ed. Washington,

DC: American Psychological Association, 1995.

Jacobs, D. G. (2006, March). "Power Culture."Smart Business Atlanta, http://www.sbonline.com/locaL/ARTCILE/8356/66/0/POWER_CULTURE.ASPX

Jacobs, K. "Georgia Power Hit With Bias Suit." *Wall Street Journal*, July 28, 2000.

James, E. H., and A.J.Merrell. "Gender and Diversity In Organizations: Past, Present, and Future Directions." *Sex Roles 45*, 45 (5/6), (2001): 243-257.

Jefferson, J., and P.R. Gerkovich. "Valuing and Leveraging Diversity." *Catalyst*, www.catgalystwomen.org.

Kalev, A., and F. Dobbin. "Best Practices or Best Guesses: Assessing The Efficacy Of Corporate Affirmative Action and Diversity Policies," *American Sociological Review, 71*, (2006): 589-617.

Kulik, C. T. "Managing Diversity in Organizations: An Exercise Based on Racial Awareness Training." *Journal of Management Education, 22* (2), (1998):193-203.

Lester, J.S. The Future of White Men and Other Diversity Dilemmas. Berkeley, CA: Conari Press, 1994.

Leverett, A. "Workforce Demographics Evolve With Changes in

Community." *The Citizen*, May 19, 2003.

Martin, K., M.A., Quigley, M. A., and S. Rogers. "Implementing A Learning Management System Globally: An Innovative Change Management Approach. *IBM System Journal, 44* (1), (2005):125-143.

McCloskey, F. "Influencing Growth Through Dialogue." *Profiles In Diversity Journal, 6,* January/February 2004.

McCloskey, F. "Insights On Advancing U.S. Corporate Diversity and Inclusion Initiatives." *Affirmative Action Review, 2009.*

McCloskey, F., and J. Barber, J. "Georgia Power Turns Crisis Into Journey. *The Diversity Factor, 13* (4), (2005):16-22.

McCloskey, F., and J. Barber. "Igniting The Spark." *Profiles in Diversity Journal, 3* (4), (2002).25-33.

McCullough, T. "Barranco Ready for Georgia Power's Diversity Challenge." *The Citizen*, August 25, 2000.

McCullough, T. "New Organization Emerges From Diversity Issues." (T. McCullough, Ed.) *The Citizen*, August 25, 2003.

McCullough, T. Ratcliffe Reflects: Move Brings Memories, Anticipation." *Highlights,* February 2, 2004.

McIntosh, S. "Diversity Initiatives Foster Change." *The Citizen*,

February 8, 2002.

Morgan, L. "Company Keeps Its Commitment To Employees With Job Selection Training." *The Citizen*, August 2009.

Morgan, L. "Efforts To Improve Job Selection Under Way." *The Citizen*, May 2008.

Mott, W. J. "Developing A Culturally Competent Workforce: A Diversity Program In Progress." *Journal of Healthcare Management*, 48 (5), (2003):337-342.

Naff, J. E., K. Naff, and E.J. Kellough. "Responding To A Wake-Up Call: An Examination of Federal Agency Diversity Management Programs." *Administration and Society*, 36 (1), (2004):62-90.

Newkirk, M. (2004, October 31). "Race Discrimination Lawsuit: Long Legal Labyrinth." *Atlanta Journal-Constitution*, October 31, 2004.

Pallerino, M. J. "Diversity Starts At The Top." *Business To Business*, (2008):1-6.

Palma-Rivas, R. M. "Current Status and Future Trends of Diversity Initiatives in the Workplace: Diversity Experts' Perspective." *Human Resource Development Quarterly*, 9 (3), (1998):235-253.

Pearcy, S. "2009 Most Respected Business Leader: Power for the Future." *Georgia Trend*, (2009): 1-6.

Poe, J. "Making Sure Diversity Gets A Chance; Up Close Harriett Watkins, External Manager of Georgia Power." *Atlanta Journal-Constitution*, September 30, 2000.

Poe, J. "Race and Business In Atlanta: Civil Rights Struggle Shifts To Legal Fight For Full Rewards of Corporate Workplace." *Atlanta Journal-Constitution, October 15, 2000.*

Profiles in Diversity Journal. "International Innovation in Diversity Awards. *Profiles in Diversity Journal, 10* (4),(2008)" 92-95.

Profiles in Diversity Journal. "2009 Internal Innovation in Diversity Awards." *Profiles in Diversity Journal*, (2009): 25-34.

Quinn, M. C. "Georgia Power Learns From Coca-Cola Bias Suit Cases Similar: Utility's Response Shows Lessons Gleaned From Soft Drink Giant's Actions." *Atlanta Journal-Constitution*, July 29, 2000.

Quinn, M. C. "Georgia Power Says Five Nooses Displayed." *Atlanta Journal-Constitution*, July 30, 2000.

Ratcliffe, D. (2002, October 21). "Culture Scan Validates Company's Commitment to Trust." *The Citizen*, October 21, 2002.

Ratcliffe, D. (2002, April 5). "Leading By Example." *The Citizen*, April 5, 2002.

Reese, K. "From The Ground Rod Up Mike Garrett." *Georgia Trend*, http://www.georgiatrend.com/site/page7164.html

Richard, S. L., O.C. Richard, O. C., and S.L. Kirby. "An Investigation of Workforce Diversity Programmes: A Multiple Perspective Approach." *Equal Opportunities International*, 15 (6/7), (1996): 17-27.

Rosenberg, M. (2005, March/April). "The Biologist At Southern's Helm." *Energy Biz Magazine*, 2005.

Rowland, D., and M. Higgs. "All Changes Great and Small: Exploring Approaches To Change and its Leadership." *Journal of Change Management*, 5 (2), (2005):121-151.

Saporta, M. "*David Ratcliffe: Corporate America Is On Trial.*" Atlanta Business Chronicle, http:??atlanta.bizjournals.com/atlanta/stories/2009/04/27/newscolumn1.html

Schraub, D. "Diverse White Men." *The Debate Link*, http:dsadevil.blogspot.com.

Shirreffs, A. "Inclusive Advocate." *Atlanta Woman*, March 2009.

Shreve, B. "*Garrett Named Executive of the Year by School of Business.*" Georgia State University Campus News, http://media.www.gscnade.com/media/storage/paper299/ne3ws/2004/0917/CampusNews/...

Sonnenschein, W. The Practical Executive, and Workforce Diversity. New York: McGraw-Hill, 1997.

Steffon McIntosh. "We Are Raising The Bar On Leadership Expectations." *The Citizen*, February 8, 2002.

The Citizen. "New Organization Emerges From Diversity Issues." *The Citizen*, August 25, 2000.

The Citizen. "Powered By People." *The Citizen*, October 19, 2001.

The Citizen. "Lawsuit Application Denied." *The Citizen*, March 22, 2002.

The Citizen. "Building A Better Company, One Individual at a Time." *The Citizen*, September 15, 2003.

The Citizen. "Management Council Members Share Personal Notes From Diversity Journey." *The Citizen*, November 3, 2003.

Thomas, D. A., and R.J. Ely. "Making Differences Matter: A New Paradigm For

Managing Diversity." *Harvard Business Review*, vol. 74, no. 5, (1996): 79–90.

Thomas, R. R., Jr. Building A House for Diversity: A Fable About a Giraffe and Elephant Offers New Strategies for Today's Workforce. New York: AMACOM, 1999.

Thomas, R. R., Jr. Building on the Promise of Diversity: How We Can Move to The Next Level in Our Workplaces, Our

Communities, And Our Society. New York: AMACOM, 2006.

Tsui, A. S., T.D. Egan and C.A. O'Reilly III. (1992). "Being Different: Relational Demography And Organizational Attachment." *Administrative Science Quarterly*, vol. 37, (1992): 549–79.

Tucker, K. H. "From Representation To Inclusion." *Georgia Trend*, June 6, 2006.

Unger, H. "Discrimination Lawsuit: Coca-Cola Accused of Company-Wide Patterns." *Atlanta Journal-Constitution*, April 24, 1999.

Vedantam, S. "Most Diversity Training Ineffective, Study Finds." *Washington Post*, January 20, 2008.

Verdigets, F., and J.R. Hipple. "The Five Elements of Transforming Corporate Culture." *The Strategist*, (2008):16-19.

Walker, R. "Mitigating the Fear of Retaliation Georgia Power Style." *Ethikos* (2008): 4-16.

Wall Street Journal. "Judge Encourages Coca-Cola To Maintain Diversity Efforts." *Wall Street Journal Online, December 1, 2006.*

Welch, M. "Style Points CEO David Ratcliffe Has Energized The Southern Company." *Business To Business*, January 1, 2007.

White, E. "Diversity Programs Look To Involve White Males As

Leaders." *The Wall Street Journal,* May 7, 2007.

Williams, M. "Better Communications Makes Us Stronger." *The Citizen, November 2006.*

Williams, M. "Task Force Works To Improve Job Selection Process." *The Citizen*, February 2008.

Woodall, S. "Management Council Approves Diversity Recommendations." *The Citizen*, December 15, 2000.

Woodall, S. "Workplace Ethics Review Shows Process On Target." The Citizen Online, August 28, 2004.

Woodall, S. "Lawsuit To Proceed." *The Citizen*, January 25, 2002.

Woodall, S. "Company Gives Green Light To Affinity Groups." *The Citizen*, May 5, 2003.

Wooten, L. P., & E.H., James. "Managing Diversity." *Executive Excellence, 18* (8), (2001):17-18.

Wooten, L.P., and E. H. James. "When Firms Fail To Learn: Perpetuation of Discrimination In The Workforce." *Journal of Management Inquiry, 13* (1), (2004):23-33.

Wooten, L. P., & E.H., James. "Leadership As (Un)usual: How To Display Competencies In Time Of Crisis." *Organizational Dynamics , 34* (2), (2005):141-152.

Wooten, L. P., & E.H., James. "Diversity Crises: How Firms Manage Discrimination Lawsuits." *Academy of Management Journal,* 49 (6), (2006):1103-1118.

Wooten, L. P., & E.H., James. "Linking Crisis Management and Leadership Competencies: The Role of Human Resource Development." *Advances in Developing Human Resources, 10* (3), (2008): 352-379.

Zendrian, A. (2008, February 27). "Diversity Unclear At Smaller Firms." *New York Times,* February 27, 2008).

About the Author

Dr. Shelton J. Goode is the president and chief executive officer of Icarus Consulting. He is a diversity leader with over twenty years of human resource and business experience. He has held executive HR positions for companies ranging in size from $300 million to $11 billion-plus. He has developed and implemented talent-management programs, performance management systems, sales incentive plans, labor relations strategies, and large-scale culture-change initiatives. As a result, he has earned a reputation as a strategic yet results-oriented HR and business leader.

Dr. Goode learned the value of diversity management firsthand by rolling up his sleeves and providing CEOs and senior executives with counsel, insight, resources, tools, and innovative ideas that helped advance their companies' strategic business goals. For the last ten years, he has leveraged his seasoned leadership and consulting skills to help companies implement diversity management initiatives that enhanced their talent acquisition, employee retention, and employee engagement strategies.

Dr. Goode has also used his knowledge and experience to teach and mentor others. In 1993, he was awarded the first-ever African American Doctoral Fellowship by Troy University and began teaching at the university in 1996. Since that time, he has been dedicated to helping adult learners achieve their educational goals. For example, as an adjunct professor at Troy University, Dr. Goode taught thousands of students in the school's master's in public administration program. His teaching excellence was recognized when he received the school's prestigious Faculty Member of the Year Award in 2005. Dr. Goode leveraged his extensive teaching experience to publish his first book, *So, You Think You Can Teach: A Guide for the New College Professor in Teaching Adult Learners*. He is also the founder and CEO of My ABD Network, an organization that helps students succeed in doctoral education programs.

Dr. Goode, a highly decorated Air Force veteran, has served the country in times of war and consistently served his community in times of need. In July 2011, the Supreme Court of Georgia appointed him to the State Bar Ethics Investigative Panel. He was one of only three non-lawyers serving on this prestigious panel. He chaired the Conference Board Diversity and Inclusion Leadership Council and has served on the board of numerous professional organizations, such as the Atlanta Compliance and Ethics Roundtable, American Association of Blacks in Energy, Society for Human Resource, Management, and Atlanta and Diversity Management Advocacy Group. The National Association of African Americans in Human Resources awarded him their HR Trailblazer Award in 2005 and 2012; he was the only person selected for the award twice. In April 2013, Georgia's Technology Association presented him with the organization's first Lifetime Achievement Award for his contributions to the field of diversity and inclusion.

Dr. Goode received his bachelor's degree from Southwest Texas State University (now Texas State University) and his master's degree in human resource management from Troy University. He obtained his doctorate in public administration from the University of Alabama. Dr. Goode speaks nationally on a variety of human resource management and diversity topics.

About Icarus Consulting

Icarus Consulting's mission is to unleash the power of human potential by helping people and organizations to defy gravity and fly. Icarus Consulting helps organizations achieve excellence through inclusion by ensuring that employees are valued, respected, and connected at every level in the organization. Icarus Consulting is nationally recognized for helping organizations develop strategies to attract, design, and retain highly skilled talent from an emerging diverse workforce and, at the same time, enhance the engagement, knowledge, and skill of their current employees. Icarus Consulting has earned the reputation for helping organizations create a workplace where their people no longer feel pressure to downplay aspects of their identity to thrive and contribute in a way that fuels the organization's bottom-line growth.

Icarus Consulting understands how important it is to empower all organization members to drive positive organizational change in today's rapidly changing business landscape. Based in Atlanta with a global capability, Icarus Consulting partners with their clients' HR, talent management, diversity and inclusion, and business leadership teams on change management organizational culture around the corner and across the globe.

Icarus Consulting uses its extensive experience to resolve client's unique challenges by developing and delivering training on unconscious bias, establishing diversity and inclusion councils, conducting a BRG Leadership Academy^SM to transform resource groups into true business partners, facilitating executive learning sessions, launching diverse mentoring programs, or providing coaching to hi-potential and emerging leaders. Icarus Consulting works with organizations at all stages of their diversity and inclusion journey.

Icarus Consulting leverages its in-house think tank, the Center for Strategy, Innovation, and Results, to research mega-trends as they apply to future work, employee engagement, and the workplace. The Center specializes in helping leaders learn what is coming and what to do to get ready today! For over ten years, the Center has researched and studied the critical organizational effectiveness trends shaping the future and the agile leaders who will make it happen.

The Center for Strategy, Innovation, and Results partners with companies, nonprofits, government agencies, associations, and communities to better understand the impact of generations on the future. The Center also provides consulting support services to consultants on mapping the "desired" future state for organizations. Lastly, the Center helps organizations and communities plan for culture change by mapping employee engagement trends impacting tomorrow, how the diverse workforces and populations impact those trends, and what agile leaders should be doing today.

The Center utilizes a Future Map, which provides insights into what is coming for an industry or community, shares the implications of trends, and presents opportunities. The Future Map is an exclusive look into our 'crystal ball' so that organizations can see the demographic and cultural trends impacting an organization, industry, or community. This tool helps the Center's clients better understand the relevant issues and adapt their culture accordingly.

"

"defensive avoidance · 150
"defensive avoidance" · 150

A

accountability · 154, 156, 160
Accountability · 148
acculturation · 198
Advisory Councils · 100
affinity groups · 163
Affirmative Action · 83
affirmative action plan · 198
ageism- · 198
Ahmaud Arbery · 193
Al Vivian · 85, 86
Ambiguity · 77
American Institute for Managing Diversity · 86, 216, 217, 218, 221, 223, 224, 226, 227
anti-oppression · 199
Authentic Leadership · 151

B

benchmarking · 100, 105
bigot · 200

Breonna Taylor · 193
bullying · 200
Burberry · 17
business resource groups · 63, 93, 191

C

case study · 24, 95, 130, 148
catalytic · 16
Charlottesville · 47
Chief Human Resource Officer · 86
civil rights · 201
class action · 156, 157, 162, 163
competitive advantage · 242
Conference Board · 250
coronavirus · 13, 14, 33, 35, 36, 39, 40
courageous conversation · 24
Covid-19 · 13
COVID-19 · 13, 15, 34, 41, 180
cultural assimilation · 202
Cultural Competence · 181, 185
cultural competency · 203
Cultural Fluency · 71
culturally competent leaders · 186

culture · 4, 130, 134, 135, 136, 138, 140, 144, 146, 147, 150, 151, 155, 157, 158, 160, 161, 162

D

Defense Department Race Relations Institute's · 83
Defense Equal Opportunity Management Institute · 82
DEOMI · 83
differential validation · 204
discrimination · 133, 134, 141, 155, 157, 158, 159, 160, 161, 162, 163
disparate treatment · 24, 113, 178
diversity · 4, 5, 6, 130, 133, 155, 157, 158, 162, 241, 243
Diversity · 2, 250
Diversity Advisory Council · 163, 182, 242
diversity climate · 205
diversity competency · 205
diversity management · 27, 202, 205, 206, 222, 249, 250
diversity- management · 130
Diversity Pioneers · 86
diversity professional · 122, 179

diversity professionals · 178, 179
dominant group · 64, 113, 114

E

Emotional intelligence · 168
empathy · **123**
employee engagement · 136, 145
Employee Resource Groups · 63, 93, 111, 191
environmental equity · 206
Equal Employment Opportunity Commission · 132, 207, 238
Equal Employment Opportunity Commission (EEOC · 207
Equifinality · 65
ERGs · 23, 63, 93, 94, 95, 96, 97
essentialism · 207
ethnocentrism - · 208
eurocentrism · 208

F

Financial Crisis · 32, 38
First Step Act. · 189
Fishbowl Practices · 68
Forbes · 13, 54, 75

G

Gallup · 125
Gap Matrix · 136
gender Characteristics · 209
Gender diversity training · 84
General Counsel · 138
George Floyd · 7, 193
Georgia Minority Business Association · 155
Georgia Minority Business Association's · 155
Georgia Power · 100, 130, 131, 132, 133, 134, 135, 136, 140, 141, 142, 144, 146, 147, 149, 151, 153, 155, 156, 157, 158, 161, 162, 163
Great Depression · 32, 33, 35, 38
Great Recession · 31, 32

H

human rights · 211
hypervigilance · 150

I

Icarus Consulting · 16, 74, 75, 95, 96, 97, 108, 109, 110, 111, 118, 192, 193, 249, 251, 252
identity group · 212, 213

inclusive language · 212
individual racism · 213
integration · 123
internal dysfunction · 178

J

Jennifer Brown · 185, 186
Jim Crow · 193

L

lawsuit · 133, 151, 155, 156, 157, 158, 161, 162, 163
LGBTQ · 57, **179**, 214, 229

M

management council · 139
Managing Differently · 89, 124
McKinsey · 135
Millennial · 95
multicultural education · 216
Multiculturalism · 84, 215

N

National Domestic Workers Alliance · 39
National Rifle Association · 47

New Paradigm Strategy Group · 46

O

oppression · 199, 201, 213, 215
Organizational Behavior Theory · 147
organizational climate · 217
organizational effectiveness · 136
organizational performance · 5, 145

P

Pan-Africanism · 218
pandemic · 13, 14, 15, 30, 32, 33, 34, 35, 36, 37, 38, 41, 178, 180
paradoxes · 24, 150
performance management · 149
physically challenged person · 218, 219
privilege · 27, 227

Q

quarantined · 13

R

race · 179, 201, 207, 208, 210, 211, 218, 220, 221, 223, 224, 226, 227
racial equity · 221
racially visible people · 218, 221
Regional Councils · 99
Religious diversity · 85
retaliation · 133, 134, 135, 136, 138, 139, 140, 141, 142, 143, 144, 145, 146, 147, 148, 149, 160, 163
Retaliation · 130, 136, 143, 144, 247
reverse discrimination · 223

S

Second Chance Policies and Initiatives · 188
segregation · 14
Self-Awareness · 167
Self-Reflection · 167
sex · 207, 209, 223, 226
sexism · 87, 214, 223, 239
sexual harassment · 178, **223**
sexual orientation · 179, 227

social justice · 126
Society for Human Resources Management · 67
Society of Human Resource Management · 49
Southern Company · 131, 144, 153, 154, 156
Southern Style · 144, 148
Succession Planning · 70
Supreme Court · 250
systemic discrimination · 225

T

transformative · 30, 67, 185
transgender · 209, 226
Tulsa Race Massacre, · 193
Twitter · 181

U

Underutilization · 68
unemployment · 13, 15, 34, 38
unhealthy behaviors · 179
United States Supreme Court · 142

V

Valuing diversity · 89

W

white fragility · 227
white privilege · 23, 70, 84, 85
work teams · 244
Workplace Ethics · 133, 134, 143
World Economic Forum · 42, 44